ALSO BY JANE AND MICHAEL STERN

Trucker: A Portrait of the Last American Cowboy
Roadfood
Amazing America
Auto Ads
Friendly Relations
Horror Holiday
Goodfood
Square Meals
Where to Eat in Connecticut
Roadfood and Goodfood

REAL AMERICAN FOOD

Illustrated by Jane Stern

Jane and Michael Stern's
Coast-to-Coast Cookbook

REAL AMERICAN FOOD

From Yankee Red Flannel Hash and the
Ultimate Navajo Taco to
Beautiful Swimmer Crab Cakes and
General Store Fudge Pie

ALFRED A. KNOPF   NEW YORK   1986

751-2600

THIS IS A BORZOI BOOK
PUBLISHED BY ALFRED A. KNOPF, INC.

Library of Congress Cataloging-in-Publication Data

Stern, Jane.
Real American food.

Includes index.
1. Cookery, American. I. Stern, Michael, [date]
II. Title.
TX715.S8387   1986   641.5973   86-45284
ISBN 0-394-53953-2

Manufactured in the United States of America

FIRST EDITION

To Martha Kaplan

CONTENTS

Introduction   ix

Acknowledgments   xi

INTRODUCTION

hen we began writing this American cookbook we knew we did not want to divide it into appetizers, entrées, and desserts. There is culinary logic to such a method, but it could never convey the adventure and good times we have had eating across the country.

America is not a land of appetizers and entrées. It is a land where people gather to eat in ways that express their regional character: the South's pig pickin' parlors, Basque hotels in the Nevada hills, clam shacks on the North Atlantic coast, and sale barn cafes throughout the Great Plains.

That is why we cluster the recipes in this book according to style of eatery. We want to paint a picture of America as we have seen it at the table, through recipes that are authentic, that duplicate at home what we have enjoyed on the road.

Why and *how* people eat what they eat are the secret spices that make regional American food so especially delicious.

We are sure you will enjoy Mama Lo's Broccoli Casserole (p. 117); but it is that much more fun when you know about Southern soul food cafes, about how Mama inscribes the daily menu every morning on a sheet of blue-lined notebook paper, about why supermarket white bread is exactly the right ingredient in the dish. Or take the California "smoothies" we describe in our chapter about Manly Food (p. 273): They're great, but even more flavorful when you know that they are the preferred drink of body builders who flock to the Orange Inn to drink them by the shakerful.

The food revolution is going strong, bringing high style to American cooking. But we cannot agree that American cuisine is something new, or even that upscale cookery represents progress. This country's culinary past is hardly the dark ages. Since the Pilgrims landed, America has been evolving an elaborate cuisine, expressive of the settlers and the melting pot, of pioneer cooks and housewives, always too off-the-cuff to get officialized and codified the way some bandwagon culinary patriots seem to want it.

Every time we go out on the road we are surprised by the depth and verve of regional cooking, so much of it unknown outside its local home. Buffalo chicken wings and pan-blackened redfish have gone mainstream, but only locals know about a Rochester garbage plate (p. 12), or a Missouri fried brain sandwich (p. 250), or Mobile Bay West Indies salad (p. 173), or a San Francisco New Joe Special (p. 286), or loosemeats from Sioux City (p. 253). Like safari hunters, we traveled into the wilds of America and came back with the trophies to share with you.

Nor would this gastronomic portrait of the country be complete without alive-and-well classics, like Yankee blueberry muffins (p. 66) and Kansas City fried chicken (p. 222). They are not unique to this book, but we believe the recipes we offer, gathered over hundreds of thousands of miles (and having tasted enough blueberry muffins to give us permanent indigo tongues), are the most authentic tastes of America.

When we first conceived of a regional cookbook, we tapped each restaurant in *Roadfood and Goodfood* for their choicest recipes. Most were generous, and many recipes worked fine straight away. Others needed fiddling to adjust them to home kitchen cooking. A few places were secretive about how they made their specialties; and that, in a way, proved the most fun. The two of us, along with test cooks Melanie Barnard and Brooke Dojny, spent many hours over the stove breaking the code of favorite dishes. If we didn't feel we got it accurately, then it was not included. If it worked, it's here. In every case, credit for the recipes belongs to cooks all across America.

Of primary importance was that every recipe work right at home, and thereby reflect the goodness of the meals we have relished on the road. To that end, each has been reworded, organized, and adjusted.

It was important to us that this book not be a duded-up fantasy of American cookery. The American food we love, as it is eaten every day across this land, needs no food stylist. It's got style to spare. This is a vibrant, of-the-people cuisine, a crazy quilt of tearoom dainties and hands-on grub, from cowboy bullmeat brisket in Texas to sunshine cake in Milwaukee, from banana cashew pancakes in the West to red flannel hash in New England. Come with us down the blue plate highway. America is a great place to eat.

ACKNOWLEDGMENTS

ost publishers and editors contribute to their authors' books from behind a desk. But those ramblin' Borzois, Bob Gottlieb and Martha Kaplan, fearlessly hit the road with us to share biscuits, prunes, and red-eye gravy in the South's real American cafes. Bob Cornfield, our friend and agent, took us on safari to his native Brooklyn in search of the perfect knish. Bob, Bob, and Martha have our thanks for sharing the journey. And thanks, too, to Mary Maguire, who puts the fun in telephoning.

Melanie Barnard and Brooke Dojny went beyond the formidable role of test cooks to offer unending enthusiasm, as well as a rare knowledge of this country's cuisine.

The restaurateurs, chefs, and home cooks who shared their recipes with us are acknowledged with their recipes in the text; real American food is theirs, and we thank them for it.

REAL AMERICAN FOOD

THE EAST

THREE KINDS OF DINERS

MID-ATLANTIC DELIS

SUGARHOUSE AND COUNTRY STORE

STREET FOOD

ff the cuff and on the hoof at corner candy stores, in sub shops, and from the ovens of roving knish wagons, street eats in the Northeast are as effervescent as the head on a freshly made egg cream. Street food is a sassy city cuisine created by vendors instead of chefs and relished with gusto by street-corner connoisseurs.

Who needs a table and chairs? China and flatware only get in the way. If you want to dine in high style in Philadelphia or New York, or at the all-night white hot wiener shops of Rochester, all you really need is a pair of comfortable shoes and an iron gut.

Street food's fun is its informality. If you have any doubt, imagine your ham and pepper hoagie being served on a Spode plate by a long-faced waiter. Distressing, isn't it? Or try to figure out how you'd use a knife and fork to eat a slice of New York pizza. Can't be done! Or conceive, if you will, of dishing out Rhode Island "wieners up the arm" the next time you have dinner by candlelight. Ludicrous!

Street food is *public*, seldom served at home. Paradoxically, that is precisely what makes it so extra-special good at home, and so much fun to cook and serve. The frisson of a cheese steak indoors, in civilized company in the dining room, gives it naughty cultural tang that transcends its flavors. What magic it is to serve warm soft pretzels to guests who come expecting ordinary snacks. Or to dish out hoagies instead of sandwiches; Fourth of July garbage plates instead of naked wieners; egg creams in lieu of dry white wine. Street food out of context is all the more exciting.

It's a thrill to bring it indoors because—let's be honest—it is the kind of junk food that most of our mothers warned us against: You don't know where the vending cart has been; nor do you know where it goes at night. Like inverted vampires, street vendors disappear when the sun goes down, reemerging the next day, their wagons loaded down with stuff to eat from who knows where.

Pat's—"King of Steaks" in South Philly—is the hub of street food culture in America, a revelation of why this chow is at once so awful and so good. Pat's is always open, round-the-clock, seven days a week, since 1930. Pat's, the story goes, invented cheese steaks as a Depression-era way to serve a lot of calories cheap. Prime time at Pat's is after midnight on a weekend. The neon-lit triangular building is surrounded by a mulligan stew of Philadelphians, from debutantes in ball gowns to prostitutes in Spandex short shorts, denizens of South Philly and of Society Hill, bums, police officers, and politicians.

They stand on a sidewalk strewn with dropped french fries, shreds of steak, and bloodlike pools of hot sauce. A few lean on ledges or against the wall, but most are freestanding in a special steak-eating posture that demands a slight forward tilt of the torso at the waist and a double-handed grip on the sandwich. That way, the loaded sandwich can be smashed into their jaws, and whatever drips out will hit the sidewalk rather than their shoes.

Street food connoisseur Eliot Kaplan documented the special language of the steak, noting that one never calls a cheese steak sandwich a "hoagie." (Hoagie implies lettuce and tomatoes, which are never put on a cheese steak, except at Mike and Carol's, a Pat's rival.) What you want is a *steak;* "sandwich" is understood. When it is ordered at the order window (and you better be quick about it, because the countermen at Pat's give no quarter), you call "cheese with," meaning steak, cheese, and onions. "Or if you're a real vet," Eliot advised, "scream 'Cheese with, and take the guts out,' which means remove the inside of the roll so peppers can be laid in."

SOUTH PHILLY CHEESE STEAK SANDWICH

No fresh cut of beef available in a butcher shop is low grade enough to accurately duplicate the sizzling thin-sliced leatherette that goes into a genuine cheese steak sandwich. Only frozen sandwich steaks will do. Yes, there are places in Philadelphia that sell upscale steaks, using choice-graded chuck roast, tender and thickly sliced, and it does make a perfectly fine beef sandwich. *But it is not a steak sandwich.*

The quality of meat stands in inverse relationship to the greatness of a steak sandwich. Oh, the meat's got to be there—plenty of it. But the point is that it shouldn't taste too much like beef. You want it more for its oily texture, its saltiness, the way the thin slices sop up the taste of grease and onions on the grill.

It's the bread that makes the steak sing. Get yourself some terrific-quality Italian bread—torpedo loaves, no more than half a day old (or to make your own, see p. 249). Then follow these directions, and you will have a drippingly good homemade facsimile of a Pat's sandwich. (Even at home, we recommend you eat it standing up.)

8 ounces Cheez Whiz (the only correct brand)
2 tablespoons butter
1 large onion
Oil or butter for frying
4 frozen sandwich steaks

2 Italian rolls, sliced lengthwise
Condiments to taste: ketchup, red and green peppers, hot sauce

Put Cheez Whiz in top of a double boiler with butter. Heat until soft and drippy. Keep warm over hot water as you prepare steaks.

Slice onion and fry it in oil or butter on a griddle. When golden brown and squiggly, scoot onions to side of grill and slap on a couple of slabs of prefab frozen sandwich steaks. When brown on one side (less than a minute), flip and cook other side, pushing onions back to mingle with meat. The steaks will be done within 90 seconds, total, but don't worry if they loiter on the grill with the onions a few extra minutes.

When ready to serve, take a sharp knife and hack steaks into helter-skelter ribbons, then scoop them up with onions and load them into the rolls. Immediately spoon on molten cheese and add desired condiments.

We recommend an order of cheese fries on the side.

Serves 2, with cheese left over for 2 orders of cheese fries.

SIDEWALK CHEESE FRIES

For authenticity's sake, cheese fries should be served in large paper cups, one cup per serving; and don't be shy about making them from frozen crinkle-cut fries.

2 fistfuls hot french fries

3–4 ounces molten Cheez Whiz

Put fries in paper cups. Drizzle on hot Cheez Whiz.

Serves 2.

REAL FRENCH FRIES

Purists will want to make their own french fries. You might even consider drizzling them with other kinds of melted cheese. Fancy cheese, however, goes beyond pure to persnickety.

Potatoes (1 per person)
Vegetable oil for deep frying

Salt to taste

Peel and cut potatoes into ¼-inch logs. Soak in cold water 20 minutes; change water; soak again 20 minutes; change water; soak 20 minutes more. Drain potatoes and blot thoroughly dry.

Heat oil in deep fryer (or deep skillet) to 380°. Lift basket (or large slotted spoon), throw in a handful of potatoes, and quickly reimmerse basket. Fry 3–4 minutes, until golden brown. Throw fries onto paper towels to drain, return basket to oil, and when oil is up to 380°, continue with a second handful of potatoes. Fries may be kept warm for a while in a 275° oven on a baking sheet lined with paper towels. Salt just before serving.

Cheese steaks haven't traveled much outside Philly, probably because other regions of the country have their own variations: Italian beef in Chicago (p. 247), French dip in the West (p. 281), beef on weck in Buffalo (p. 42). But no place has pretzels to compare with Philadelphia's.

We don't mean the hard kind of pretzel that you casually eat by the handful with a six-pack, or the sticks that get heaped into TV party mix with the nuts and Rice Chex. No, we are talking *serious pretzel*, a pretzel worthy of focused concentration. In the summer, Philadelphians eat them gripped in napkins, chomping down with gusto other cities save for hot dogs. In the winter, held in a warm mittened hand, they are as comforting as a hot water bottle.

A soft pretzel is a hefty chaw, as fat as a bagel. Its skin is rugged, not slick or crusty, but tough, with a markedly bitter taste. Glistening across its surface like a spill of diamond chips are grains of hard, coarse salt.

And the corker, the twist that turns this beauteous gnarled knot of bread into something uniquely Philadelphian, is mustard. A bright yellow ribbon along the top, following each bend, neatly applied with a steady squirter. Only sunny yellow mustard from a squeeze or squirt bottle is correct, its sheen a foil to the tan surface of the dough.

The best of Philadelphia's pretzels—"The Good Ones," according to signs on vending carts from the Italian market to Rittenhouse Square— are produced by the Philadelphia Soft Pretzel Company on North Third Street. Forty to sixty thousand are hand twisted every day (some bakeries, shame on them, stamp them out). But serious pretzophiles don't wait for them to arrive at the carts; they stop at the bakery before noon and buy bagfuls, hot from the tunnel-shaped oven.

We asked Jeanne and Dan Sidorick, who run the bakery, what their secret is. "The city's awful water," Jeanne grinned. "Everyone complains about it, but that's what makes them special. That's why you can't make a Philadelphia pretzel anywhere else."

Maybe so, but this recipe comes close—by purposely polluting the water in which they're boiled. Traditionalists use lye, but that was too scary for us. Baking soda does the trick, giving these pretzels' skin their Philly tang.

PHILADELPHIA SOFT PRETZELS

1 package dry yeast
1 teaspoon sugar
1 cup tepid water (110°)
2 cups all-purpose flour
½ cup gluten flour

1 teaspoon salt
2 tablespoons baking soda
½–1 tablespoon coarse salt,
    depending on taste

Dissolve yeast and sugar in ¼ cup of the tepid water.

Combine flours, add salt; stir in remaining ¾ cup water. When yeast mixture is foamy, add it to flour and mix thoroughly. Turn out onto floured board and let rest 2–3 minutes while you clean and oil bowl. Knead 10 minutes, until dough is silky and resilient, adding flour if necessary. Return to bowl, cover with a double layer of plastic wrap; let rise 1 hour, or until doubled in size.

Punch down dough. Cut it into 8 pieces, then roll each piece into a thin tube 18–24 inches long. To form a pretzel, grasp each end of the dough, forming a horseshoe with the curved part away from you. Twist the ends around each other and press each firmly onto the loop of dough beneath them.

Let pretzels rest 10 minutes under a towel on a lightly floured board. Preheat oven to 450°.

Simmer a quart of water with baking soda in a large skillet. Poach pretzels two or three at a time, 30 seconds on each side. Remove pretzels, pat dry, and place on baking sheet lightly dusted with cornmeal. Sprinkle pretzels with coarse salt.

Bake 10–12 minutes, until light brown. (For crustier pretzels, run them under broiler for 30 seconds just before baking.) Serve warm, with squeeze bottle of mustard.

Makes 8 large pretzels.

The subject of hoagies is a Pandora's box: You can find as many ways to make one as you can permutate cold cuts and chefs. A hoagie almost always has lettuce and tomatoes, unless it's a hot *sub*, in which case it might have tomato sauce. Cold hoagies are usually sprinkled with olive oil (directly on the bread, before the cold cuts are layered on). The bread, as on a cheese steak sandwich, must be a small loaf (or half a large loaf) of the highest quality—crisp-crusted, sturdy, fresh.

Hoagies in the Northeast go by many names, including subs, heros, torpedos (the Bronx), grinders (Connecticut), wedges (Westchester County), bombers (upstate New York), and zeps (western Pennsylvania). But it is as a hoagie, in the Delaware Valley from Philadelphia to Atlantic City, that the stuffed Italian loaf has attained perfection.

Its apotheosis has a lot to do with the way it's treated—not as an appendage to a pizzeria, but as a *cause célèbre*. And we do mean *célèbre*. No hoagie shop worth its olive oil is without a roster of celebrity clientele. It's a peculiar phenomenon (true of cheese steaks too, and to a lesser degree of New York delis): Hoagies are a magnet for famous people's endorsements. The logic is that the overstuffed sandwiches are people's food. If you can *get down* and chomp a hoagie, you're a regular guy or gal.

The *ne plus ultra* hoagie is found at Ragozzino's on the south side of Philadelphia: a sandwich so effulgent that it is nearly impossible to eat without napkins and a flat, stationary surface. A table or the hood of a car works equally well.

ARCHETYPAL DELAWARE VALLEY HOAGIE

The ingredients of a hoagie are limited only by the chef's imagination. Let us, for the sake of order, limit this one to cold cuts, the classics: salami, ham, and cheese. We cannot stress too strongly the importance of making a hoagie on *fresh*, hard-crusted, fluffy-inside Italian bread. (The torpedo rolls on page 249, although relatively small, are the proper consistency.) Cold cuts should be imported, bought at an Italian grocery store, not the supermarket.

1 loaf Italian bread, 1–2 feet
Olive oil
Genoa salami
Capicola
Provolone cheese
Iceberg lettuce, shredded

Beefsteak tomatoes, sliced
Roasted red peppers (see
   p. 248)
Italian salad dressing
Oregano

Slice the loaf lengthwise. If you like your sandwich heavy on the cold cuts, you may want to scoop out some of the bread's insides to make way for the ingredients. Sprinkle both halves generously with olive oil. Layer the cold cuts in a floppy, bent, and twisted pile so that there is some spring between individual pieces (i.e., don't lay them flat on top of each other). Heap on the lettuce and tomatoes, then peppers. Sprinkle with Italian dressing and plenty of oregano. Place the top on the sandwich, but don't squish it, lest everything slither out.

Hot dogs are all-American, but only the East has evolved a mature frankfurter cuisine. It is a cuisine without chefs and almost without cooking techniques. Its stars are its vendors, and its methods are those of *assembly* in the field, rather than toil in the kitchen.

In every stand and store that makes hot dogs a specialty, the dogs are a *given*, from the factory. (Although the given varies tremendously from Rochester to New York to Providence.) How they are cooked and served, what they are called, and with what they are dressed determines the shape of the cuisine.

Baltimore has frizzled hot dogs (split and fried in oil); Washington has half-smokes (sultry sausages dished out in convenience stores); New Haven has the split wiener (griddle fried, at Savin Rock).

Perhaps the strangest branch of frankdom is Rhode Island, home of New York System, an enigmatic label found on storefront shops throughout the state. Clearly, "New York" refers to the hot dog's spiritual (if not actual) home on the boardwalk of Coney Island. We have yet to get a definitive answer from any vendor as to whether "system" means the hot dogs themselves, or the way they are cooked en masse, or some other elusive "system."

Rhode Island Coney Islands are sawed-off wieners barely three inches long served in spongy little rolls, topped with chili (known as Coney sauce; see p. 245). When you want a lot of them, you order "wieners up the arm," which refers to the server's technique of lining a dozen or more dogs along his arm, wrist to shoulder, and efficiently applying the desired condiments.

In New York City, you can eat crackly-skinned all-beef kosher dogs in every (nondairy) delicatessen, and boiled Sabrett's dogs on nearly every street corner. But these are nothing you cannot get elsewhere. What distinguishes New York City wiener culture is the dominance of sauerkraut as a condiment.

The New York City dog is overshadowed by upstate frankfurter fanaticism. Buffalo, Rochester, Syracuse—these are where the hot dog is enthroned as the king of street foods. In Buffalo, they begin with an ordinary pork and beef hot dog. It is cooked over a hot charcoal fire, just like on a picnic. But Buffalo tube steaks get special treatment: As they cook, the grill man pokes them with his fork, hacks them with a knife, mashes them down, and rolls them hard against the grate. The result is a tube steak that by virtue of its lacerations absorbs maximum smoke flavor and develops a charred, crusty skin. At Ted's in Tonawanda, these brutalized beauties are swallowed up with superior hot relish and sided by shaggy onion rings.

They char-grill in Rochester too, but what distinguishes Rochester (and Syracuse) is the popularity, along with red hots, of white hot wieners. White hots, made with veal, ham, and beef, are mild and lean, easy on the garlic but with a dash of mustard. Genuine Rochester white hots and red hots (as well as fantastic hot sauce) can be ordered by mail from:

Zab's Backyard Hots, Inc.
1504 Scottsville Road
Rochester, NY 14623
(716) 436-4890

Once you get your upstate wienies, you will want to grill them over coals, as described above. What you probably should do next is to put them into buns, ladle on the hot sauce and/or mustard, and whale them down.

Or you can decide to throw caution to the wind, to go insane, wienerwise, and turn your grilled hots into an authentic Nick Tahou garbage plate.

Nick Tahou is a Rochester original, dishing out the dogs round-the-clock since 1918. It is a democratic greasy spoon with pinball machines up front, booths along the wall, and a counter. Place your order and wait, then carry it to a seat. The menu lists Texas hots (red), pork hots (white), burgers, eggs, potatoes. What the menu does not list is what a large portion of Nick Tahou's clientele comes to eat: a garbage plate, which is nothing less than the Assumption of the upstate hot dog.

ROCHESTER GARBAGE PLATE

Let us reassert that the essence of hot dog cookery is not so much technique as assembling the right ingredients and organizing them in a proper manner. This recipe, therefore, is more a shopping list than a cooking lesson. With the exception of the sauce, the rest of the components are garden-variety supermarket items. We find an ice cream dipper invaluable in measuring out the various elements.

The first thing you have to do to make a garbage plate is to cook up a batch of sauce:

1 medium onion, chopped fine	1 teaspoon black pepper
1 clove garlic, minced	¼ teaspoon cayenne pepper
1 tablespoon cooking oil	1 teaspoon chili powder
1 pound chuck, triple ground	½ teaspoon ground cumin
until ultra-fine	½ teaspoon allspice
1 cup water	¼ teaspoon cinnamon
¼ cup tomato paste	¼ teaspoon ground cloves
2 tablespoons brown sugar	1 teaspoon salt

In a large skillet fry onion and garlic in oil until soft. Add meat, stirring constantly with fork to keep its texture fine. Once it browns, add water and tomato paste. Simmer 10 minutes. Add sugar and spices and simmer 30 minutes more, adding water if necessary to keep it moist (but not soupy).

Makes enough for 6–8 garbage plates.

Note: This is also excellent as a topping for hot dogs or hamburgers.

Now make some home-fried spuds, as follows:

6 medium boiling potatoes
4 tablespoons butter, or 2
   tablespoons butter plus 2
   tablespoons bacon grease

Boil potatoes until they can be pierced with fork. Remove from water, peel, and cut into ½-inch chunks.

Melt butter in a heavy skillet. Throw in potatoes, tossing to coat with butter. Cook until brown and crusty, stirring occasionally so they don't stick together. Add more butter if necessary. Keep warm over lowest possible heat setting. Season to taste.

We are quite certain that whenever Paul Bocuse makes a garbage plate, he cooks the baked beans from scratch (see p. 103). But we recommend buying them by the jar, already cooked.

Each garbage plate is constructed from:

1 scoop baked beans, at room temperature
1 scoop home-fried potatoes
1 tablespoon diced raw onion

2 red hot dogs, split and grilled
1 tablespoon prepared mustard
½ cup sauce

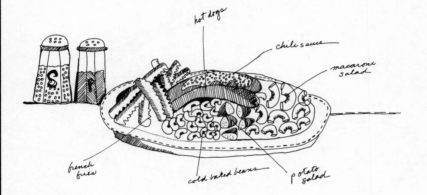

On a heavy cardboard plate, plop one scoop each of baked beans and home-fried potatoes, side by side. Sprinkle onions over both scoops. Lay hot dogs across scoops, pressing down to flatten beans and potatoes beneath dogs. Spread dogs with mustard. Ladle sauce over everything. Serve with bread and butter and macaroni and cheese on the side.

The logic of street food cuisine goes haywire in New York City, where every kind of food imaginable is eaten all day long, sitting, standing, and on the run. Street food is everywhere, hawked at you from pushcarts, storefronts, and outdoor cafes. It is sold in smelly subway stations, in office building lobbies, and from roving vans dispensing egg creams and pretzel rods.

New York pizza is sold from holes in the wall that display their hot cooked pies out in the open, as close to pedestrian traffic as possible. When you order a slice (and you always just say "slice"; pizza is understood), it is slapped on a rectangle of wax paper that does nothing but speed the orange oil slick off the slice and onto your cuff. Each slice is so self-contained that you can flip it over, cheese side down, and nothing will fall off. It has a distinctly rank odor, not bad, just distinctive; and it is topped with tomato sauce and white mozzarella that are intermingled to the point of inseparability. The crust is thin and leathery.

There is only one right way to eat such a slice. Grasp the outer edges of the crust with thumb and middle finger, then press hard onto the center with your index finger, creasing it and enabling you to fold the wedge, like the first step of making a paper airplane. Now, walk like hell up the avenue, pushing your way gruffly through the crowd, without dropping a crumb or missing a step.

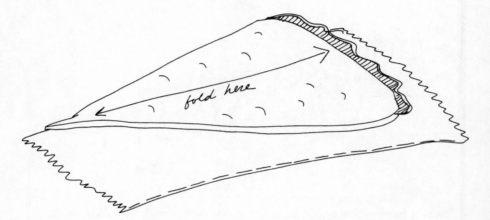

NEW YORK PIZZA BY THE SLICE

Do not compare New York pizza with Italian pizza, not even with Chicago or Boston pizza. It is a dish unto itself. Even though many sidewalk pizzerias do offer additional ingredients, such as mushrooms or pepperoni, forget them. For one thing, they weigh down the pie, making it difficult to eat while maneuvering through a crowd. More important, the beauty of the true New York pizza is its simplicity.

For a tough but light-bodied crust, you need a pizza stone or a screen to form a porous oven "floor" for this pie. You also need a long wooden paddle known as a baker's peel. If you don't mind a slightly damper crust, the pizza can be made on an ordinary cookie sheet, generously greased with vegetable oil.

½ package dry yeast
1 teaspoon sugar

1¼ cups tepid water (110°)
3 cups flour

1 teaspoon salt
¾ cup drained canned
   tomatoes
1 teaspoon oregano
2 cloves garlic, minced fine
½ pound low-moisture
   mozzarella, grated

¼ cup grated Pecorino
   Romano cheese
Dash olive oil
Crushed red pepper

Combine yeast and sugar with ¼ cup of the water.

Combine remaining cup of water with flour and salt. When yeast mixture is foamy, add it to flour and stir vigorously. Turn out onto a floured board and let dough rest while you clean and oil bowl.

Knead dough 10 minutes, adding flour if necessary to create a smooth, silky mass. Return to bowl, cover with a double layer of plastic wrap, and let rise until double in bulk, about 2 hours. Punch down dough. Knead again 3 minutes. Cover and let rest.

Preheat oven (with pizza stone or quarry tiles in oven) to 500°. Dust baker's peel with a sprinkle of flour. (If using an ordinary cookie sheet, preheat oven, grease sheet well with vegetable oil, but don't put it in oven. Prepare pizza as instructed below, and simply lay full-size pizza dough onto greased cookie sheet. Bake until crust is light brown.)

If your pizza stone is 12–14 inches, divide dough in half to form 2 pizzas. Flour a board and flatten dough out on it. Pressing with the heel of your hand, work dough into a circle. When it is about ½ inch thick, pick it up and use your fists underneath to stretch it further. Proceed slowly and patiently, letting the weight of the dough do most of the work. When pizza is full size, lay it on flour-dusted peel.

Pulverize tomatoes with oregano and garlic until you have a smooth sauce. Spread sauce on pizza nearly edge to edge. Sprinkle on mozzarella and Pecorino cheese, then olive oil. Using a quick jerking motion, slide pie from peel onto stones.

Bake 10 minutes, or until crust is light brown. Remove from oven with peel and put on metal serving tray. (If using a cookie sheet, serve directly from sheet.)

Cut in triangles and serve, accompanied by shakers of crushed red pepper.

Serves 3–4.

New York's first pizzeria opened in 1895; it was not until decades later that it evolved into common snack food. Among its once-popular street-corner antecedents were roasted yams (sold for a penny, as a combination hand-warmer and snack in cold weather), chestnuts (still around), and, on the Lower East Side, knishes.

Yonah Schimmel began selling knishes from a pushcart in the early 1900s, when Houston Street (say "House-ton") was the gateway to the Jewish ghetto. You can still find an occasional street-corner knish, but in our book, Knish Central has moved indoors, to Yonah Schimmel's bakery and restaurant, presided over by Mr. Schimmel's great-granddaughter, Lillian Berger.

Mrs. Berger's knishery (which recently opened a branch uptown) looks as it did a half century ago, a little old bakery under a stamped tin ceiling, with rows of polished wood tables occupied by knish-nibbling coffee drinkers who seem not to have moved all day. As you nosh, occasional knishes ride up from the basement bakery on an ancient dumbwaiter, and take-out customers come in to buy *muhn* (poppy seed) cake, potato pudding, and cheese bagels.

Unlike the square, Brooklyn-style knishes sold in most New York delis, Yonah Schimmel's have a hand-formed look. They are working-man's food, peasant fare for sustenance and comfort. The classic kosher knish is filled with potatoes. You can also stuff them with spinach, sweet potatoes, kasha (buckwheat groats), or cabbage. Nonkosher knishes are sometimes filled with liver. We found this recipe for chicken knishes in our *Tempting Kosher Dishes* cookbook, published in Cincinnati in 1930.

BIG KNISH

If you use chicken fat along with oil, these will have the monumental avoirdupois that marks an authentic knish. Prepare your fillings first, so they are ready when the dough is.

2½ cups sifted flour
1½ teaspoons baking powder
½ teaspoon salt
2 eggs, well beaten
⅔ cup vegetable oil, or ⅓ cup

oil plus ⅓ cup rendered chicken fat
2 tablespoons water
Additional oil to brush on dough

Preheat oven to 375°. Sift flour, baking powder, and salt together. Make a well in center; add eggs, oil, and water. Mix with hands until smooth. Turn out onto a lightly floured board, knead a few times, then roll dough out to ¼ inch thick. Brush with oil.

Cut 6-inch circles of dough and put 2–3 tablespoons of filling in each. Draw the circumference of the dough up to a point and pinch it together firmly, creating a seamless pocket.

Place on greased baking sheet and bake 30–35 minutes, until nicely browned.

Makes 8–10 knishes.

POTATO FILLING

1 cup chopped scallions
6 tablespoons chicken fat or
    butter
2 cups mashed potatoes

2 tablespoons sour cream
1 teaspoon salt
¼ teaspoon pepper

Sauté scallions in chicken fat. Combine with potatoes, sour cream, salt, and pepper.

Enough for 8–10 knishes.

CHEESE FILLING

1 cup chopped scallions
4 tablespoons butter
2 cups pot cheese

2 eggs
1 teaspoon salt
¼ teaspoon pepper

Sauté scallions in butter. Combine with cheese, eggs, salt, and pepper.

Enough for 8–10 knishes.

CHICKEN FILLING

1 cup finely chopped cooked
    chicken meat
2 matzohs, crumbled fine
1 egg

¼ cup chicken gravy (canned is
    fine)
Salt and pepper to taste

Combine all ingredients, adding enough gravy so mixture is moist, but thick enough to hold together as a lump when squeezed.

Enough for 8–10 knishes.

For many New Yorkers, the champagne of street food is an egg cream. To appreciate its mystique, you have to understand the New York candy store. In Manhattan, Brooklyn, Staten Island, or the Bronx, "candy store" does not mean a dainty little pink and gold boutique selling marzipan bunnies and hazelnut truffles.

A candy store is a place to hang out, usually a mom-and-pop place, a street-corner supplier of newspapers, ball-point pens, Hav-a-Hanks, and

Hershey Bars. It is to Gotham what general stores are to rural areas: a social center for shmoozing and kibbitzing. To those who grew up with candy stores, then moved away, they signify a nostalgic sense of *neighborhood*. And the humble food associated with candy stores evokes a time of gastronomic innocence.

All good candy stores have a fountain, if only a tiny one with a single seltzer squirter. The best of them, like Hoft's on Burke Avenue in the Bronx, offer a rainbow of syrups for flavored Cokes and sodas. Hoft's even makes its own ice cream and chocolate-dipped graham crackers, and sells sandwiches and burgers, accompanied by icy double-chocolate malts, Broadway flips, or Hobokens.

Hoft's also makes a classic egg cream. By its name, you might logically guess that an egg cream is made with eggs and cream. Wrong. An egg cream is a fool-the-mouth drink that only tastes as luxurious as eggs and cream. In fact, it is made from seltzer water, milk, and syrup.

Egg cream magic is fleeting. It must be dispatched with utmost speed, within three minutes of being made. Otherwise, it loses its head; it turns flat, and becomes no more appealing than a glass of watery chocolate milk. That is why it is perfectly proper to *gulp* an egg cream and why egg creams seldom accompany a meal. The only good companion for an egg cream is a pretzel. A long pretzel rod, crisp and salty, for chewing between swallows.

Our recipe is for home kitchens, without soda fountain equipment. If you have a Three Stooges–style seltzer bottle, use it to add the seltzer and minimize stirring (which breaks up the head).

CORNER STORE EGG CREAM

2 tablespoons chocolate syrup (Fox's U-Bet brand is preferred)

⅓ cup ice-cold milk
⅔ cup ice-cold seltzer

Put chocolate syrup in bottom of a 12-ounce glass. Add milk and stir. Slowly add seltzer, stirring quickly, but no more than necessary to get a good head going.

Serves 1.

Like hot dogs, ice cream is all-American food, the most common of street eats. But with a logic that no one has plumbed, it is most popular in New England, where the average yearly consumption is twenty-three quarts per person per year—enough for a cone every other day. (In contrast, the national average is fifteen quarts.) No ice cream–loving traveler we know has yet been able to explain this American paradox: The warmer the climate, the less likely it is you will find good ice cream to eat.

All the great moments in ice cream history happened in the East (except for the invention of the sundae, in Wisconsin—not exactly a tropical paradise itself). It was in Philadelphia that George Washington first tasted the stuff, and liked it so much he spent $200 one summer making ice cream in the presidential kitchen. The first Howard Johnson's was in Quincy, Massachusetts. Hot fudge was invented in Boston (at Bailey's). And to this day, America's ice cream trends are set in New England. Cookie-flavored blends and Steve's "mix'ins" come from Boston. Ben and Jerry's of Vermont popularized dastardly mash. Connecticut is home of the Harbor Bar and Mousse du Jour.

Connecticut is also the home of prune ice cream: a specialty of the Griswold Inn in Essex, Connecticut, "for about 200 years," according to innkeeper Bill Winterer. It is a strange, musty-flavored, coffee-colored custard, just faintly sweet, its creamy nature not quite blending with the oily tang of the dried fruit. Undeniably dowdy, serious, yet at the same time profoundly luxurious, prune ice cream is the perfect way to end a Saturday supper of pork and beans and brown bread.

200-YEAR-OLD PRUNE ICE CREAM

An ice cream freezer, hand-cranked or electric, is required.

12 ounces pitted prunes	⅔ cup sugar
1½ cups water	Pinch of salt
3 cups cream	3 egg yolks

Soak prunes in water 24 hours. Simmer 10–12 minutes, until prunes are soft and liquid is reduced by one-third. Drain, and cool liquid, reserving it. Chop prunes fine.

In a double boiler heat cream with ⅓ cup of the sugar and salt, stirring to dissolve sugar.

Whisk egg yolks with remaining ⅓ cup of sugar. Add juice from prunes. Slowly pour in about ½ cup of the warm cream, continuing to whisk. Slowly stir egg mixture into cream.

Cook over boiling water, stirring frequently, until mixture thickens enough to coat back of a spoon. Strain into metal or glass bowl. Cool. Cover and place in refrigerator at least 1 hour, until fully chilled.

Mix in chopped prunes and freeze in ice cream machine according to manufacturer's directions.

Makes 1–1½ quarts.

Sometime long ago, northern New England fell in love with Grape-Nuts. Why or how it happened remains undocumented, but the fact becomes quickly apparent to any dessert lover on an eating trip north of Massachusetts. Throughout Vermont, New Hampshire, and Maine, menus almost always include Grape-Nut pudding on their pudding roster. (There is always a roster of puddings in a true New England restaurant.) And at Cole Farms, a giant diner-restaurant in Gray, Maine, they make Grape-Nut ice cream.

When we saw it on the menu, we assumed it meant that the ice cream was sprinkled with crunchy Grape-Nuts as a topping. No, this is ice cream with the Grape-Nuts mixed in and frozen with the cream, so that by the time it is served, they have softened considerably. The crunch is muted, but you still get a nubby feeling on the tongue, and the grainy taste of the cereal is a lovely complement to plain vanilla.

GRAPE-NUT ICE CREAM

An ice cream freezer is required.

2 cups half-and-half   2 teaspoons vanilla extract
⅔ cup sugar   1 cup cream, chilled
Pinch of salt   ½ cup Grape-Nuts cereal
4 egg yolks

Over boiling water in top of a double boiler heat half-and-half with ⅓ cup of the sugar and salt.

Whisk egg yolks with remaining ⅓ cup of sugar. Slowly add ½ cup of the warm half-and-half, continuing to whisk. Pour egg mixture into warm half-and-half, continuing to whisk. Cook over boiling water, stirring, until mixture thickens enough to coat a spoon. Strain into metal bowl and cool. When cooled, add vanilla, cover, and refrigerate at least 1 hour, until fully chilled.

Stir cream into custard and freeze in ice cream machine according to manufacturer's directions. When nearly frozen, add Grape-Nuts.

Makes 1 quart.

As a street food lagniappe, we offer one last ice cream recipe, based on a flavor invented by Dr. Mike's Ice Cream Shop in Bethel, Connecticut. Making it requires a shopping expedition to a gourmet shop or fine gift store for a very special candy called Chocolate Lace (made next to Bethel, in Danbury).

Chocolate Lace, created by a Russian immigrant named Eugenia Tay, is a hard-spun candy web that looks like lace and tastes like New England's Sugar-on-Snow (p. 96), but with a coat of the most astounding bittersweet chocolate. If you don't know where to find Chocolate Lace, the manufacturer will direct you to their nearest outlet; call (203) 792-8175.

Dr. Mike's former owner Peter Seltzer got the idea to mix broken-up Chocolate Lace into plain ice cream (*plain*, not vanilla); when Robert Allison took over the business two years ago, he changed the formula only by adding more Chocolate Lace. As far as we're concerned, it is impossible to have too much candy in this ice cream.

The recipe that follows is our interpretation of the theme, a simple formula, as are all Dr. Mike's recipes. What makes Dr. Mike's ice cream so extraordinary, other than the fact that it is made every day from nothing but sweetened cream and the best flavorings money can buy, is the quality of the cream itself: fresh, superrich, high butterfat content. Robert Allison told us he gets his from a special herd of dairy cows in Massachusetts. If you don't have your own personal cow, try to use ordinary heavy cream, not the ultra-pasteurized variety.

CHOCOLATE LACE AND CREAM ICE CREAM

An ice cream freezer is required.

⅔ cup corn syrup
3 cups heavy cream, well
    chilled

1 7-ounce box Chocolate Lace
    candy, crumbled coarse

Mix corn syrup into cream, blending thoroughly. Pour into ice cream machine and freeze according to manufacturer's directions. Just before ice cream is firm, add Chocolate Lace.

Makes 2 pints.

Street food is by nature urban. The country hasn't any streets; it has roads. But there is one rural New England foodstuff that fills the street food bill in every way: fried dough.

Although fried dough "flippers" are popular on Cape Cod, New England's southern shore is Doughland. Consider the region's unbounded passion for doughnuts—also known as drop cakes, dumfunnies, twisters, jumbles, and symballs. Nowhere else in America will you find doughnuts as good as those sold in dozens of small shops throughout Connecticut and Rhode Island. The southern shore is the home of clam fritters and doughboys (unsweetened fried dough to accompany fish dinners). Here is where you will find fried dough in its purest form—known with stark Yankee logic as fried dough.

Living in New England, we are accustomed to fried dough and sometimes forget just how catastrophic it sounds to visitors. Not a very elegant name, fried dough; a real gut-buster. The reality of good fried dough is that it is puffy, flaky-crusted, steamy inside, with a gentle cakey chaw.

Every county fair and flea market in southern New England has a fried dough wagon among its booths, sending forth the golden disks spread with cinnamon-sugar or tomato sauce. Although fried dough is served on paper plates, no utensils are provided; in true street food style, it is eaten on the stroll.

The established toppings are confectioners' sugar, cinnamon-sugar, or tomato sauce. At a restaurant called Corky's in East Hartford, Connecticut, they offer fried dough spread with sweetened peanut butter. Our favorite topping is maple butter, applied while the dough is still slightly warm.

FRIED DOUGH WITH MAPLE BUTTER

If you are going to serve your fried dough with maple butter, make the butter in advance.

1 cup flour
1 teaspoon baking powder
½ teaspoon salt
1 tablespoon vegetable
    shortening or lard

⅓ cup warm water
Oil for frying

Mix flour, baking powder, and salt. Cut in shortening until mixture is mealy. Slowly stir in water to form a ragged dough.

Turn dough out onto a floured board and knead 2 minutes, or until smooth. Cover with a towel and let rest 15 minutes.

Heat oil in a deep skillet to 375°. Divide dough into 4 equal-size balls and roll the first one out into a 5-inch circle. To keep it from puffing like a giant *sopaipilla*, use a sharp knife to cut 4 or 5 1-inch-long slits through dough. (Or if you want a balloonlike pastry, don't cut it!)

Ease circle of dough into hot fat. Cook 30 seconds until brown, then turn it and cook other side until golden brown. Drain on paper towels. Cook other circles and serve immediately.

Makes 4 fried doughs.

MAPLE BUTTER

6 tablespoons sweet butter   2 tablespoons maple syrup

Cream butter and syrup together. Chill. Remove from refrigerator 30 minutes before serving.

EAT IN THE ROUGH

at in the rough" is a Massachusetts term for a dining style unique to the summer and to the shore. Eat in the rough means open-air informality: no printed menus, no silverware or tablecloths, no service whatsoever. Place your order at the kitchen window, then wait for your number to be called. Stake out a table, carry your own food (served in cardboard containers and Styrofoam cups on corrugated trays). For ambience, eat in the rougheries offer the smell of the ocean, plus seagulls hovering overhead, waiting to swipe a french fry.

Although the term is Massachusetts's, eat-in-the-rough values apply to the best Yankee seafood all along the coast. From the humblest clam stand in Connecticut to the grand dinner halls of Rhode Island and the dockside lobster pounds of Maine, New England's shoreline gastronomic pleasures are aggressively casual.

This T-shirt and cut-off cuisine is suitable for picnic tables and the bench seat of cars in parking lots. Its kitchen techniques are hardly more than frying, boiling, and steaming.

The heart of eat-in-the-rough country is the North Shore of Massachusetts: "the fried clam belt" (a term we've used with trepidation ever since a fashion-conscious listener once called a radio show to ask us where she could purchase her own fried clam belt). It was on the North Shore, in Essex, that Lawrence Woodman invented fried clams on July 3, 1916, to serve along with the Saratoga chips he sold at his raw bar.

To this day, Woodman's of Essex is Fried Clam Central. It is crowded, noisy, boisterous, with an indoor dining room and a tent out back, yet never enough tables for the summer hungries who swarm to it for platters piled higher-than-wide with mountains of fried clams and just about everything else that will fit into a Friolator: shrimp, scallops, oysters, fish, potatoes, and onion rings.

Woodman's clams are full and tender, their crust light gold, gently seasoned, just a wee bit oily; but for a short while in the early 1980s, even these heavenly squiggles of ocean nectar were surpassed by the clams dished out at the Clam Box in neighboring Ipswich.

The Clam Box was (and still is) a real charmer, built in 1938 to look exactly like a *clam box*, the trapezoidal cardboard container in which pints of fried clams are served to take-out customers. There was a boardwalk around the box, and over the years a small indoor eating area was added, but its architectural integrity remained.

When we discovered it nearly ten years ago, the Clam Box was run by Skip and Cindy Atwood, who knew a thing or two about frying clams. Before they sold the business, they gave us their recipe.

CLAM BOX FRIED CLAMS

Littlenecks or cherrystones taste fine, but they do not have the same ring-and-belly shape as the soft-shelled Ipswich clams used in all true clamatoria.

½ cup evaporated milk
¾ cup whole milk
1 egg
½ teaspoon vanilla extract
Dash salt and pepper

4 dozen freshly shucked clams
½ cup cake flour
1½ cups yellow cornmeal
Oil for frying

Combine evaporated and whole milk, egg, vanilla, salt, and pepper. Soak clams in liquid, then dredge clams in combination of cake flour and cornmeal, fluffing them in the flour mix for light but thorough coverage. Shake off excess flour.

Fry at 365–375° until golden brown and crisp, about 5 minutes. Do not crowd clams in oil. Drain on paper towels, salt to taste, and serve immediately with french fries, onion rings, and coleslaw.

Serves 4.

What the pig is to Southern cookery and the cow to Texas, so the clam is to coastal New England. Served fried or on the half shell, steamed, baked, stuffed, or broiled, or as the topping of a thin-crusted garlic-and-oil New Haven–style pizza, clams are the soul of shoreline Yankee cooking.

They are at their fullest glory in an old-fashioned clambake, an Indian ritual borrowed by hungry Pilgrims. A true clambake is defined less by specific ingredients than by primitive technique—food cooked over hot stones layered with seaweed. Clams, fish, and potatoes are tucked among the weed by a bakemaster, then covered with canvas and left to steam amidst the funky ocean plants for a few hours. Toward the end of the process, sweet corn (in the hull) is thrown in too.

A few restaurants (including Woodman's of Essex) manage to put together a modified clambake, cooked over wood instead of cumbersome stones, and usually including lobsters (not part of the original formula). One of our favorite stops for just such a modernized clambake is an open-air, summer-only establishment called the Place in Guilford, Connecticut. It is nothing more than an organized picnic, with tree stumps for chairs, construction spools for tables, and an open-air wood fire providing plenty of atmospheric smoke. The specialty of the Place is roasted littleneck clams, brushed with hot sauce, sweet corn on the side.

OPEN-AIR CLAMS

2 tablespoons butter
2 tablespoons olive oil
1 clove garlic, minced
1 onion, diced

½ cup ketchup
1 tablespoon horseradish
1 tablespoon Worcestershire
 sauce

5 drops Tabasco sauce, or more   2–3 dozen littleneck or
   to taste   cherrystone clams
Salt and pepper to taste

First, make sauce. Melt butter in saucepan, and add oil. Add garlic
and onion and sauté until soft. Stir in ketchup, horseradish,
Worcestershire, Tabasco, salt, and pepper. Adjust seasonings to
taste.

   Scrub clams in clean water and place on a wire rack over an
open wood or charcoal fire. As soon as the clams begin to open,
about 3–5 minutes, remove from fire and pry off top shell. Cut
clams free from shell, return to rack, brush with sauce, and roast
until sizzling, about 2 minutes.

Serves 4–6 as hors d'oeuvres.

The sloppiest, easiest way to cook and serve clams is to steam them.
Served warm and dripping moist in a large bowl, with accompanying
dishes of broth and melted butter, steamers are the preferred beginning
to any serious shore dinner. Some highfalutin restaurants, unsatisfied
with the briny savor of the clams' own juices, steam them in wine. That,
we assure you, is not the Yankee eat-in-the-rough way to go about it. Plain,
clear water (salt water, or salted fresh water if desired) allows the natural
smack of the clam to blossom without competition.

STEAMED CLAMS BY THE BUCKET

Although any small, relatively tender clam can be steamed, the
best steamed clams are made from the variety known in fish markets as steamers—technically soft-shell clams, although their
shells are actually very brittle. As an appetite-whetter to precede
a shoreline feast, about a dozen per person will suffice.

Clams   Melted butter
Salted water

Scrub clams with a brush and rinse. Repeat until clams are thoroughly clean. Discard any clams that aren't tightly closed.

   Place clams in a large kettle with about ½ inch of salted water
at the bottom. Cover kettle and simmer until clams open, 5–10

minutes. Remove from heat, discarding unopened clams. Serve immediately. Strain broth through cheesecloth and serve in a wide dish, suitable for dunking, alongside clams and a dish of melted butter, also for dunking. (Or you *might* want to try the recipe we found in *Secrets of New England Cooking* [1947], which calls for serving the clam broth garnished with a spoonful of salted whipped cream!)

South of prime fried clam territory, from Wood's Fish Pier in Plymouth, Massachusetts, to the Sand Bar in Saybrook, Connecticut, nearly every posted clam shack menu lists "stuffies." Stuffies are one step up the ladder of refinement from fried clams and steamers because they require a utensil.

They are made from quahog (say *co-hog*) clams, too big and tough to eat whole. The quahogs are scooped out, chopped up, mixed with some form of stuffing, then repacked in the shell. At the Common's lunchroom in Little Compton, Rhode Island, each stuffie is then topped with the other half of its shell, keeping the insides moist and warm. The more common way of serving stuffies at clam stands is to send them out the window on the half shell, with a plastic fork plunged into the clammy stuffing.

STUFFIES

12 large quahog clams	4 tablespoons butter
2 tablespoons minced onion	½ teaspoon prepared mustard
2 tablespoons minced green or red bell pepper	1 teaspoon minced parsley
⅓ cup minced celery	¾ cup cracker crumbs
	2 teaspoons lemon juice

Scrub and wash clams well. Steam them in a large covered pot with ½ inch of salted water. When clams open, 5–10 minutes, remove them from pot, reserving liquid. Strain liquid through cheesecloth to remove any grit.

Remove clams from shell. Wash and reserve shells. Chop clams fine.

In a large saucepan sauté onion, pepper, and celery in butter until tender. Add mustard, parsley, crumbs, chopped clams, lemon juice, and ½ cup of the strained clam juice. Stuff mixture into half shells and bake at 350° 20 minutes.

Makes 14–16 stuffies.

In the vicinity of Portland on the coast of Maine, a favorite way with clams—especially as a side dish to a boiled lobster—is clam *cakes*. Clam cakes take us even higher on the food chain than stuffies, because they are often served indoors at real restaurants (such as Cole Farms in Gray), and they are sturdy enough to require a utensil heavier than a plastic picnic fork.

That said, we must confess that our favorite clam cakes are the ones we enjoyed at the Two Lights Lobster Shack in Cape Elizabeth, as casual an eatery as any traveler could hope to find, overlooking a misty surf. The day we dined at Two Lights, eating in the rough meant that we had to compete for our dinner with saline breezes whipping in off the ocean. As we ate, lightening the weight on our cardboard plates, the wind would pick them off the picnic table and spirit them away, strewing fried clams across the rocky coastline. What a happy food fight that was; and you ought to know that all through it, as long as even a couple of bites of clam cake remained on the plate, that plate held fast in our camp.

PORTLAND-STYLE CLAM CAKES

2 cups shucked clams	½ cup milk
2 cups flour	¼ cup clam juice, strained
1 teaspoon baking powder	1 medium onion, diced fine
2 eggs, beaten	Butter and Crisco for frying

Reserve juice from clams and chop clams fine.

Sift flour and baking powder together. Add eggs, milk, and clam juice. Mix in clams and diced onion, and enough extra milk to yield a thick but pourable pancakelike batter.

Drop by heaping tablespoonfuls and fry in a skillet in equal amounts of butter and Crisco. When crisp and brown on one side, 3–4 minutes, flip and cook other side.

Makes 18–20 clam cakes.

Rhode Island has never heard of griddle-fried clam cakes. In the Ocean State clam cakes mean just one thing: balls of dough, laced with minced clam, deep fried and eaten with one's hands along with other fried food or chowder.

This geogastronomic fact supports our long-held contention that New England from Massachusetts south is the fried dough capital of America. Sure, you'll find baked goods—muffins, breads, and hermits—but the dough of choice, especially in Rhode Island and Connecticut, is always *fried*. Around Narragansett Bay, every shore dinner, large or small, is accompanied by clam cakes.

These fritters, sometimes served with a pitcher of maple syrup, lend unmistakable elegance to the concept of fried dough. Never mind that they are eaten by hand, usually out of a cardboard box or grease-stained paper bag: Clam cakes are the class of the dough world. Brittle-crusted, puffed up with baking powder, laced with pearlescent morsels of moist clam, they are fried in golf ball–size rounds, gnarled and knobby from the shock of the batter hitting hot oil.

RHODE ISLAND CLAM CAKES

2 teaspoons baking powder
2 cups sifted flour
2 eggs, beaten
⅔ cup milk
4 tablespoons butter, melted

2 cups chopped clams
¼ teaspoon salt
⅛ teaspoon pepper
Oil for deep frying

Combine baking powder, flour, eggs, milk, and butter and stir into a smooth, thick batter. Sprinkle clams with salt and pepper and stir them into batter. (A dash of clam juice may be added if batter is too thick to drop easily from a tablespoon.)

Heat oil in a deep fryer to 365°. Drop clam batter in by tablespoonfuls and fry 2–3 minutes, or until a rich golden brown.

Makes 24–28 clam cakes,
enough to serve 6–8.

Nobody in Rhode Island eats clam cakes as a solitary dish. They are an essential part of a shore dinner; and they are served with chowder as a down-size version of shore dinner known, with true Yankee logic, as "clam cakes and chowder." More than bacon and eggs or lox and bagels, clam cakes and chowder are an established, inseparable duo. Ocean State eaters regularly judge their seaside restaurants not on their clam cakes alone, nor on their chowder, but on their *clam cakes and chowder*. At the Rocky Point Park Shore Dinner Hall in Warwick, a section of the hall is reserved for people who come to eat only clam cakes and chowder.

Ah, but what kind of chowder are they having? Vast quantities of hot air are expended among Eastern gastronomes debating this unanswerable question: What constitutes proper clam chowder? So much of the argument has centered on the issue of tomatoes (do they or don't they belong in chowder?) that some other rather fine regional distinctions have been ignored.

The obvious difference is between New England and Manhattan

chowder. New England's is a simple milk or cream brew, made with salt pork, potatoes, and clams, but without even a hint of tomatoes. Manhattan's, which one irate Rhode Island chef described to us as "yesterday's vegetable soup with clams thrown in," is milkless, tomato-based, and spicy. Furthermore, it is often eaten in sit-down restaurants, rather than standing up outside an open-air shack. The distinction between the two is simple enough.

But the picture gets cloudy when you consider that many of Rhode Island's most esteemed chowderdromes sell a creamy pink-shaded chowder that has tomatoes *and* milk and is therefore true to neither definition. Furthermore, every Rhode Island clam cake and chowder restaurant sells a vast number of their clam cakes along with a fourth style of chowder, made with neither cream *nor* tomatoes. It is a bracing steel gray clam juice–based broth, made with not much more than salt pork, clams, and a few chopped potatoes. This salty stuff, according to chowder maven

Carolyn Wyman of New Haven, is true Rhode Island chowder. As far as we're concerned, it is the only right companion for clam cakes, its sharp ocean zip perfectly counterpointing the cakes' avoirdupois.

For an authentic Rhode Island recipe, we turned to an authority on native foods: Eleanor Dove, a Narragansett Indian and founder of the Dovecrest Restaurant in Arcadia, where the seminal connection between American Indian and Yankee cooking is expressed in a menu that offers some of each, and many dishes that are *both*.

DOVECREST QUAHOG CHOWDER

An elemental recipe. It can, of course, be jazzed up with any number of herbs and seasonings: rosemary, thyme, bay leaves, parsley, sherry. But we believe simplicity is this soup's charm.

¼ pound salt pork, diced
1 large onion, diced
2 large potatoes, diced
   (2 heaping cups)
2 cups water

2 cups very finely diced
   shucked quahog clams
2 cups clam juice
2 tablespoons butter

In a 1-gallon stockpot fry salt pork until fat is rendered. Add diced onion and cook until light brown. Add diced potatoes and just enough of the water to cover. Cook until potatoes are pierced easily with a fork. Add quahogs, clam juice, butter, and remaining water. Simmer 15–20 minutes.

Serves 4–6.

Note: This chowder tastes better when refrigerated overnight and reheated the next day.

Before getting on to other chowders, we will suggest an alternative to clam cakes as a companion to Eleanor Dove's soup: Rhode Island jonnycakes. They are another culinary subject to which controversy seems unduly attracted: How is jonnycake spelled? What is its etymology? Should jonnycakes be cooked thick or thin?

Some historians say they got their name because, once made, they stayed edible during a trip. Others speculate that they were called journey cakes because they were so quick and easy to make while one traveled. All that was needed was a bag of meal, water, and fire. Or if the travelers were in a fancy mood, they sometimes took a hint from native Indian chefs and mixed pumpkin pulp or squash into the batter.

Purists can buy granite-ground jonnycake meal from:

> Kenyon Corn Meal Company
> P.O. Box 221
> West Kingston, RI 02892
> (401) 783-4054

A five-pound bag is $6.25 plus shipping. We have found that Eleanor Dove's recipe works pretty well with white cornmeal from the supermarket shelf.

PRINCESS PRETTY FLOWER'S JONNYCAKES

1 cup white cornmeal
1 teaspoon sugar
¼ teaspoon salt
¾ cup *boiling hot* water

1 tablespoon butter, melted
2 tablespoons milk
Vegetable shortening to grease
   griddle

Combine cornmeal, sugar, and salt. Stir in boiling water quickly. Add melted butter and milk, stirring to form a batter that is thicker than pancake batter but a bit thinner than mashed potatoes. Let stand 3 minutes.

Grease griddle with shortening. (We recommend cooking jonnycakes on a lightly greased nonstick surface. Because they remain on the griddle 30 minutes, ordinary surfaces will require more oil, and the jonnycakes will be heavier.) With griddle on medium heat, drop batter by heaping tablespoonfuls. Smooth top of each patty with a knife, leaving them about ½ inch high. Cook 15 minutes. Turn and cook 15 minutes more.

Makes 8–10 small jonnycakes.

The other kind of Rhode Island chowder, a mongrel mix that nobody seems to want to talk about, is in fact an essential element in the most exemplary shore dinner hall: Rocky Point Park. The reason chowderhounds don't like to talk about it, we reckon, is that it has tomatoes; chowder with tomatoes has been so vilified and stereotyped that pink chowder chefs are afraid of being called New Yorkers.

This creamy bisquelike tomato/clam soup, unique to Rhode Island, is always served at shore dinners at the same time the clam cakes are brought out.

THE OTHER RHODE ISLAND CLAM CHOWDER

¼ pound salt pork, diced
1 onion, sliced
2 cups sliced potatoes
    (2 potatoes)
1–2 cups boiling water
2 cups chopped quahog clams
½ cup pulverized stewed
    tomatoes

⅛ teaspoon baking soda
1 cup milk
Salt and pepper to taste
2 tablespoons butter
Saltine crackers

Fry pork in a skillet until crisp. Remove pork, leaving fat. Fry onion in fat until soft, about 3 minutes. Pour fat and onion into stockpot. Add potatoes. Add enough boiling water to cover potatoes, and simmer until potatoes begin to soften.

Add chopped clams. Mix tomatoes and baking soda and add to stockpot. Simmer 5–10 minutes, until potatoes can be pierced easily with a fork. Add milk, bring to a simmer just long enough to heat through (but do not boil). Add salt and pepper. Swirl butter into soup to melt just before serving.

Saltine crackers should be put at bottom of each soup bowl, with chowder poured over them. Salt pork cracklings may be served as a garnish for soup.

Serves 4–6.

Heading north from Rhode Island there is no ambiguity about chowder. Inland, you might find corn chowder; and fish chowders abound, made with cod, salt cod, and (in some Portuguese fishing towns) pickled cod. But when it comes to clam chowder, no Down East chef will give you any argument about the following time-honored recipe we derived from the Union Oyster House (America's first restaurant) in Boston:

TRUE YANKEE CLAM CHOWDER

Old-timers speak of *building* a chowder, a reference to arcane formulas for heavyweight layered stews of salt pork, potatoes, fish, and crackers. This creamy classic is built around salt pork (all chowders' foundation), but without crackers in the soup, you can eat it with a spoon instead of a knife and fork.

2 large potatoes, diced (about 2 cups)	8 tablespoons butter
2 cups clam juice	4 tablespoons flour
2 cups chopped quahog clams	Salt, pepper, Worcestershire
¼ pound salt pork, diced fine	sauce, and Tabasco sauce
1 large onion, chopped (⅔ cup)	to taste
1 rib celery, diced (½ cup)	1½ cups milk, warmed
	1½ cups cream, warmed

Cook potatoes in clam juice until tender. Add clams and bring to a boil. Set aside.

In a heavy stockpot cook salt pork until rendered. Add onion and celery; sauté until soft. Melt in 4 tablespoons of the butter, then add flour slowly to create a roux. Stir over medium heat until flour mixture is a rich gold, about 3 minutes.

Add potato and clam mix, stirring until thickened. Add seasonings to taste. Stir in milk and cream and simmer very gently (but do not boil) 5–10 minutes. Remove from heat and allow chowder to become tepid. Heat up again when ready to serve, topping each bowl with an extra pat of butter, using remaining 4 tablespoons of butter.

Serves 4–6.

The penultimate eat-in-the-rough experience is a Maine lobster pound. It needn't be in Maine (although the majority of them are), and it doesn't have to be adjacent to the moorings of the lobster trawlers, but the basic point of a worthy lobster pound is the minimum distance (and short time) between the lobster skimming on its ocean floor and diners picking at its cooked carcass.

That is why we like lobster eating in locations like Beal's Lobster Pier in Southwest Harbor, Maine. Surrounding its picnic tables are lobster traps, hauled in for repair. Surrounding the pier on which the picnic tables sit are lobster boats, rocking easily in their berths for the night. The day's catch of lobsters, preceded by buckets of steamers or bowls of quahog chowder and followed by chunks of blueberry cake on paper plates, are boiled in seawater while you wait.

BLUEBERRY CAKE FOR AFTER LOBSTERS

8 tablespoons butter	½ teaspoon salt
1 cup sugar	¾ cup milk
1 egg	2 cups blueberries
2½ cups flour	2 teaspoons cinnamon
2½ teaspoons baking powder	1 teaspoon nutmeg

Preheat oven to 375°. Butter a 9 x 12-inch baking pan generously.

Cream 4 tablespoons of the butter thoroughly with ⅔ cup of the sugar. Beat in egg. Sift together 2 cups of the flour, baking powder, and salt. Add sifted ingredients alternately with milk, beating after each addition. Fold in berries.

Cream remaining 4 tablespoons of butter with remaining ⅓ cup of sugar. Combine remaining ½ cup of flour with cinnamon and nutmeg and mix into butter-sugar combination to form a crumbly topping.

Spoon batter into prepared pan and sprinkle crumb mixture on top.

Bake 35 minutes, until a cake tester comes out clean. Cool 10 minutes. Cut into squares while still warm.

Serves 6–8.

Nunan's of Cape Porpoise is a Quonset hut built for lobster eating, with sinks and rolls of paper towels placed in convenient locations along the wall. Its windows open onto marshland, but on cool nights they're closed and the room is warmed by a lineup of antique space heaters. Tables are rimmed, to catch lobster shells and juices. Lobsters are carried from the kitchen on metal trays, accompanied by a bag of potato chips, a roll, and a pat of butter. Soda or beer is supplied by a large refrigerator out in the open. "We're not frilly," Bertha Nunan says. Amen.

HOW TO COOK A LOBSTER

Bertha Nunan comes from a long line of lobster fishermen, and she claims that her lobsters taste better than others because she learned how to cook them from her lobsterman grandfather, Captain George Nunan. The technique is to put 2 inches of water in the bottom of the lobster pot, salt it generously, and bring it to a boil. Drop in the live lobster (or lobsters), put the lid on, and simmer them for exactly 20 minutes. Serve with drawn butter and, to cut the richness, a little dish of vinegar for an occasional dip. (If additional lobsters are to be made, Bertha advises, pour out the water, clean the pot, and start again with fresh, newly salted water.)

Cracking the shell and eating it is the only perfect way to have a lobster; so we probably ought to stop at that. But we won't, because there is one other pretty wonderful eat-in-the-rough dish that lobster fanciers with jaded palates ought to know about. That is a rarity called the hot lobster roll.

HOT LOBSTER ROLL

Having enjoyed them for years in our home state, at Jimmie's of Savin Rock and Abbott's Lobster in the Rough (at Noank Harbor), we thought hot lobster rolls were unique to Connecticut. Every lobster roll we had encountered elsewhere was an awful lobster *salad* roll, in which the sweet pure lobster meat was gunked up with mayonnaise, camouflaged behind lettuce and celery, and hidden under a spongy bun. Yuk!

Then one day, while driving north up the coast, we discovered the Maine Diner in Wells, specializing in an item that the menu immodestly described as "FANTASTIC." Sure enough, it was a hot lobster roll, as we have come to love it in Connecticut—nothing more than large chunks of warm, fresh-picked lobster meat, bathed in butter, piled into a grilled frankfurter bun, chips and pickle on the side.

It is easy to make this golden drippy bun of luxury. Brush the inside of an ordinary store-bought frankfurter roll with plenty of butter and grill it on a griddle or skillet until golden brown. Remove it to a plate, toasted side up. Then melt a few more tablespoons of butter in the pan and briefly sauté about half the meat (large, whole chunks preferred) from a cooked 1–1¼-pound lobster. Pile the meat into the bun and try to eat it.

Impossible! If you have used enough butter, the drippy lobster meat will quickly soak into the bun. That, plus the meat's weight, nearly dissolves the bread to the point that eating the sandwich becomes a matter of picking, slurping, mopping, and licking, i.e., lobster eating without the fuss of the shell.

The top of the line eat-in-the-rough experience is a Rhode Island shore dinner hall. Once common along the shore of Narragansett Bay, true shore dinner halls have become mementos of a nearly vanished way of plowing into food—with unbounded gusto.

Our favorite location for shore dinner is the pristine little dining room at Aunt Carrie's, on the beach between Point Judith and Narragansett. Half of Aunt Carrie's is an open-air clam shack, selling pints and platters to sun worshipers and denizens of the parking lot.

The other half is an indoor dining room overlooking the beach. There aren't more than a dozen tables, plain aged wood. The staff of waitresses dresses all in white, like nurses. Although it is swept by ocean breezes, this room has a protected aura about it, a quiet that makes it look more like a snapshot from the 1940s than a three-dimensional restaurant. Along with such outré items as "peas and mashed potatoes" and "homemade bread and butter" (heavy-crusted cinnamon bread), the menu offers "Rhode Island Shore Dinner." It includes chowder, clam cakes, steamers, broiled fillet of sole, sweet corn, a lobster, brown bread and butter, and a choice of desserts: watermelon, ice cream, or Indian pudding.

Indian pudding is as old-fashioned as a clambake, a dark duff with centuries of character in every rough-grained spoonful. All recipes for it are pretty much the same. The significant variable is the darkness of the molasses. Light molasses yields a custardy porridge. Use blackstrap molasses and you get a pungent, crusty pudding like they make at Durgin-Park in Boston. (True homestyle Indian pudding is baked in the brick oven adjacent to the center chimney. It is put in the oven midday Saturday to be ready for Sunday breakfast.)

INDIAN PUDDING

½ cup molasses
¼ cup dark brown sugar
2 eggs
Dash salt

¼ teaspoon baking soda
5 cups milk
⅔ cup yellow cornmeal
4 tablespoons butter

Preheat oven to 300°. In a large saucepan mix together molasses, brown sugar, eggs, salt, baking soda, and 3 cups of the milk. Bring to a boil and add cornmeal slowly, stirring constantly. When fully mixed and thick, stir in butter, then remaining 2 cups of milk until blended. Pour into a well-oiled 2½-quart casserole set in a larger pan of water and bake, uncovered, 1 hour. Reduce heat to 275° and bake 4–6 more hours, until crusty brown, adding hot water to larger pan to maintain level.

Serve warm, with a scoop of vanilla ice cream on top.

Serves 8–10.

BAR FOOD

ar food has a bad reputation because most of it appears to be floating in formaldehyde; you have to be pretty drunk to find glass crocks filled with pickled hard-boiled eggs appetizing. Nouvelle bar food, such as defrosted potato skins, is no improvement. Anyone more interested in eating than drinking stays away from taverns. After all, people who forgather for the purpose of swilling mugs of suds are unlikely to care about the virtue of angel food cake.

The mid-Atlantic states are an exception, where some of the best authentic regional food is available exclusively in places devoted to drinks. There is nothing low-down or mean about these establishments. Most are neighborhood taverns set up to serve the solidest of citizens. At Schwabl's in West Seneca, New York, where they specialize in bar food like chicken wings and beef on weck, the menu boasts, "We cater to a nice homey family trade."

From upstate New York to St. Marys County, Maryland, the taverns of the East are sanctuaries for culinary traditions that have no other place to go. Not fine enough to be served at home or in a restaurant, the bar food in which they specialize constitutes a ragtag cuisine of snacks and sandwiches, crab cakes and stuffed ham.

In Buffalo, if you want local specialties, head for the Anchor Bar or Eckl's. You cannot imagine eating what they serve without quaffing great quantities of American beer, or (on Saturday night) highballs and lowballs, old-fashioneds and Rob Roys. These beer and beef taverns are treasuries of Eisenhower-era food and drink, laden with local color.

Their decor is knotty wood panels and decorative rugs showing twelve-point bucks and poker-playing bulldogs. Stout men in leisure slacks converse with ladies in doubleknit pantsuits of springlike pastels, their hair sculpted into firm frosted crowns. Waitresses favor textured white nylon uniforms; bartenders and hosts wear the short, shiny jackets of a barber or dentist. Among the staff, name tags are popular, especially name tags dolled up with a pipe cleaner poodle pin or a flowery hanky.

In this straight-shooting part of the world, beef was never dethroned from its preeminent place as The Only Good Food. At Eckl's or Schwabl's, or a dozen other taverns in the Buffalo area, the specialty is the sandwich known as "beef on weck." "Weck" is the abbreviation for kummelweck, a salt-encrusted caraway seed–flavored hard roll. The roll is cut, dipped in juice, then wrapped around a couple of inches of rosy red thin-sliced roast beef.

Purveyors of beef on weck all work from the same basic formula; competition is based on subtle variation. Hand slicing—when the sandwich is ordered—is crucial if a beef house is to be taken seriously; and natural gravy is *de rigueur*. At Eckl's, which is listed in the yellow pages as "Eckl's Beef & Weck Restaurant," the meat is outstanding: no chemical tenderizers, no cryonautic meat malarkey. Just a great haunch of cow, slow roasted to perfection.

If you are preparing beef on weck for a crowd (a good idea, considering it seems a bit self-involved to make a roast entirely for oneself), we recommend following the example of Schwabl's in West Seneca, where the beef is set out in a prominent place and sliced with panache for all to see. With a sharp carving knife and a pile of salty rolls, this makes a grand centerpiece for a party.

BEEF ON WECK ROAST BEEF

Use your favorite roast beef—even the best. A standing rib roast or chateaubriand makes great beef for sandwiches. Rump or eye of round is good, too. If using a rump or eye of round roast, do not cook it much beyond rare or it will toughen.

Eye of round roast, 4–6
    pounds, at room
    temperature

Salt and ground black pepper
Flat beer

Preheat oven to 500°. Place roast on a rack, fat side up, in a shallow, lightly greased pan. Rub well with salt and pepper. Place in oven. Reduce heat to 350° immediately and roast until rare. Baste with flat beer. Time will vary depending on thickness of roast: 20 minutes per pound for a thick one, as little as 10 for a thin one. If in doubt, ask your butcher, or use a reliable meat thermometer; 135° is rare, just about right for beef on weck sandwiches.

Remove roast from oven and allow to settle.

Taste the natural juices in the roasting pan. Add salt and pepper to taste, so that kummelweck rolls can be dipped in the juice (if desired) before sandwiching the beef.

Slice roast thin, with a very sharp knife.

*Makes enough beef for 10–12
hefty sandwiches.*

Now the weck. It must be spongy enough to sop the gravy, yet tough enough to stay intact. Kummelweck rolls are shockingly salty—big salt patches stuck all over their tops like a pretzel. That's the way Buffalonians like it, perhaps because it goes so well with beer.

GIANT WECK ROLLS FOR BEEF SANDWICHES

2 packages dry yeast
1½ cups tepid potato water (110°) (save water when you boil potatoes)
2 teaspoons sugar
1 cup mashed potatoes
1 cup milk
8 tablespoons butter, melted

2 teaspoons salt
2 tablespoons caraway seeds
7–8 cups flour
1 egg white, beaten with 1 tablespoon water
Coarse salt to taste
Caraway seeds for sprinkling on top

Mix yeast with ½ cup of the potato water and sugar.

Combine mashed potatoes, remaining cup of potato water, milk, butter, salt, and caraway seeds. When yeast mixture is foamy, stir it in. Add 7 cups of the flour, cup by cup, stirring until dough comes away from bowl. Turn out onto a floured board and let rest while you clean and butter bowl.

Knead dough 10 minutes, adding flour if necessary to create a smooth dough. Return to bowl and roll dough around to coat it with butter. Cover and let rise in a warm place until double in bulk, about 2 hours.

Punch down dough, knead again 1–2 minutes. Roll out and divide into 12 pieces. Form each piece into a smooth ball. Then flatten ball slightly so that it's roll-shaped. Set 2 inches apart on lightly greased cookie sheet. Cover loosely with towel and let rise until double in bulk, less than 1 hour.

Preheat oven to 375°. Brush rolls with egg white mixture and sprinkle with desired amount of coarse salt and caraway seeds. Bake 15 minutes. Reduce heat to 325° and bake 15–20 minutes more, until rolls are medium brown. Remove from oven and cool on baking rack.

Makes 12 giant rolls.

If you're not a beef on weck eater, Schwabl's will set you up with another upstate sandwich: ham. Ham a New York specialty? You bet, when served as it is here, in a pool of sweet-and-sour red tomato gravy redolent of cloves, on a pallet of white bread, with pungent warm potato salad on the side.

WEST SENECA HAM SANDWICH SAUCE

Start with a boiled ham, at room temperature. Slice it thin (by hand) and spread it across 2 square slices of supermarket white bread for each serving. Then ladle on plenty of this sweet-smelling sauce.

4 scallions, including some of the green tops, sliced thin	1 cup apple cider
4 tablespoons butter	¼ cup brown sugar
2 tablespoons flour	1 tablespoon tomato paste
¼ cup cider vinegar	⅛ teaspoon ground cloves

Sauté scallions in butter until tender. Stir in flour until thoroughly mixed. Add vinegar, cider, sugar, and tomato paste. Add cloves. Simmer until thick, about 5 minutes, adding more cider if too thick. Serve warm, spooned over open-faced ham sandwiches.

Makes 1⅓ cups,
enough for 4 sandwiches.

BUFFALONIAN HOT POTATO SALAD

Hot potato salad, served on the side of ham sandwiches at Schwabl's, is winter fare that goes well with pork roasts and whole hams too.

6 medium boiling potatoes	1 egg, beaten
2 hard-boiled eggs, chopped	4 tablespoons vinegar
4 slices thick-cut bacon, cut into 1-inch lengths	1 teaspoon dry mustard
¼ cup minced onion	1½ teaspoons salt

Boil potatoes until pierced easily with a fork. Drain, peel, and dice while still warm. Mix in chopped hard-boiled eggs.

Fry bacon with onion until cooked but not crisp. Remove bacon and onion with slotted spoon and add to potatoes. Reserve bacon fat.

Beat warm bacon fat gradually into beaten egg. Then beat in vinegar, dry mustard, and salt. Combine with potato mixture.

Serve warm, with an ice cream dipper, on top of the pool of West Seneca Ham Sandwich Sauce (preceding recipe).

Serves 6–8.

A few years ago, nobody outside Buffalo had heard of Buffalo chicken wings; but this did not matter to Buffalonians, whose passionate loyalties to one wingery or another show just how strongly they feel about what is, for the rest of the country, peripheral bar food.

It was Teressa Bellissimo of the Anchor Bar who invented them one night in 1964 when her son Dom and a bunch of his hungry friends came into the tavern for something to eat. Teressa didn't have anything but wings, which she was saving for soup. So she improvised . . . and Buffalo chicken wings were born.

Teressa's wings became an Anchor Bar attraction every Friday. They were halved, sopped in a melted butter hot sauce, deep fried, and served with bleu cheese dressing and celery stalks to cool the tongue.

Their popularity spread to other upstate New York taverns, to the extent that now all a tavern owner need do is put a sign in the window announcing "Wings," and everybody knows exactly what he means: the same Anchor Bar configuration of miniaturized drumsticks in their hot sauce, with cool bleu dressing and celery on the side. Wings still reign supreme at the Anchor Bar, where the Bellissimos go through over thirteen tons a month.

BUFFALO CHICKEN WINGS

Most taverns offer wings mild or hot, with extra sauce on the side, if requested. They come in a small wooden bowl capped with a second wooden bowl (for bones), and the dressing is served in a white paper cup, into which one can dip either celery or wings. Buffalo wings are easy to make and fun to eat. They should be fried just before serving.

24 chicken wings, rinsed and patted dry
5 tablespoons butter
2–3 tablespoons bottled Louisiana-style hot sauce (Tabasco, etc.)
Oil for deep frying

Paprika
Celery sticks
Bleu cheese dressing (bottled supermarket variety is fine; or make your own— following recipe)

With a butcher's cleaver hack wings in half at joint. Discard tips. Place wings in a bowl.

Melt butter in a saucepan. Add hot sauce, stirring until well mixed. (Start with 2 tablespoons and taste; 3 tablespoons makes a very hot sauce.)

Pour hot sauce over wings. Stir thoroughly to make sure wings are coated. Let sit 30 minutes, stirring occasionally.

Heat oil to 365°. Fry wings 5–6 minutes, until crisp and golden. Drain on paper towels. Sprinkle with paprika. Serve with celery and bleu cheese dressing. (If desired, extra hot sauce can be made by combining more melted butter and hot sauce.)

Serves 4–6 as hors d'oeuvres.

ICONOCLASTIC BLEU CHEESE DRESSING

We have yet to eat bleu cheese dressing in a Buffalo bar that tasted any different from what comes in bottles from the supermarket shelf. Fine. And yet we must confess that there are times when a certain gourmet itch leads us to make this tangier companion to wings (also good on top of green salads).

1 cup yogurt
1 tablespoon wine vinegar
1 teaspoon sugar

Juice of ½ lemon
1 clove garlic, minced fine
½ cup crumbled bleu cheese

Combine all ingredients thoroughly except bleu cheese. Fold in cheese gently, so as to keep it lumpy.

Makes enough dressing for 4 orders of wings.

"Stop in any bar in Binghamton," Roadfooder Joe Manning wrote us six years ago, "and ask for spiedies. I think you'll like what you find." Although we had no idea what he was referring to, we had gotten some pretty hot tips from Joe in the past (including one that led to the best grinder in Connecticut), so we were on our way to Binghamton.

We cruised through the Polish and Ukrainian parts of town, noting a sign advertising a weekend special on "spiedie sticks" in the window of a hardware store. It was spring, and the stoops of the homes were populated with women in housecoats, enjoying the good weather. Among the rows of solid homes, we found a neighborhood tavern named Sharkey's. Men sat at the bar, some of them fresh from the barber shop next door, their broad pink necks newly denuded. Women in support hose had staked out a center table and sat together debating orthopedic insoles. And the smell of charcoal grilling lamb filled the air.

Spiedi, we later learned, means "stick" in Italian. Binghamton spiedies (pronounced *speedies*) are chunks of meat (beef, pork, or—most often —lamb) that are marinated in vinegar and herbs, threaded onto skewers, and roasted over charcoals.

Most taverns in town have their own recipe for spiedie sauce, its flavors reflecting whether the cook is Italian, Greek, Ukrainian, or Polish. When you are served spiedies at Sharkey's, you are given a basket of sliced French bread, which is designed to be used as an edible hot mitt for deskewerizing the meat and getting the whole fistful sandwich into one hand (so the other hand is free to lift your mug of beer).

If you want to make true Binghamtonian spiedies, send away for a "Spiedie Survival Kit" (marinade plus spiedie sticks) to:

Rob Salamida Company
133 Washington Avenue
Endicott, NY 13760
(607) 785-4391

Or make your own marinade, as follows:

SPIEDIES

Spiedies require a good long soak in their marinade. We recommend a full 4 hours, or even overnight.

¾ cup olive oil
½ cup red wine
½ cup red wine vinegar
4 cloves garlic, minced fine
1 teaspoon freshly ground
    pepper

1 teaspoon thyme
½ teaspoon allspice
3 fresh mint leaves, crushed
1 bunch fresh parsley
2 pounds lamb, cut into 1-inch
    chunks

Combine all marinade ingredients and pour over lamb. Toss to coat all pieces and cover. Chill at least 4 hours, rearranging meat occasionally so it all soaks equally.

Thread on metal skewers and cook over charcoals about 8 minutes.

Serve on skewers, with thinly sliced French bread.

Serves 6–8 as hors d'oeuvres.

When we lived in New Haven, Connecticut, we owned a bulldog but were not especially rah-rah in any other way. In fact, we never set foot inside the Yale stadium. But we did enjoy an undying romance with a tavern named George and Harry's, the place Yalies used to go for a beer and a square meal.

There were two George and Harry's, one of which was beautifully decorated with carved wood and stained glass windows of *Lux et Veritas* crests. The other one (our place) served booze and real food and was almost magical in its aversion to modernity. For a decade, its storefront window displayed the same scene: a row of empty gallon liquor bottles and plastic flowers gray with dust. The old square clock on the wall ticked away, the toothpick dispenser was refilled but never replaced, and the green leather booths took on a gleam from the friction of a million Ivy League behinds.

One of the things we loved about George and Harry's was that even if there was only one customer in the place, the kitchen staff hustled as if they were preparing the president's inaugural dinner. In the somnambulistic darkness of the old tavern, their pace was set by a pint-size counterman named Angelo.

Angelo was a romancer of all the food he served. No matter what appeared at the kitchen window, it was always cause for rhapsody. Crooning about the deliciousness and magnificence of the lamb stew (every Thursday) or chicken Maryland (Tuesday), he sounded on the verge of tears, like a father at an only daughter's wedding.

When Angelo saw us walk in the door, he called out, "Two Greeks!" The call referred not to us but to our order for two Greek salads. Although many Greek-run kitchens make it, we think this one is definitive.

GEORGE AND HARRY'S GREEK SALAD

It was possible to customize a "Greek" at George and Harry's by asking them to omit the anchovies, but it seemed almost sadistic to do so. Angelo's cry of "Greek—no anchovies" would set the chef spinning on his heels, looking frantically around the kitchen, as if for some ancient anchovy-extraction tool to remove the fish from our platters.

Salad

Equal mix of iceberg lettuce and escarole, torn into bite-size shreds
1 tomato, cut into wedges

½ green bell pepper, seeded and diced
½ red onion, sliced translucent-thin

6–10 Kalamata olives
4 ounces feta cheese, crumbled
    coarse

4 anchovy fillets

Dressing

½ cup olive oil
2 tablespoons red wine vinegar
1 teaspoon salt
½ teaspoon coarse-ground
    black pepper

½ teaspoon dry mustard
1 teaspoon oregano
1 clove garlic, crushed
Dash sugar

Arrange salad ingredients on a wide oval plate, with anchovy fillets in a parallel pattern across the top. Mix dressing ingredients and pour over salad. Serve with a dinner roll and a pat of butter.

Serves 2.

When Angelo saw that we were just about through with the Greek salads, he reached into the glass-fronted dessert case for two custard cups. How he loved to serve caramel custard! He grabbed a small knife reserved for custard loosening only and ran it into the cup between china and custard. Then he put a saucer on top, inverted the cup, and shook them together like a bartender with a shakerful of hooch. When he had pumped enough, he set it down, saucer on the bottom, and with a dramatic flourish, lifted off the cup. Caramel sauce spilled out as the cup rose, drenching a perfect thimble of smooth ivory custard, quivering in the center of the saucer. "Beooootiful," Angelo intoned, "two carmelacustas."

CARMELACUSTA

To make caramel custard the George and Harry's way, you need individual custard cups. It can also be made in a single mold, if desired.

5 egg yolks
1 cup sugar
½ teaspoon vanilla extract

Dash salt
1½ cups whole milk
1 cup evaporated milk

Preheat oven to 350°. Place a pan of water in oven. The pan should be large enough to hold 4 custard cups.

☞

Beat together yolks, ½ cup of the sugar, vanilla, and salt. Scald whole milk and evaporated milk and stir very slowly into egg mixture.

Melt remaining ½ cup of sugar in a heavy skillet over medium heat until it caramelizes. Pour it into 4 6-ounce custard cups and swirl it around to coat bottom and sides. Pour custard mixture on top of sauce. Place custard cups in pan of preheated water in oven. Bake 35–40 minutes, or until a sharp knife inserted into center of custard comes out clean. Chill until ready to serve.

To serve, run a knife around sides of custard, shake, and unmold onto a saucer.

Makes 4 6-ounce custards.

The closing of George and Harry's saddened but did not surprise us. It was a shot-and-a-beer relic in a world of blow-dry "gathering places" serving funny-named drinks made with ice cream. We never expected to have an honest tavern meal again. Then in 1984 we wandered into Brandy Pete's in Boston.

Brandy Pete's began as a pool hall and was bought in 1935 by "Brandy Pete" Sabia, whose wife made spaghetti dinners to sell with his bootleg booze. Pete is dead, and they've had to change locations, but Pete's son Joe runs the place just as it has been run for half a century.

The saloon is overseen by a portrait of Pete declaring, "The customer is always wrong." Its clientele is a mix of financial district types and peripheral characters who look as if their mothers' milk might have been on draft. The staff of waitresses is of the combat-ready school of service: Don't try to give them any lip, unless you want a thumb in your mashed potatoes.

The cuisine is hot lunch deluxe: turkey and dressing, pot roast and gravy, fish cakes and baked beans. And a wonderful Pete specialty listed on the menu as "gravy meat and spaghetti." This dowdy rib-sticker is a big plate of well-cooked spaghetti noodles topped with a mountain of fall-apart tender pot roast in sweet tomato sauce.

GRAVY MEAT AND SPAGHETTI

6 cloves garlic, diced as fine as
  possible
1 cup chopped onion
2 cups canned whole tomatoes,
  drained
1 cup tomato paste
1 cup tomato sauce
½ cup water

1 teaspoon ground black
  pepper
1 tablespoon salt
2 pounds boneless chuck roast
¼ cup sugar
12–14 ounces spaghetti
Olive oil

Combine garlic, onion, tomatoes, tomato paste, tomato sauce, water, pepper, and salt. Bring to a boil in a pan large enough to hold roast. When boiling, add roast and reduce to a simmer. Cover. Simmer 3½ hours, stirring every 30 minutes to keep roast from scorching on bottom.

Remove roast. Add sugar to sauce in pan and simmer another 30 minutes.

Cook spaghetti in boiling salted water until tender. Drain and add enough olive oil to keep it from being sticky.

Arrange spaghetti on a plate, top with slices of roast, then top roast with gravy.

Serves 6.

Rhode Island has us stumped. Why is it called Rhode *Island* when it is fully attached on three sides to the rest of the country? How can it be that this smallest state in the union is the easiest (for us, anyway) to get hopelessly lost in, wandering for hours without seeing civilization? And what explains all the enormous restaurants specializing in meals that look as if they were scaled for Gargantua?

Archie's Tavern, for example, is approximately twenty times larger than any other tavern you have ever seen. It is a tavern/eating hall, where Rhode Islanders gather en masse to put on the feed bag in a manner unheard of outside the Ocean State. The specialty of the house is a "neanderthal caveman cut" prime rib, of which the menu boasts, "We serve over two tons every week!" An order of pork chops consists of three. You can get "hungry man's porterhouse," the "large Italian platter," or family-style chicken served in vast platters to long communal tables.

The host patrols the multiple dining rooms wearing a pink jacket and a white carnation, just like at the Junior Prom. When he came our way we flashed him our brightest smiles, trying to conceal chipmunk cheeks full of yeasty cinnamon rolls (doled out to tables by the basketful).

RHODE ISLAND CINNAMON ROLLS

Years ago, Rhode Islander Frank Muhly pointed out that we ought to investigate what he called the "chicken-with-a-cinnamon-sweet-roll-on-the-side sweepstakes," an undeclared competition among Rhode Island's chicken dinner halls. At Archie's Tavern the rolls are served with family-style chicken, as with every dinner in the house. They are baked fresh, every hour, so they always arrive warm at the table.

1 package dry yeast	6 tablespoons butter, melted
¼ cup plus 1 teaspoon granulated sugar	1 teaspoon salt 3–3½ cups flour
¼ cup tepid water (110°)	½ cup brown sugar
½ cup warm milk	1 teaspoon cinnamon
2 eggs	

Dissolve yeast and 1 teaspoon of the granulated sugar in water. Dissolve remaining ¼ cup of sugar in warm milk. Add eggs and 4 tablespoons of the melted butter. Mix salt into flour. Stir milk mixture into 2½ cups of the flour. Add yeast mixture, stirring vigorously. Turn out onto a floured board and let rest while you clean and butter bowl.

Knead dough just long enough for it to become smooth, adding up to ½ cup of flour as needed (no more than 2–3 minutes are required). Cover dough with cloth. Let dough rest on board 10 minutes, then knead again 5 minutes. Return to bowl, cover, and let rise until double in bulk, about 2 hours.

Punch down dough and roll it out on a lightly floured board in an 11 x 14-inch rectangular shape, about ⅜ inch thick. Brush with remaining 2 tablespoons of melted butter, leaving a little butter to brush tops of rolls. Mix brown sugar and cinnamon and spread over dough, patting it with your hand. Roll dough up into a long tube like a jelly roll and use a serrated knife and quick, sure strokes to cut it into 1-inch slices. Place slices on buttered cookie sheet, brush with butter, cover with towel, and let rise until round and puffy, about 1 hour.

Preheat oven to 375°. Bake 15 minutes, or until golden brown. Remove and cool buns on a rack.

Makes 12 rolls.

Even the humblest clam shack in Rhode Island will likely list snails on its menu. Not smelly *escargots*, but clean, cool conch, either sliced or chopped in a zesty marinade. At Archie's, buy them as an appetizer and you get what seems like a full quart. They are sliced thin, served on top of lettuce with Tabasco sauce on the side. Their marinade has a strong Mediterranean punch.

SNAIL SALAD

½ pound conch out of shell, or
    8 conch in shell
½ cup olive oil
¼ cup lemon juice
1 teaspoon dried oregano, or 1
    tablespoon fresh, minced

2 cloves garlic, halved
Salt and pepper to taste
Lettuce leaves

If using conch in the shells, boil 3 minutes in salted water, then remove meat from shells and discard soft entrails. Simmer meat 20–25 minutes in salted water. Cool and slice thin.

    Whisk together oil and lemon juice, adding oregano, garlic,

salt, and pepper. Add conch. Cover and chill 4–8 hours. Discard garlic.

Serve spooned atop lettuce leaves with toothpicks or small forks on side.

Serves 8 as hors d'oeuvres.

ALL-YOU-CAN-EAT CHICKEN

The best chicken dinners in Rhode Island differ from those in the Midwest and South in that the chicken isn't fried in lard. It *is* skillet cooked, but there is no batter, and the medium is butter. The result is pure butter-flavored sautéed chicken—drippingly juicy, with a crisp skin but no crust.

3 whole chicken breasts, cut in half
Salt and pepper to taste

6 tablespoons butter
½ cup chicken broth

Preheat oven to 375°. Wash and dry chicken. Sprinkle each piece with salt and pepper.

Melt butter in a large skillet with a cover. Place breasts in butter skin side down and fry over medium heat. Turn after 2 minutes. Turn again after 2 more minutes. Continue turning as chicken turns light gold. (Use gentle tongs, so as not to pierce the chicken as you turn it.)

After 10 minutes, cover pan and place in oven. Bake 15 minutes. When a thermometer inserted into breasts reads 140°, chicken is done.

Remove breasts with slotted spoon and place on serving platter. Return skillet to top of stove over medium-high heat. Add chicken broth. Bring to boil and simmer 2–3 minutes. Pour over chicken.

Serves 4–6.

Tavern hopping is essential for any eater who wants to taste the specialties of St. Marys County, Maryland, between the Chesapeake Bay and the Potomac. To drive this land of river coves, tobacco fields, and old plantation homes is to enter another century.

Stop in a tavern like Hill's Club in Mechanicsville or the Willows in Leonardtown and you encounter a way of life in which the pub is the heart of social life. Not just for beerhounds and barflies, but for people as upright as the town priest (whom we watched at the Willows, having lunch with five ladies from his congregation).

As in Virginia to the west, the pillars of St. Marys country cuisine are crab and ham: hard crabs from the bay and cured country ham, aged and smoked until it develops elegant piquance. Ham connoisseurs prefer the old, rank hams; and so it is that autumn has become the time for ham stuffing—a full year after the hogs are slaughtered and the hams hung up to cure.

The idea of stuffing ham—like so much Southern cooking—came about as the slaves' way of decorating the second-rate parts of the hog they were relegated. They stuffed jowls and ears with turnip greens or kale; the result was so good that the technique worked its way up the social ladder to the dearest of pig parts, the whole ham.

Ham stuffing is a ritual for which every St. Marys County tavern seems to have its own special recipe. In Mechanicsville, at Hill's Halfway House, the ham contains a center core of crunchy, high-spiced greens; at Hill's Club (next door, but no relation), the greens are soft and oily; while at Copsey's, just up the road, the ham is stuffed with small pockets of kale and cabbage and is not the least bit spicy. Karla Keller of Courtney's, on the water in Ridge, told us her mother's recipe (which she makes only between September and March) uses cabbage and is *very* spicy.

ST. MARYS COUNTY SPICY STUFFED HAM

Because of the expense of a whole country ham, as well as the considerable amount of work involved in stuffing one, we recommend this as a centerpiece for a special occasion party. To order country ham by mail, see page 163; or for an authentic Maryland-cured country ham (hickory smoked, sugar cured), contact:

Roy L. Hoffman & Sons
Route 6
Box 5
Hagerstown, MD 21740
(301) 739-2332

1 country ham (about 15 pounds)
2 cups finely chopped kale
2 cups finely shredded cabbage
3 cups washed and coarsely chopped spinach
½ cup finely chopped scallions
½ cup finely chopped celery

6 tablespoons butter
½ teaspoon cayenne pepper
½ teaspoon ground black pepper
½ teaspoon dry crushed red pepper
½ teaspoon salt

Cover ham completely with water and soak at least 12 hours. Change water, and bring to a boil. Simmer ham 1 hour. Remove from water, allow to cool. Cut off rind and all but a thin (⅛-inch) layer of fat.

Put 2–3 inches of water in a large stockpot and bring to a boil. Add kale, cabbage, and spinach, reduce heat to lowest possible setting, cover, and simmer 4–5 minutes, until greens become limp. Drain in a colander.

In a saucepan large enough for greens, sauté scallions and celery in butter until soft. Add cooked greens and seasonings. Stir until mixed.

Cut 10 4-inch-deep pockets all around ham with a sharp knife. Have a helper pull apart each hole so you can stuff it with greens. Wrap the ham thoroughly in a double layer of cheesecloth and sew cloth together tightly.

Put ham in a large pot, cover with water, and bring to a boil. Reduce heat, cover pot, and simmer 3 hours. (Make sure ham is covered fully with water as it simmers.)

Remove ham from water and allow to cool. Refrigerate overnight, still in cheesecloth. Remove from refrigerator, remove cheesecloth, and allow ham to reach room temperature. Serve in very thin slices.

Serves 20.

Every eatery that sells stuffed ham in the cool weather also offers crab cakes year round; but until we hit the tavern trail, we had never met a crab cake we liked. In other parts of the country, crab cakes seem like a sly method of extending a few threads of crab, via wads of bready stuffing. But the bar food crab cakes of St. Marys County are plush patties of aromatic crab, bound together in a gossamer web and grilled until crusty brown.

One of our favorite crab cake stops is Copsey's on Route 5, where whole crab feasts (crack them yourself) are dished out on tables topped with brown wrapping paper, accompanied by pitchers full of beer. Mrs. Copsey stuffs a fine ham; her son was the 1980 oyster shucking champion; and she told us that 90 percent of the restaurants in the county buy their seafood from the Copsey family fish business. So you can see these people know a thing or two about local culinary specialties. Mrs. Copsey's crab cakes are sweet and creamy textured with a buttery crust.

BEAUTIFUL SWIMMER CRAB CAKES

Do not crush the hunks of crabmeat any more than mixing demands. The larger they are, the juicier and crabbier the cake.

½ cup pulverized cracker
   crumbs
1 pound lump crabmeat, free
   of shell
1 tablespoon mayonnaise
1 tablespoon cream
1 tablespoon prepared mustard

1 egg, beaten
1 tablespoon minced parsley
1 teaspoon white pepper
½ teaspoon salt
½ teaspoon Worcestershire
   sauce
Butter

Mix crumbs into crabmeat. Combine mayonnaise, cream, mustard, egg, parsley, pepper, salt, and Worcestershire. Add to crabmeat and stir only enough to blend. Shape mixture between your hands into 6 hamburgerlike patties.

Heat 4–6 tablespoons of butter in a large skillet. Set crab cakes in hot butter and sauté about 3 minutes on each side, until crisp and brown. If cooking crab cakes in batches, add more butter for second batch.

Serves 6.

Cakes are a way of accentuating the palliative possibilities of crabmeat; soup shows another potential—the ability of crab to hold its own as the central character in a fiery mélange. Maryland crab soup is bright orange, pepper hot, and thick as gumbo.

FIERCE CRAB SOUP

1 medium onion, chopped
½ green bell pepper, chopped
4 tablespoons butter
4 cups fish stock (clam juice may be substituted if no fish stock can be had)
¼ cup rice
1 large tomato, peeled and diced

½ teaspoon Worcestershire sauce
1 pound lump crabmeat, free of shell
2 teaspoons chili powder
½ pound fresh okra, sliced
½ teaspoon sugar
Salt and pepper to taste

In a 2-quart pot sauté onion and pepper in butter until onion is soft. Add fish stock and rice. Boil easily 15 minutes. Add tomato, Worcestershire, crabmeat, chili powder, and okra. Simmer 20 minutes. Stir in sugar, salt, and pepper.

Makes 4 2-cup servings.

THREE KINDS OF DINERS

With its cast of sassy waitresses, brawny truckers, honky-tonk angels, and midnight ramblers, the diner is part of the folklore of the American road.

As its image ascended into archetype, the diner's reality petered out. A true blue plate special dog wagon, dishing out honest meals of meat loaf and mashed potatoes or liver and onions, succotash on the side, is a rare find. Most of the Navy chefs (whose expertise at working in a galley made them perfect for limited-mobility diner kitchens) have retired; with them, the masculine cuisine of the roadside diner has lost its punch.

Diners have become so outré that urban pioneers resuscitate them as museums of nostalgic food. At an aqua blue diner-style eatery in Chicago named Ed Debevic's, corned beef hash and sloppy joes are served amidst neon signs by young hipsters pretending to be old hashslingers. It is diner as dinner theater—with valet parking outside.

Debevic's and its callow brethren notwithstanding, shreds of true and original diner culture remain, untouched by gentrification—especially in the East, where diners were invented.

Diners were born in the 1890s when Boston, New York, and Philadelphia junked their horse-drawn trolley cars in favor of electric ones. The discarded cars, available cheap, were converted easily into mobile beaneries. Their shape defined the diner look.

The father of the diner as an architectural tour de force was a New Rochelle, New York, manufacturer named Patrick J. "Pop" Tierney, known to hash house historians as "the man who brought the toilet inside." Tierney made a point of calling his lunch cars *diners* because in the 1920s and '30s, train travel was about as swanky as you could get. He modeled his cafes out of metal, oak, enamel, and tile, introduced booths so women could dine in a ladylike manner, and gave his diners locomotivelike names such as "The Comet," "The Skyliner," or "The Philadelphia Flyer."

You might come across a stray chrome beauty in an Indiana cornfield, or in the West along Route 66, but the wide-open spaces have never been the diner's natural habitat. From its earliest days, the diner has been a social place, in or near the city and well-traveled routes.

The design and cuisine of a diner are almost always correlated. There are three basic types: the antique wooden dining car, the silver streamliner, and the post-Hellenic mutation.

The really ancient dining cars, made of wood or enameled metal, tend to serve the most primitive diner meals. Most of them are found in north country New England and along the coast of Maine, and their kitchens are storehouses of regional archaism: New England boiled dinner, red flannel hash, hermit bars and dumfunnie doughnuts, puddings and cobblers.

Almost all of these items are on the menu seven days a week at a thriving roadside survivor named Moody's in Waldoboro, Maine. Here is dinerism in its purest form, before stainless steel flourishes, and before menus grew long enough to please every taste.

Moody's food is Yankee to the soul. Among its rare and true New England specialties is a fast-disappearing dish called American chop suey.

What we like about American chop suey is the hopeless nerdishness of its name. Unlike fiddlehead ferns or cod cheeks or other such recently "discovered" arcane regionalia, American chop suey is simply too mundane in taste and too debased in theory to ever get chic. You can hardly find a more accursed and hopelessly unfashionable genealogy: the penurious Yankee cook's knock-off of a discredited pseudo-Chinese dish.

Many natives of New England remember American chop suey as school lunch food, or as Mom's home cooking when Mom wasn't in the mood to cook. All of this is some explanation of why it has disappeared from most home tables, and from all but the most hoary diner menus. And yet, and yet . . . we are here to stand up for American chop suey. Isn't there room in the world for dumpy food too?

Dumpy is what the old-fashioned wooden diner eating experience is all about. That is why this Moody's-inspired meal is centered on American chop suey.

WOODEN DINER DINNER

Inland Corn Chowder

American Chop Suey

Harvard Beets

Grape-Nut Pudding

INLAND CORN CHOWDER

Although chowder usually means fish or clams, farmhouse chowders can be made from the leftovers of yesterday's chicken dinner, a garden abundance of sweet corn and beans (succotash chowder), even hard-boiled eggs. What Eastern chowders share is a salt-pork base, plus a thrifty soul that makes the most of humble ingredients.

Corn chowder is on the menu nearly every day at Cole Farms, a big wooden lunchroom in Gray (inland), Maine. Cole Farms' kitchen is a bastion of Yankee diner food, including five different kinds of pudding, eleven pies every day, American chop suey, and Portland-style clam cakes ("we make our own"). Their chowder recipe is simplicity itself, scarcely more than corn, onions, potatoes, and milk. For this recipe we have gone retro on them and suggest starting the chowder the old-fashioned way, with salt pork. If you can scrape the kernels off some fresh ears of corn (about 6), this soup sings.

4 ounces salt pork, diced	3 cups sweet corn kernels
1 onion, diced	1 cup milk
2 medium boiling potatoes, peeled and diced	1 cup cream
	4 tablespoons butter
2½ cups water	Salt and pepper to taste

Fry salt pork in a stockpot over low heat until fat is rendered, about 15 minutes. Add onion and fry until onion is soft and begins to brown. Add potatoes and water, cover, and simmer until potatoes can be pierced with fork. Add corn, milk, and cream. Bring to ☞

a simmer but do not boil. Add butter and add salt and pepper carefully. (The salt pork makes this quite salty without additional salt.)

Serves 4 as a main course;
serves 6 as a first course.

AMERICAN CHOP SUEY

Some of our vintage 1930 cookbooks list American chop suey as being made with rice. That would explain its name, but in New England, at Moody's and Cole Farms and all the other diners in which we've seen it, American chop suey always contains noodles —elbow macaroni in particular. How it came to be called chop suey is anybody's guess. We speculate that it was simply a fanciful name for a dish of stirred-together small-size ingredients, "chop suey" implying any higgledy-piggledy combination of oddments.

This recipe is based on a 1936 *Boston Cooking-School Cook Book* (Fannie Farmer). Is it a surprise that the recipe was dropped from the revised edition?

8 ounces elbow macaroni
2 cups canned tomatoes,
    drained
¼ pound Cheddar cheese,
    grated
1 onion, diced

2 tablespoons olive oil
¾ pound lean ground beef
1 rib celery, cut in 2–3-inch-
    long fine strips
½ teaspoon soy sauce
Salt and pepper to taste

Cook macaroni in 2 quarts boiling salted water until soft. Drain and return to kettle. Stir in tomatoes and cheese and stir until cheese is melted. Cook onion in olive oil until it softens, about 3 minutes. Add meat and stir, cooking until it is browned. Add celery and soy sauce, then add meat mixture to noodles. Stir well, adding salt and pepper. Serve hot.

Serves 4.

HARVARD BEETS

American chop suey is a meal in itself and hardly needs accompaniment. But let's have a small bowl of this dowdy diner favorite (named for its crimson color) to add a sugary subtext to our paleo-gastronomic menu.

Beets—always plentiful and cheap—are critical ingredients in New England cooking. Aside from their appeal to a thrifty spirit, their very nature seems to match the Down East temperament. They are tough enough to require a good hard boil to soften; and they are drab looking outside, but colorful when opened up. No boiled dinner is complete without them; they are the soul of red flannel hash.

Classic Harvard beets are *not* orange flavored.

½ cup sugar	6–8 large beets, cooked,
1½ teaspoons cornstarch	peeled, and sliced
¼ cup water	3 tablespoons butter
¼ cup vinegar	Salt and pepper to taste

Mix sugar and cornstarch. Add to water and mix well. Combine with vinegar and boil 5 minutes. Add beets and let stand (with heat off) 30 minutes. Before serving, bring to a boil and add butter. Season with salt and pepper.

Serves 4–6.

GRAPE-NUT PUDDING

While we have never seen it served south of Connecticut or west of the Hudson River, we also can't remember a single wood-sided diner north of Massachusetts that doesn't feature Grape-Nut pudding on the menu every day. It is a balmy not-too-sweet custard, the Grape-Nuts softening into a pillow of brown cereal hidden beneath jiggly ivory cream.

2 cups whole milk	Dash salt
1 cup evaporated milk	1½ teaspoons vanilla extract
½ cup sugar	¾ cup Grape-Nuts cereal
3 eggs plus 2 yolks, beaten together	

Preheat oven to 325°. Set a shallow pan (large enough to hold the baking dish) filled with water in the oven. Butter a 1½-quart casserole generously.

Warm whole milk and evaporated milk together.

Mix sugar into eggs, then add warm milks very slowly, stirring constantly. Add salt and vanilla. Strain into casserole, then stir in Grape-Nuts.

Put casserole in pan in oven and bake 1 hour, or until a knife inserted in custard comes out clean. Serve tepid.

Serves 6–8.

There are a few more wood-diner dishes that cannot be ignored: boiled dinner, red flannel hash, and the classic morning muffin. All three are, in truth, closer to the spirit of home cooking, or perhaps inn food; but few home cooks take the time anymore. And although muffins have enjoyed newfound popularity, only relic eateries are square enough to serve plain boiled corned beef. (The Homestead in Sugar Hill, New Hampshire, is one such landmark.)

Anchored by a corned beef, surrounded by well-cooked (not *al dente!*) vegetables, boiled dinner is another frugal New England notion: a way to take advantage of the fire you have to keep going all day to warm the house. So you throw in the corned beef, then the vegetables, and let them cook half a day until tender. Thursday evening is the customary time for Vermonters to sit down to what they sometimes call the "bil'd dish."

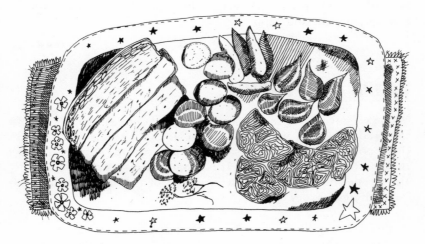

THURSDAY EVENING BOILED DINNER

Even this version would be considered revisionist by hidebound Yankee chefs, who insist on cooking all the vegetables together with the beef, so the beets color everything. This recipe calls for each item to be prepared separately. It requires a lot of pots, but we think it makes a prettier dinner. The next day, set the beets' dye loose when you make your hash.

5–6-pound corned beef	6 carrots, peeled
10 medium beets, with stems	1 tablespoon butter
2 tablespoons ginger preserves	1 tablespoon brown sugar

10 small white onions, peeled	2 tablespoons maple syrup
12 new potatoes, peeled	1 tablespoon whole cloves
30 fresh green beans, ends snipped	½ head cabbage, quartered
1 tablespoon Dijon mustard	Butter to taste

Rinse beef, place in large pot, and cover with water. Boil gently 4–5 hours, or until tender to a fork. As beef boils, periodically remove scum that rises to surface of water. Replenish water as it boils away.

As beef cooks, prepare vegetables. Clip beets, leaving 2 inches of stem. In large pot, cover with water and boil until tender, about 40 minutes. Let cool and slip off skins. Cut into wedges, return to saucepan to warm with ginger preserves.

Cut carrots into thirds, then in half lengthwise. Boil until tender yet firm. Melt 1 tablespoon butter in skillet, add brown sugar, and simmer until blended. Add carrots and swish around until coated. Cover and set aside.

In separate saucepans boil onions, potatoes, and beans until cooked but not mushy.

When beef is cooked, remove it from pan, reserving briny water. Transfer beef to ovenproof platter. Mix mustard and maple syrup and paint on beef. Stud beef with cloves and place under broiler 5 minutes.

Cook cabbage about 15 minutes in water reserved from cooking beef. *(Note: If planning to make red flannel hash [following recipe] save about a cup of this liquid.)*

Transfer beef to serving platter and place warm vegetables around it clockwise in this manner: beets at twelve o'clock, onions at two o'clock, green beans at four o'clock, carrots at six o'clock, potatoes at eight o'clock, and cabbage at ten o'clock.

Serve with mustard and horseradish on the side, and extra butter melting on the potatoes and green beans.

Serves 6–8.

There is always too much boiled dinner, which is good, because that means you have the makings for red flannel hash the next day. The source of the name is apparent as soon as you mix in the beets.

Hash and diners go way back to the earliest night-owl days when the sleazy eateries were pejoratively known as hash houses, the implication being that you never quite know what went into their hash. With a logic known only to editors of slick cooking magazines, hash suddenly became chic again a few years ago. In the kitchens of New England diners, it never lost favor. Hash has always been the sensible thing to make from leftovers.

RED FLANNEL HASH

Coarsely chop all leftovers from boiled dinner (see preceding recipe), making sure there are approximately twice as many potatoes as beets. (If not, you should boil a few extra potatoes.) Add just enough reserved boiled dinner stock to barely moisten.

Render a few ounces of salt pork in a large iron skillet. Dump in chopped dinner. Flatten hash to fill pan. Cover and cook over medium heat until bottom is brown and crusty, 20–30 minutes. Flip, cook other side, and serve. Top with poached or fried eggs, if desired.

TRUE BLUEBERRY MUFFINS

Muffins were invented as a quick breakfast breadstuff to serve on the day when yeast bread was being made—and as a way to use up spoiled milk. Although they can be made ahead and refrigerated, they are really good only when eaten within a half hour of being baked. In our book, the ideal muffin should be fragile enough to pull apart with the slightest coaxing. It should be so delicate that only softened butter can be used, dropped gently on a steaming half and allowed to melt before the first bite is taken. The way to get muffins like that is to hardly mix the dry and liquid ingredients. Just stir them together into a lumpy batter and pour into muffin tins right away.

2 cups flour	4 tablespoons butter, melted
⅓ cup sugar	and cooled
1 tablespoon baking powder	1 cup lightly floured fresh
½ teaspoon baking soda	blueberries (tiny wild
½ teaspoon salt	lowbush berries from
2 eggs, beaten	Maine are preferred)
1 cup buttermilk	

Preheat oven to 400°. Grease 12 2½-inch muffin cups (even nonstick tins should be greased lightly).

Sift together flour, sugar, baking powder, baking soda, and salt. Mix together eggs, buttermilk, and melted butter. Stir liquid ingredients into dry ingredients, mixing with a fork only enough to moisten. Batter will be ragged. Stir in berries gently.

Plop into prepared muffin tins, filling each cup nearly to the top, and bake 18–22 minutes, until light brown on top. Serve immediately with softened butter on the side.

Makes 12 muffins.

The sleek stainless steel and Formica diners, built during the 1940s and '50s, are usually one step higher on the ladder of culinary evolution than the wooden ones. Silver streamliners tend to serve archetypal blue plate square meals: beef stew, meat loaf, chicken croquettes, 99¢ breakfast specials, and crumb-top apple pie. While wooden diners are at home in northern New England, most of the silver beauties belong to New York State, New Jersey, and Pennsylvania.

In Pennsylvania, many of them have a discernible regional accent. At Zimmie's in Mifflintown or the Dutchman's Diner in Reamstown, the universal meat and potatoes menu is ballasted by a mother lode of Pennsylvania Dutch cooking: scrapple for breakfast, shoofly pie for dessert. "Dutch," by the way, has nothing to do with Holland; it is a corruption of *Deutsch*, Germany being where the settlers came from.

Their cookery, designed to provide plenty of calories for hard-working farmers, is a natural match with the culinary philosophy of the non-Dutch stainless steel diner—so succinctly captured by the motto of the Tick-Tock in Clifton, New Jersey: "Eat Heavy."

PENNSYLVANIA STAINLESS STEEL DINER DINNER

Tom-Ev Rivel Soup
Pepper Relish
Deviled Beef Ribs
Filling
Funeral Pie

TOM-EV RIVEL SOUP

Of all the silver diners in the Dutch belt of Pennsylvania, the now-departed Tom-Ev of Shoemakersville was the archetype, a perfect marriage of Lancaster County cooking and diner ambience. When we found it in the mid-1970s, it was all pink Formica and ribbons of chrome, but instead of liver 'n' onions or stew, Tom-Ev served superlative shoofly pie, scrapple, and potato filling along with old-fashioned viscera such as beef heart or pig stomach. (The heart comes sliced like a roast, not the ticking heart-shaped horror movie mass that we had feared.)

What caused us to veer off Route 61 was Tom-Ev's mobile highway sign advertising rivel soup, a broth in which tiny dumplings —known as rivels—masquerade as rice.

4 cups chicken broth	2 cups sifted flour
¼ teaspoon salt	2 eggs, beaten

Heat broth to boiling.

Stir salt into flour. Mix beaten eggs into flour, rubbing into tiny rice-size dough balls. Slowly add rivels, stirring constantly. Simmer 10–15 minutes.

Serves 4.

PEPPER RELISH

Pennsylvania Dutch dinners are always sided by galaxies of relishes. At the Dutchman's Diner in Reamstown, family-style meals in the Salt and Pepper Room are accompanied by side dishes of corn fritters, apple fritters, hot lettuce, pepper cabbage, chowchow, apple butter, bread filling, and red cabbage. Even at humble Dutch diners, like Tom-Ev's, the sweet-and-sour ritual is honored with at least one extraordinary relish alongside every meal.

1 large green bell pepper, diced fine	1 cup finely chopped celery
1 large red bell pepper, diced fine	4 teaspoons salt
	2 tablespoons mustard seed
2 cups finely chopped cabbage	2 tablespoons brown sugar
	1 cup cider vinegar

Combine peppers, cabbage, and celery. Stir in salt. Let stand overnight in refrigerator. Rinse and drain thoroughly. In a saucepan stir mustard seed and brown sugar into vinegar and heat to boil. Pour over drained vegetables in an earthenware crock. Cool and refrigerate overnight. Serve within 2 days.

Makes 3 cups.

DEVILED BEEF RIBS

At a Lancaster County dinner, the main course is usually chicken or ham, sometimes fish; it is almost always a perfunctory offering, so that one has an excuse for all the side dishes (some of which, like chicken and dumplings or *schnitz und knepp*—ham, apples, and dumplings—are as hearty as any main course). In order to have a relatively clear note to play harmony against the basso profundo filling that comes on the side, we suggest anchoring this meal with these sharp-flavored bones, which because of their low cost are a staple diner menu item. This recipe is our recollection of the ribs they used to serve at a bustling truck stop diner named Muller's outside Stroudsburg on Route 209, once known to truckers as the Ho Chi Minh Trail for all its wicked switchbacks.

1 onion, chopped fine
3 cloves garlic, minced
2 teaspoons salt
½ teaspoon black pepper
Juice of 1 lemon (about 2
    tablespoons)

4 tablespoons prepared hot
    mustard
¼ cup light vegetable oil
4 pounds short ribs of beef

Combine all ingredients except beef and marinate ribs at room temperature 2–3 hours. Stir two or three times to make sure ribs are evenly marinated.

Preheat oven to 425°. Lay ribs on roasting rack fat side up. Bake, uncovered, 15 minutes. Reduce heat to 350° and roast 1½ hours, until meat is tender.

Serves 4.

FILLING

Filling is to mashed potatoes what sumo wrestlers are to other athletes. It is the ultimate extreme starch, the spuds augmented by bread and fat and eggs. And yet, as it bakes, this filling puffs into a nearly soufflélike cloud. At Zimmie's diner in Mifflintown, it is served *alongside* mashed potatoes . . . and fried chicken . . . and dinner rolls . . . and roast beef, stewed tomatoes, applesauce, and gravy. Whew!

3 eggs, beaten
2½ cups milk

15 slices white bread,
    pulverized into crumbs

2 cups mashed potatoes
1 onion, chopped fine
3 tablespoons butter (or

chicken fat, if available),
melted
2 teaspoons salt

Combine eggs and milk and pour over bread. Stir in mashed potatoes. Add onion, butter, and salt. Empty into well-buttered 1½-quart casserole, cover, and bake 40 minutes.

Serves 8–10.

FUNERAL PIE

A staple in the Pennsylvania repertoire—and a diner chef's favorite, because of its long-lasting qualities—is raisin pie, once known as funeral pie because it could be kept on hand for days in a cool cellar, in anticipation of family occasions, from weddings to wakes.

2 cups raisins
2 cups water
½ cup sugar
3 tablespoons flour
½ teaspoon salt
3 tablespoons lemon juice

1 teaspoon grated lemon rind
1 tablespoon butter
1 baked 9-inch pie shell (see
    p. 123)
Whipped cream (optional)

Combine raisins and water in saucepan and simmer gently 20 minutes, stirring frequently. Remove from heat. Combine sugar, flour, and salt and stir into raisins. Return to heat and simmer 2 minutes, stirring. Add lemon juice and rind. Remove from heat and add butter. Cool thoroughly.

Pour into baked pie shell. Serve topped with whipped cream, if desired.

Serves 8.

Nouvelle diners, still manufactured by the Kullman Dining Car Company in Avenel, New Jersey, are barely recognizable as diners. But you know one when you see it. They are what one might call post-Hellenic diners, structures of Moorish or Mediterranean design, some with walls that look as if they were dipped in glue then rolled in terrazzo. They've got curtains on the windows, chandeliers hanging from the ceiling, and ambitious menus longer than your arm listing hundreds of entrées ranging from lox and bagels to duck à l'orange.

But like a streetwalker in a coronation gown, their true character is broadcast to every passerby. First of all, they are open all (or most of the) night. They still have a counter inside, and although the hashslinger and grillman have been sequestered in a back room, replaced by mottled mirrors and busts of ancient philosophers, you would still never mistake them for an Atlantic City casino. Even the most elaborate nouvelle diners are essentially down to earth.

Almost all (in fact every one we have ever been to) are Greek-run, and the best things to eat in them are the Greek specialties. At the Silver Star, a mega-diner of the future in Norwalk, Connecticut, the Savvidis brothers sell a showstopper souvlaki sandwich designed to give garlic breath that will kill mosquitoes ten yards away with one whistle.

POST-HELLENIC DINER LUNCH

Souvlaki on Pita with Garlic Cream
20-Pound Cheesecake

SOUVLAKI ON PITA WITH GARLIC CREAM

Ordinary store-bought pita breads will suffice, but they don't have the oomph provided by a homemade flatbread. As for the lamb (or sometimes pork), there is no need to start from scratch: warmed-over leftovers will provide the chewy, well-done effect of diner souvlaki.

BREAD

1 package dry yeast	1 teaspoon salt
1 teaspoon sugar	Cornmeal
2½ cups tepid water (110°)	Butter
6 cups flour	

Mix yeast and sugar with ¼ cup of the water. Mix remaining water with flour and salt. When yeast mixture is foamy, add it to flour mixture, mix well, and place dough in a covered bowl to rise in a warm place 3 full hours.

Preheat oven to 450°. Divide dough into 8–10 balls. On a lightly floured board, roll each out with a rolling pin to a circle 8–10 inches in diameter. Place on preheated baking stone or baking sheet sprinkled with cornmeal. Bake 5 minutes, until puffy and barely brown. If bread has ballooned, deflate it by pricking. Spread immediately with just enough butter to moisten, then let cool. Serve warm.

Makes 8–10 breads.

MARINATED LAMB FOR SOUVLAKI

1 cup olive oil
⅓ cup lemon juice
¼ cup Dijon mustard
2 cloves garlic, minced

1 teaspoon ground cumin
2 pounds lamb from leg or
   shoulder, cut into chunks

Combine all marinade ingredients and marinate lamb chunks overnight. Thread lamb on skewers and brush with remaining marinade. Broil or cook over charcoal, turning once or twice, until lamb is pink inside, about 10 minutes.

Spread lamb chunks across warm pita bread and serve accompanied by garlic sour cream.

Makes enough for 4–6 souvlakis.

GARLIC SOUR CREAM FOR SOUVLAKI

2 cups sour cream
4 cloves garlic, minced fine

½ teaspoon salt
4–6 fresh mint leaves

Combine sour cream, garlic, and salt. Cover and refrigerate several hours. Garnish with mint. This should be *very* garlicky.

20-POUND CHEESECAKE

One of the thrills of dining in a post-Hellenic diner is watching the pastry case revolve. The new-breed diners all seem to be in competition to create pies and cakes bigger and more elaborate than any that have gone before. Foot-high meringue pies, *croquembouches*, cream-puff swans, and Paris-Brests abound, displayed on mirrored shelves, bathed in rosy lights. It almost seems a shame to eat one. In fact, it *is* a shame to eat one, because these pastries are almost all *hideous*, loaded with old oil and preservative gums.

So in the spirit of largesse that animates the pastry chef (but preferring to offer a recipe that is not only impressive but tasty too), we offer our own ultra dessert, guaranteed to put a point on the meal. After the high spices of souvlaki, this mellow-flavored cheesecake is just the balm one needs.

☞

1½ cups graham cracker crumbs (12 full crackers)
1 cup sugar
8 tablespoons butter, melted
½ teaspoon cinnamon
1 8-ounce package cream cheese, softened
1 cup sour cream
1 cup heavy cream
¼ teaspoon salt
3 eggs plus 2 yolks
1 teaspoon lemon juice
¼ teaspoon vanilla extract

Preheat oven to 350°. Mix cracker crumbs and ¼ cup of the sugar. Stir in butter and cinnamon until crumbs are moist. Pat evenly onto bottom and sides of an 8-inch springform pan. Bake 10 minutes and remove from oven. Let cool.

Reduce oven heat to 275°. Combine remaining ¾ cup of sugar with remaining ingredients and mix with electric beater until smooth. Pour into crust and bake 1½ hours, or until cake is set. Remove from oven and cool until sides pull away from springform pan. Unmold and chill in refrigerator, covered loosely, until 30 minutes before serving.

Serves 10.

MID-ATLANTIC DELIS

ou don't have to be Jewish, or a New Yorker, to know the format and features of a deli. Its cuisine and its cast of characters have become Americana. But no place in the country has delis as pure in spirit (or with rye bread so good) as the mid-Atlantic states.

A deli is foremost a meat store, the classic arrangement providing a glass case, nose-high, up front where you walk in. The case is filled with beef tongues, turkey breasts, smoked fish, and pans of egg salad; nearby are metal cases venting stinky clouds from pastramis and corned beef briskets held hot and moist; and along one wall (or in the front window) hangs a knublewurst curtain—beef and garlic salamis of various lengths, some new and plump, other aged specimens wrinkled and hard as kosher rawhide.

Even if they are young, the deli staff seems old and weary (orthopedic shoes are part of the uniform). When the countermen make you a sandwich, their work is laden with angst. If it's a table-service establishment, you deal with the shleppers in their mustard-colored jackets, a towel draped on their arm for wiping tables. They stand impatiently, order pad in hand, addressing all men in glasses as "doctor" or "professor," carrying plates of food with what seems like sloppy ineptitude (but is actually stylized apathy), then retiring to lean against the wall and complain to their comrades-in-ennui.

Then there are smaller neighborhood delis staffed with waitresses

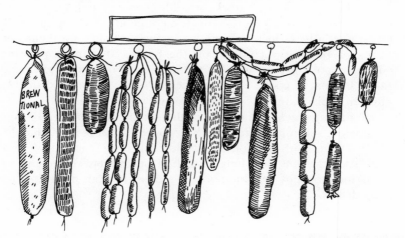

who are not nearly as abrasive as their male counterparts. But they manage to kvetch quite nicely as they treat their customers like characters in a Jewish mother joke: "Oy," says one at Fine & Schapiro on 72nd Street in New York, speaking to the dining room at large about a slender diner who leaves one matzoh ball in his soup bowl. "He's so thin, and he doesn't finish his soup."

Deli fanciers wouldn't have their service any other way. A deli is a place to which people retreat for the primitive security that such parental kibbitzing offers, accompanied by Jewish soul food like gefilte fish, chopped liver, and chicken in the pot.

CHICKEN IN THE POT

Chicken in the pot is the full-dress cousin of chicken soup. What makes it different is how it is served—*in the pot*, to be shared. Each person should have a wide soup bowl into which he can put pieces of chicken and vegetables, matzoh balls, or knedlach, then bathe them with ladles of stock from the serving dish. (Traditional cooks make their chicken stock from feet, necks, and cockscombs.)

1 4–5-pound fowl or chicken, disjointed
8–12 cups chicken stock
1 cup minced onion
6 carrots, peeled and cut into 2-inch lengths
4 ribs celery, cut into 2-inch lengths
3 cloves garlic, crushed
1 bay leaf
2 teaspoons salt
1 teaspoon coarse-ground pepper
8 ounces egg noodles or 8 matzoh balls (optional; see following recipe)

Place chicken in a large stockpot, adding enough chicken stock to cover. Add remaining ingredients (except noodles). Bring to a boil. Cover partially, reduce heat, and simmer 2–3 hours, until chicken is tender but not yet falling off the bones. (If using a roasting chicken, cooking time will be 1–1½ hours. Fowl is tougher and takes longer to cook, but produces a more flavorful dish.) As chicken cooks, skim fat from surface every 30 minutes.

If making chicken in the pot with noodles, add noodles 10 minutes before serving and turn up heat to a boil. Serve immediately.

If serving with matzoh balls, add cooked matzoh balls 5 minutes before serving, just long enough to warm them thoroughly.

Bring stockpot to table and serve directly from pot into wide soup dishes.

Serves 4–6.

2ND AVENUE MATZOH BALLS

Our recipe for matzoh balls came from Abe Lebewohl of the 2nd Avenue Deli, where chicken in the pot is made with both matzoh balls and noodles. Abe's recipe was simplicity itself, nothing more than matzoh meal, eggs, baking powder, salt, and oil. But if we are making matzoh balls for a plain chicken broth, we like to give them extra pizazz in the form of beef marrow, parsley, and a hint of onion—as follows. (If matzoh ball soup is desired, cook the matzoh balls in chicken stock and serve directly from pot, with the stock in which they have been cooked.)

4 eggs
¼ cup light oil, or marrow
    from cooked beef bone
½ teaspoon baking powder
1–1½ cups matzoh meal

2 teaspoons grated onion
2 teaspoons finely chopped
    parsley
¼ teaspoon salt

Set a saucepan half full of salted water (or chicken stock) to boil.

Beat eggs. Add oil or marrow, beating well. Add baking powder, and add matzoh meal slowly, mixing until the consistency of peanut butter. Mix in onion, parsley, and salt.

Wet hands and shape mixture into golf ball–size rounds. Drop into simmering water and cook, partially covered, 20 minutes, or until firm in center.

Makes 16 matzoh balls.

Deli service is always fast (albeit grudging), and many customers come for a quick sandwich and a Manhattan Special (coffee soda), then go on their way; and yet, delis are famous for their lingerers.

Observe the scene on the Lower East Side at Katz's (where enigmatic signs outside read "Katz' That's All" and "Wurst Fabric"). Shmoozers and newspaper readers sit at side-by-side Formica tables, offering commentary on world news and Lower East Side street life just outside the door. The noise level is high; without any partitions between tables, the bright eating hall hums with across-the-aisles movement. Nothing seems to have changed in decades, certainly not the sign above the cash register that implores visitors to "send a salami to your boy in the army."

Along with cold-cut sandwiches, Katz's denizens drink deli drinks like Dr. Brown's cel-ray or cream tonic. Old men tarry nursing hot tea served *à la russe*—in a glass tumbler equipped with a silver handle. (The Old World way is to put a sugar cube in your mouth and drink the tea through the cube.)

The fun at Katz's is getting sandwiches from the countermen: piled-high portions of corned beef or brisket, sided by amazing french fries—the secret of which, one counterman told us on the sly, is a generous portion of schmaltz (rendered chicken fat) in the frying oil. Katz's is also the place for great kosher hot dogs—all-beef, crinkle-skinned, loaded with garlic and smothered under mustard and sauerkraut. But the singular specialty, and one of the transcendent dishes of the nonkosher deli kitchen, is salami and eggs.

HOUSTON STREET SALAMI AND EGGS

Houston Street was once the border that divided the Jewish population of the Lower East Side from the rest of the world. The language of the streets has gone from Yiddish to Spanish, but the place still brims with multiethnic color. Laundry hangs between tenement walls, sidewalk vendors hustle their wares, and well-heeled uptown ladies sneak down to shop for bargains.

You can stop in the bakeries for rye bread that displays its kosher seal, or at Russ & Daughters for pickles lolling in their brine in wooden barrels and lox sliced with surgical precision. And at Katz's, you can go to heaven with a plate of this classic Jewish (but nonkosher) omelette.

To give it the powerhouse flavor it packs on Houston Street, be sure to use all-beef salami with plenty of garlic, known as knublewurst. If there isn't such a salami where you live, order one directly:

Katz's
205 E. Houston Street
New York, NY 10002
(212) 254-2246

4 slices salami, ⅛ inch thick, cut into strips
1 tablespoon butter

2 eggs, beaten with 1 tablespoon water
Salt and pepper to taste

Sauté salami in butter in an omelette pan. When salami begins to brown, pour eggs into pan. Cook over low heat until eggs are barely set. Flip and cook other side, no more than 30 seconds. Salt and pepper to taste.

Serves 1.

East of Katz's, at the foot of the Williamsburg Bridge on Delancey Street, you will find New York's venerable kosher dairy restaurant—Ratner's. The original Ratner's opened in 1905, selling 25¢ meals to the neighborhood. From the beginning it was a strict vegetarian kitchen, which was a guarantee of cleanliness in the days before refrigeration, when meat was too likely to spoil.

Unbridled sociability reigns at Ratner's tables. Next-door customers have no qualms about asking if they might, please, have a taste of your potato pancake to see if they would like to order one. And during Passover (when matzohs replace bread on every table), they don't mind reaching for a *shmeck* of matzoh off your table if they've run out.

Although matzohs are Passover bread, they are eaten in Jewish delis all year round, especially in the egg dish called matzoh brei.

MATZOH BREI

Erroneously described as a matzoh omelette or eggs-and-matzoh, matzoh brei—at its best—is closest in character to good French toast. What we mean is that the eggs must play a secondary role to the matzoh. They coddle it, they are the medium in which the matzohs fry, but it is imperative that they not overwhelm the dish. Otherwise, the matzoh gets all wet, and all you've got is a mealy omelette. The secret to delicious matzoh brei—*pace*, Dr. Pritikin, R.I.P.—is plenty of butter and salt.

6 matzohs (onion flavored, if desired)	¼ cup cream or milk
	4–6 tablespoons butter
2 eggs, beaten	Salt to taste
2 tablespoons sour cream	Sour cream as garnish

Break matzohs up in a large bowl, but do not crumble them. Fill bowl with water and drain water immediately. You want the matzohs wetted, but not soaked.

Add eggs, sour cream, and cream or milk. Stir gently, coating matzohs but trying not to pulverize them.

Melt 3 tablespoons of the butter in a large skillet over medium heat. Pour in matzoh and spread out evenly in butter. Dot top of matzoh with additional butter. Salt generously. When underside is browned, flip and brown top. Don't be concerned if you have to break up the "pancake" to flip it. Matzoh brei is best served in ragtag pieces.

Serve with additional sour cream.

Serves 2.

FLAMINGO PINK BORSCHT

Although many of us think of borscht as a soup, to be eaten warm out of a bowl, New York's dairy restaurants also serve it cold, in a glass. This gorgeous borscht is, of course, made without meat.

1 bunch beets, peeled and grated (1½ pounds)	1½ quarts water
	1 egg
1 tablespoon salt	1 cup sour cream
Juice of ½ lemon	Salt and pepper to taste
⅓ cup sugar	Sour cream as garnish

Combine grated beets, salt, lemon juice, sugar, and water in a stockpot. Bring to a boil, reduce heat, and simmer 20 minutes.

Beat egg and sour cream and gradually add 2 cups of the hot borscht, enough to warm them. Then slowly add warmed egg mixture to hot borscht and simmer over low heat, stirring constantly, about 5 minutes. Do not boil. Chill. Add salt and pepper and serve in large glasses, dolloped with additional sour cream.

Makes 5 large glasses.

LEADBELLY LATKES

Latkes, as potato pancakes are known by their Jewish friends, are a dairy restaurant specialty, but they go well with just about any hot lunch: beef brisket, stuffed derma, roast chicken. And with twin bowls of spicy applesauce and sour cream, they are a kosher meal unto themselves. This recipe is based on Ratner's, where the latkes are cooked long enough so that they are coarse-crusted, but still creamy inside. For that extra *je ne sais quoi*, we recommend adding a few tablespoons of schmaltz (rendered chicken fat) to the oil in which they are fried.

6 potatoes (about 2½ pounds)
1 medium onion
2 eggs, beaten
1½ teaspoons salt
½ cup flour

2–3 tablespoons schmaltz
Oil for frying
Sour cream and applesauce as garnish

Peel potatoes and grate into cold water (a food processor speeds this up handily). Let stand 30 minutes.

Grate onion very fine. Mix with eggs, salt, and flour.

Drain potatoes, squeezing out all liquid. Combine with batter.

Heat ½ inch of oil in a large skillet. Drop batter by heaping tablespoonfuls into oil and flatten each blob immediately into a 3- to 4-inch pancake. Fry over medium-high heat until dark golden brown and crisp, 4–5 minutes. Turn and brown other side. Drain on paper towels. Serve at once, with sour cream and applesauce.

Makes 18–21 pancakes,
enough to serve 6.

At the Carnegie Deli in midtown Manhattan, stand-up comedians gather late at night around the second table from the back to trade *shtik* over double-decker sandwiches and blintzes with sour cream. Like a Jewish coffeehouse, the Carnegie Deli is a home away from home for the borscht belters.

Although the pickled meats have a piercing spice fragrance as you heft them in a sandwich, the air at the Carnegie is redolent of just one thing: kosher dills. Briny green pickles and tomatoes, crocked with garlic cloves, peppercorns, mustard seeds, and maybe onions—they are definitive deli food, wrapped by the spear with every sandwich, set in silver bowlfuls on the tables. No pickle ever sold in a grocery store could compete in breath-destroying strength with those given away at the Carnegie Delicatessen, where they are manufactured in the basement by deli man Leo Steiner.

SUPER GARLIC KOSHER DILLS

A good delicatessen meal should always begin with a generous allotment of dill pickles and dilled green tomatoes to set the gastric juices running. They are for noshing as you wait, as well as startling taste buds mid-sandwich. Dill pickles are not difficult to make, but they do require patience.

5 pounds blemish-free pickling
   cucumbers, washed
2 bunches fresh dillweed,
   preferably with flower
   heads (without flower
   heads, add 1 additional
   tablespoon of dillseeds to
   recipe)

2 cups white vinegar
1 tablespoon pickling spice
1 tablespoon dillseeds
24 cloves garlic, crushed
⅓ cup kosher salt

Place cucumbers and dillweed in a large ceramic bowl or crock.

In a large kettle bring remaining ingredients to a boil. Take off heat and let mixture cool to lukewarm, then pour over cucumbers.

Let pickles stand at room temperature 24 hours. Cover and refrigerate at least 3 days before using. Taste after 3 days and add more crushed garlic cloves, if desired.

Pickles will keep, covered in refrigerator, 3–4 weeks. Serve at room temperature.

Makes 10–15 large pickles.

The signal dish of all true delis is the cold-cut sandwich—corned beef or pastrami at the pinnacle of honor, followed by brisket, turkey, chopped liver, salami, and perhaps (as at the Carnegie Deli) "very dry hard salami."

Good cold cuts are essential, but the secret of the sandwich is the bread: rye bread with sour tang and crusty bite, loaded with caraway seeds. Leo Steiner of the Carnegie Deli wouldn't even tell us which *borough* his rye bread baker worked in, lest we track him down and procure some of the Carnegie's perfect rye bread for ourselves. So we brought home a loaf, dissected it, and with the help of supercook Melanie Barnard, devised a recipe.

No doubt about it: Making true Jewish rye bread at home is a major operation; but if you enjoy bread making, the results are magnificent. What an alluring loaf this is warm from the oven—sour-smelling, shiny-crusted, freckled with caraway seeds.

JEWISH RYE BREAD

Starter

1 package dry yeast
2 cups tepid water (110°)

Pinch of sugar
2¼ cups rye flour

Sponge

1 package dry yeast
¾ cup tepid water (110°)
Pinch of sugar

1 cup rye flour
1 cup all-purpose flour

Bread and finishing

1 tablespoon salt
4 tablespoons plus 2 teaspoons
    caraway seeds
2½ cups all-purpose flour

Yellow cornmeal
1 egg white, beaten with 1
    teaspoon water

To make the starter, dissolve yeast in water with sugar in a mixing bowl. Add rye flour and stir until smooth. Cover lightly and let stand at room temperature 24 hours until sour smelling.

To make the sponge, dissolve yeast in ¼ cup of the water with sugar and let stand 10 minutes until foamy. In a large mixing bowl combine starter, dissolved yeast, both flours, and remaining ½ cup of water. Stir until smooth. Cover lightly and let stand about 3 hours. Stir down.

To make bread, stir salt and 4 tablespoons of the seeds into the

☞

sponge. Beat in all-purpose flour to make dough. Turn out onto a lightly floured surface and knead 8–10 minutes until smooth and elastic, adding enough all-purpose flour to keep dough from sticking.

Place dough in a greased bowl, rolling it around to coat entire surface. Cover lightly and let rise until double in bulk, about 1½ hours. Punch down and divide in half.

Sprinkle a large baking sheet with cornmeal. Form each piece of dough into a foot-long cylinder on baking sheet. Let rise about 1 hour, until double in bulk.

Preheat oven to 425°. Place a shallow pan of hot water in bottom or on bottom rack of oven.

Brush loaves lightly with egg white mixture and sprinkle with remaining 2 teaspoons of caraway seeds. Bake 20 minutes. After 10 minutes, open oven quickly and mist both loaves briefly with a plant atomizer. After 20 minutes at 425°, lower heat to 375° and bake 15–20 minutes longer, until loaves are browned and sound hollow when tapped. Remove to racks and cool completely before slicing. Loaves may be wrapped securely and frozen.

Makes 2 loaves.

Assemble good rye, sharp mustard, and a serious dill pickle, and you have the crucial building blocks of a great deli sandwich. Then the major decision—cold cuts. Nobody cures their own corned beef or pastrami or tongue (that's what delis are for). So let us suggest a deli sandwich shopping list based on these deli combinations from Leo Steiner's menu at the Carnegie Deli. All sandwiches, unless otherwise noted, are served on caraway-seeded rye bread.

LEO'S DELIGHTNIN

Triple-decker turkey, corned beef, and tongue, with coleslaw and Russian dressing.

BEEF ENCOUNTER

Triple-decker roast beef, chopped liver, and Bermuda onion.

LONG JOHN

Liverwurst, Bermuda onion, sliced egg, and tomato.

BROADWAY DANNY ROSE

Corned beef and pastrami (2 inches of each).

CARNEGIE HAUL

Triple-decker pastrami, tongue, and salami, with relish.

NOVA ON SUNDAY

Nova Scotia salmon, smoked lake sturgeon, Bermuda onion, lettuce, tomato, and cream cheese (suggested on a toasted bagel).

In concert with pastrami, layered with hard-boiled eggs and onions, or alone between rounds of fresh sour rye, chopped liver is definitive sandwich food. And although every deli sells it, chopped liver is one dish that accomplished Jewish cooks (grandmothers in particular) insist on making at home. Every chopped liver cook we know has her or his own private recipe or special chopped liver bowl, their common goal being the production of a thick, grainy paste, unctuous and perfumed with onions.

The secret of great chopped liver, the taste that makes it so powerfully *maternal*, is schmaltz. Schmaltz is to the Jewish cook what olive oil is to the Italian—the crucial ingredient in thousands of recipes, the essential taste. Plenty of schmaltz is what gives chopped liver its silky texture.

From-scratch cooks can make their own schmaltz by boiling the subcutaneous fat from a heavy chicken with a few tablespoons of water, until the water is boiled away and the schmaltz is clear. Throw in some shreds of chicken skin and finely sliced onions while the fat boils, and when the skin turns brown and crisp, you have the lacy delicacy called *griebines*—like fried onions, but infinitely more luscious. (For a great counterpoint of smooth and crunchy texture, pile the *griebines* onto the chopped liver in a sandwich.)

It takes a lot of fat chickens to make a little schmaltz, so we usually buy ours in a jar at the supermarket, where it sits on a very unkosher shelf side by side with lard and salt pork. Serious schmaltz lovers eat it straight, slathered on a slice of pumpernickel, with a little salt on top. (If you intend to try it that way, we recommend having antacid tablets within easy reach.)

Chopped liver mavens that we are, we labored for years under the misconception that it was made only from chicken livers. When we got the authentic recipe from Abe Lebewohl, owner of the 2nd Avenue Deli, we discovered that it is beef liver, combined with chicken liver, that gives the real McCoy its chunky authority.

SCHMALTZY CHOPPED LIVER

Traditionally, chopped liver is chopped by hand, but a food processor makes it ridiculously easy. Touch that pulse button carefully, though; you don't want the liver too smooth. A grainy texture, with bits of unground liver, is best.

2 pounds beef liver
½ pound chicken liver
1 large onion, sliced
½ cup vegetable oil
2 hard-boiled eggs

1 teaspoon salt
½ teaspoon black pepper
5 tablespoons rendered chicken
  fat (schmaltz)

Broil liver until well cooked. Sauté onion in vegetable oil until soft. By hand, in a meat grinder, or in a food processor combine liver, onion, eggs, and vegetable oil in which onion has been cooked and grind coarsely. Add salt, pepper, and chicken fat. Blend until you achieve a rough, pasty texture. (We found 20 pulses in the food processor was just about right.)

Cool in refrigerator. Mixture will stiffen as it cools. Serve on lettuce, garnished with red onion slices, extra chopped hard-boiled egg, and sour kosher dill pickles. Spread on rye or pumpernickel.

Walk past Barney Greengrass at Amsterdam and 86th Street any morning, and you can smell the smoked fish specialty of the house wafting out the door each time someone comes or goes. The breakfast of choice in this Upper West Side deli is an omelette recipe passed down from Barney to his son Moe.

Omelettes are popular in delis, the eggs scrambled and poured over strips of frying salami or pickled tongue and cooked until they become a firm pancake. At Barney Greengrass, the eggs are laced with large, silky nuggets of lox, and for their sweet aroma as well as taste, strands of sautéed onion.

LOX OMELETTE IN THE MANNER OF BARNEY GREENGRASS

2 tablespoons butter
½ small onion, sliced
2 ounces smoked salmon, cut
   into small nuggets

2 eggs, lightly beaten

Melt butter in an omelette pan. Sauté onion until it begins to brown. Add salmon, tossing until it begins to brown. Stir in eggs. Continue stirring as eggs firm up around lox and onion. Do not overcook.

Serves 1.

Delicatessens sometimes have long dessert lists, including puddings and babka, honey cake and marble cake. Most of them—let's be frank—are items that taste better when made by Mom at home. Whether it's because Mom is actually a better cook, or because one craves a maternal touch about one's cakes and puddings, desserts are *home* food. Delis have never been known for their sweets (except the halvah they sell).

On the other hand, no mom we've ever met knows how to make a baked apple like the ones they used to serve at Dubrow's cafeteria on Seventh Avenue. This bastion of institutionalized Jewish cooking dished out what had to be the largest baked apples in North America. But what was really wonderful about them wasn't their size; it was the glaze: a nearly iridescent sticky sheen so absolute that it made them look as if they could stay on the dessert shelf in the cafeteria for weeks without deteriorating. Yet beneath the translucent shroud, the apples were meltingly gentle.

BIG APPLE BAKED APPLE

1 cup sugar
1½ cups water
¼ cup red cinnamon candies
   (Red Hots, Cinnamon
   Imperials, etc.)

4 very large, tart, firm apples,
   peeled and cored

☞

Preheat oven to 375°. In a medium saucepan bring sugar, water, and candies to a boil, stirring to dissolve sugar. Simmer 5 minutes. Place apples in a baking dish and pour syrup over. Bake, uncovered, 20–40 minutes (depending on apple variety), until tender.

Remove apples with a slotted spoon to 4 serving dishes. Boil syrup 5–10 minutes more until it reaches 236° on a candy thermometer. Let cool slightly, then spoon over apples. Serve at room temperature.

Serves 4.

Baked apples are fine, but everybody knows that there is only one definitive deli dessert: New York cheesecake. And there is only one true recipe: Lindy's original.

Yes, cheesecake is often cooked at home; but we maintain that it is, in its soul, restaurant food. Home cooks tend to fancy cheesecake up, lacing flavoring into the cheese or topping the cake with fruit. True deli cheesecake is distinguished by its plainness.

According to *Knife and Fork in New York*, our 1948 guidebook to Manhattan restaurants, Lindy's (two locations) was notable as a "clearing house of news of Broadway, the theater, Tin Pan Alley, the radio world, and Hollywood. . . . The shutting down of the bar at 4am goes unnoticed by the gabbers consuming coffee and cake till ejected at 5am."

Lindy's recipe is subtle flavored but devastation rich, silky, smooth, heavy as a block of alabaster, and unadorned. Although many delis offer cheesecake topped with fruit glaze, such window dressing is for rubes and tourists. Deli aficionados want only the pure and real article, one thin slice thereof, eaten in tiny increments, accompanied by several cups of coffee, long into the night.

TRUE NEW YORK CHEESECAKE

Cookie crust

1 cup flour
¼ cup sugar
1 teaspoon grated lemon rind
Dash vanilla extract

1 egg yolk
8 tablespoons sweet butter,
  softened

Filling

20 ounces cream cheese	1 teaspoon grated lemon rind
¾ cup sugar	1 teaspoon grated orange rind
3 eggs plus 1 yolk	1½ tablespoons flour
2 tablespoons heavy cream or sour cream	⅛ teaspoon vanilla extract

To make crust, combine flour, sugar, lemon rind, and vanilla extract in a large bowl. Make a well in the center and add egg yolk and butter, working ingredients into a soft dough, adding a dash of ice water if necessary. Wrap in wax paper and chill 1 hour.

Preheat oven to 400°. Butter bottom and sides of a 7-inch springform pan. Using a floured rolling pin on a lightly floured board, roll out dough ⅛ inch thick. Using springform pan as a guide, cut a circle to fit the bottom, carefully scrape circle off board, and press it onto bottom of pan. Press remainder of dough onto sides of pan in an even ribbon, joining seams and sides to bottom neatly. Bake 15 minutes, until dough begins to brown at edges. Remove from oven and cool. Reduce oven temperature to 250°.

Beat cream cheese until smooth, then beat in remaining filling ingredients. Pour into cooled crust. Bake 1 hour, turn off oven, open oven door partially, and let cake sit 15 minutes on oven shelf. Remove from oven and cool completely. Release and remove side of springform pan. Cover cake with a loose sheet of plastic wrap and cool in refrigerator 1 hour before serving.

Serves 8.

SUGARHOUSE AND COUNTRY STORE

New England has five seasons: spring, summer, fall, winter, and mud. Mud season is maple sugaring time.

Travel through New England during mud season and you see stands of maple trees hung with buckets. Walk into the woods in the early morning as the sun begins to warm them, stand silent, and you hear a steady ping, ping of sap hitting the buckets' bottoms. Later in the day, steam begins to rise from hundreds of sugarhouses in the woods, where men and women stand over their evaporators, tending the delicate transformation of tree sap into maple syrup.

Sugaring off cannot be cultivated or modernized. It obeys only nature's rules; the weather determines how the sap will flow. Everything depends on a delicate conjunction of cold nights, when maple tree roots absorb moisture, and warm days, when the trees' internal pressure forces sap out the tap holes. At the first signs of spring, sugar men travel through their sugar bush tapping each mature tree with small metal spigots hung with gathering pails.

When the sap starts to flow (actually it never does more than drip fast), the pails are harvested into barrels that get snaked through the woods on sleds pulled by tractors or oxen. It is then returned to the sugarhouse and boiled down into syrup. It takes forty gallons of sap to make one gallon of syrup. And because the trees cannot be hurried, the price is dear.

Fifty years ago, when "Sugar Bill" Dexter opened Polly's Pancake Parlor (named for his wife) in Sugar Hill, New Hampshire, he could hardly give the stuff away. He built a pancake parlor onto his sugaring operation as a way to demonstrate the versatility of maple syrup in hopes of convincing travelers to take some home. The Dexters served pancakes (all you can eat) for 50¢.

In what used to be the carriage shed of an 1830 barn, Polly's dining room overlooks dewy meadows and the trees of the Hildex Farm sugar bush. Approach on the narrow winding road early in the morning, and you smell the coffee perking even before you see the red-trimmed building. Then, as you walk along the quiet path to enter, you begin to smell corn-

cob-smoked bacon sizzling; maple-scented muffins, warm from the oven; and pancakes on the griddle.

Every table is equipped with servings of syrup, maple sugar, and maple spread (the consistency of peanut butter). It is still possible to get an all-you-can-eat bonanza, served in batches of three: buckwheat, corn-meal, whole wheat, or plain, filled with coconut, blueberries, or walnuts, if desired.

For a catalogue of maple products, including syrup, pancake mix, and tiny hand-painted maple scoops, write to:

Polly's Pancake Parlor
Hildex Farm
Sugar Hill, NH 03585

POLLY'S PANCAKES

Blueberries (or other chopped fruit) may be added to either of these pancakes as soon as they are poured on the griddle. Sprinkle berries into the freshly poured batter, and when the pancakes are browned on the bottom, flip them over.

WHOLE WHEAT PANCAKES

2 eggs, beaten
1¾ cups milk
2 cups whole wheat flour
2 tablespoons granulated
    maple sugar (or light
    brown sugar)

1 tablespoon baking powder
1 teaspoon salt
3 tablespoons butter, melted

Combine eggs and milk. Stir in flour, maple sugar, baking powder, and salt. Add melted butter. (If batter seems too thick, add a bit more milk.) Drop in 3-inch circles on a lightly greased griddle.

Makes 18–20 pancakes.

CORNMEAL PANCAKES

2 eggs, beaten
1¾ cups milk
1 cup yellow cornmeal
1 cup flour

¼ cup sugar
1 tablespoon baking powder
1 teaspoon salt
3 tablespoons butter, melted

Combine eggs and milk. Stir in cornmeal, flour, sugar, baking powder, and salt. Add melted butter. (If batter seems too thick, add a bit more milk.) Drop in 3-inch circles on a lightly greased griddle.

Makes 18–20 pancakes.

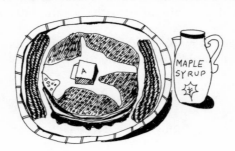

Just to be contrary one spring, we decided not to eat pancakes at Polly's. The decision came after six years of pancake-packed visits; but we did feel that duty demanded we try some of the other things on the menu. French toast it would be. The toast, like the pancakes, turned out to be extraordinary. We later learned that it was made with bread cut from loaves of what Nancy Aldrich (Sugar Bill's daughter) calls "Roger's Basic White Bread."

ROGER'S BASIC WHITE BREAD

Basic—hah! A wink of maple syrup provides an elusive rumor of sweetness to set one's taste buds wandering; the addition of cooked oatmeal gives the loaf a tender crumb.

4 tablespoons butter	1 teaspoon sugar
1/3 cup maple syrup	1/2 cup tepid water (110°)
2/3 cup water	1/3 cup cornmeal
1 1/3 cups skim milk	3/4 cup cooked oatmeal, cooled
1 tablespoon salt	to lukewarm
2 packages dry yeast	7–7 1/2 cups flour

Melt butter in a large saucepan and add maple syrup, 2/3 cup water, skim milk, and salt. Heat to 115°—no more!

Dissolve yeast and sugar in 1/2 cup tepid water. When foamy, add it to saucepan.

Combine cornmeal, oatmeal, and 7 cups of the flour in a large mixing bowl. Add liquid ingredients from saucepan, stirring vigorously until combined. Turn out onto a floured board and let rest while you clean and butter bowl.

Knead dough 15 minutes, adding flour if necessary to create a smooth, pliable mass. Return to bowl and roll around to cover with butter. Cover with a double layer of plastic wrap and let rise in a warm place until double in bulk, about 1 1/2 hours.

Punch down dough, turn out onto a lightly floured board, and shape into 2 large loaves. Place in greased 9 x 5-inch bread pans, cover loosely, and let rise to top of pans, about 45–55 minutes.

Preheat oven to 400°. Bake 30–35 minutes, until loaves sound hollow when tapped on bottom.

Turn out of pans and cool loaves on wire racks.

Makes 2 loaves.

BASIC BREAD FRENCH TOAST

This recipe works with any old bread, but what a difference Roger's maple-flavored slices make.

3 eggs
¼ cup milk or cream
4 slices day-old basic white
    bread, sliced thick

Butter for frying

Beat eggs and milk or cream together. Float bread in liquid, flipping it to make sure it is sopped thoroughly. Fry both sides in butter over medium-high heat until golden brown.

Serves 2.

In the spirit of "Sugar Bill," Nancy Aldrich still dazzles customers with novel ways to eat maple—maple mousse, maple fudge, maple nut cake, and this mapleized version of an old Yankee favorite:

MAPLE BROWN BETTY

Brown Bettys are mealy layered puddings made with cracker crumbs and molasses or white sugar. (More recent brown Betty recipes call for cornflakes.) Who Betty was or how this dessert got its name is an unsolved question of culinary history.

1 cup dry bread crumbs
2 tablespoons butter, melted
2 cups cored, peeled, and
    chopped tart apples
½ cup maple syrup

¼ teaspoon cinnamon
¼ teaspoon nutmeg
Juice and grated peel of 1
    lemon
⅓–½ cup hot water

Preheat oven to 350°. Mix bread crumbs with melted butter. Spread half the chopped apples in a well-buttered 10-inch baking dish, cover with half the bread crumbs, and add half the maple syrup. Sprinkle with half the spices and half the lemon juice and peel. Arrange a second layer. Pour hot water over top. Bake until apples are tender and top is crisp and lightly browned, about 30 minutes.

Serves 6.

MAPLE BAVARIAN CREAM

This featherweight way to savor the taste of maple is from Polly's menu. Spoons glide through it like props at a séance. The strength of its flavor depends on the grade of syrup used. Light amber yields a subtle cream; darker syrups mean more punch.

1 tablespoon unflavored gelatin	1 cup maple syrup
¼ cup cold water	1 cup cream, whipped
⅓ cup boiling water	¼ cup chopped pecans as garnish

In a mixing bowl soak gelatin in cold water until soft. Add boiling water, stirring to dissolve gelatin. Add syrup, stirring well. Set bowl in a pan of ice water and stir until mixture begins to thicken, 5–10 minutes. Fold in whipped cream. Pour into individual glasses, cover, and chill in refrigerator at least 4 hours. Serve garnished with nuts.

Serves 4.

Old-timers such as Meldrim Thomson, former governor of New Hampshire, know all the tricks to keep the sap boiling right. Surrounded by maple-scented steam in his wood-fired sugarhouse, he showed us how a drop of heavy cream clears the foamy head off the syrup in the evaporator. As we watched he dropped a few whole eggs into the boiling liquid: That, he explained, is a sugarman's technique for making lunch while on the job. He also explained how a sugarman knows that the season is over: When the peepers (tree frogs) are born and start their song, that signals the end of the sap.

As befits the primitive nature of the maple sugar-making process, breakfast at Governor Thomson's Mt. Cube Farm is a plain Yankee meal, served to friends, neighbors, and cross-country skiers on paper plates at card tables set with blue-checked cloths. When the sap is running, the little dining area hums with the sound of the evaporator working in the back room.

Sugaring is all-day work, but it is not without some immediate rewards, like a "sugar on snow" party. After the sap has been boiled down, it is put into a pot atop a stove or campfire and boiled again until it thickens. Then it is poured in a thin stream over clean packed snow, where it cools to a golden taffylike candy known as "frogs" or "leather aprons." To accompany the maple treat, sugar makers serve plain raised doughnuts and, for reviving a tired sweet tooth, sour dill pickles.

SUGAR ON SNOW

Clean freshly fallen snow or
    crushed ice
1 quart pure maple syrup
12 plain Raised Doughnuts
    (following recipe)

12 sour pickles
Coffee and/or hot chocolate

Prepare snow or ice: If using snow outdoors, it must be freshly fallen. Go to a clean bank and brush off top layer of snow. Use a spatula to pack down clean snow below. It is possible to gather clean snow in pans, well packed, and bring it indoors. If using ice, it should be finely crushed, well packed into metal or ceramic pans.

In a heavy-bottomed saucepan over medium heat cook maple syrup slowly until it reaches 232° and will form a soft ball when dropped in cold water.

Drop hot syrup by the tablespoonful onto snow or ice, allowing it to "splash" into patterns. Serve immediately, still in its tray, giving each person a fork to wind their pieces up off ice.

Accompany candy by doughnuts, pickles, and hot coffee and/or hot chocolate.

Serves 6.

RAISED DOUGHNUTS

For those accustomed to sweet cake doughnuts, raised doughnuts are shockingly plain. But you don't want any other sweetness competing with the maple. At Governor Thomson's farm, these doughnuts, made by a lady who lives down the road, are served with small cups of maple syrup for dunking.

1 package dry yeast
½ cup plus 1 teaspoon sugar
2 tablespoons tepid water
    (110°)
1 egg, beaten

1 cup milk
2 tablespoons butter, melted
3½–3¾ cups flour
Oil for deep frying

Combine yeast and 1 teaspoon of the sugar in water. Let stand 5–10 minutes until foamy. Meanwhile, combine remaining ½ cup of sugar, egg, milk, and melted butter. When yeast is foamy, add it, then mix vigorously into 3½ cups of the flour to create a smooth but somewhat sticky dough. Add more flour if dough is very soft.

Place dough in a buttered bowl, brushing top with butter.

Cover with a double layer of plastic wrap and let rise until double in bulk, 2–3 hours.

Working with half the dough at a time, roll out on a lightly floured board to ½ inch thick. Cut with a 2½–3-inch doughnut cutter (rerolling scraps), put on a lightly floured wooden board, cover loosely with a towel, and allow to rise again, 1–1½ hours.

Heat oil in a deep fryer or large kettle to 375°. (It is very important when frying doughnuts to keep oil at this temperature. A lower temperature means oily doughnuts; too high, and they will fry unevenly.) Fry doughnuts until brown on one side, turn and complete frying, about 4 minutes total. Remove and drain on paper towels. Serve immediately, while still warm. (These doughnuts do not keep well.)

Makes about 15 doughnuts and 15 holes.

To look at them, you might never guess they are royalty, but in a recent letter to us the Clukay family said that ever since they won first prize in the statewide New Hampshire maple sugar contest in 1974, they have been considered "state maple syrup kings." No longer content with simply producing the best syrup in the land, the royal family wanted to broaden their empire. So in 1977 they bought the Waterwheel Sugarhouse in Jefferson and set to work cooking pancakes, pies, muffins, and doughnuts.

The taste of maple is ubiquitous in the Waterwheel kitchen. You can get a maple milk shake, baked beans flavored with maple, and bowls of maple sugar-sweetened oatmeal. One of the dishes we liked most at the Waterwheel was this classic north country pie:

NORTH COUNTRY MAPLE CREAM PIE

1 unbaked deep 9-inch pie shell (see p. 123)
2½ cups cream
4 eggs, well beaten
½ cup maple syrup
Dash salt
¼ cup granulated maple sugar

Preheat oven to 400°. Prick bottom of pie shell with a fork and place in oven. Bake until very light, 8–10 minutes—don't cook fully. Remove from oven and cool; reduce oven temperature to 325°.

Scald 1½ cups of the cream. Combine eggs and maple syrup and drizzle cream into egg mixture *very* slowly, stirring vigorously as you pour. Add salt and pour into semibaked crust. Bake 30 minutes, until pie is set (but still a bit jiggly in the center). Remove from oven and cool.

Whip remaining cup of cream, adding granulated maple sugar as it stiffens. Spread top of cooled pie with maple whipped cream.

Serves 8.

Country stores, like sugarhouses, are repositories of rural tradition. The Vermont Country Store in Weston, with its potbellied stove in the middle of the front room and shelves of merchandise that long ago passed into oblivion everywhere else, is the Platonic ideal. You need a pair of red flannel long johns with a trapdoor in back? A vacuum cleaner from the days when vacuums looked like the *Hindenburg*? Old-fashioned mattress ticking from before the time beds got sheathed in sleazy satinette? The Vermont Country Store has them all.

Plus it has a vast supply of foodstuffs nearly impossible to get anywhere else: stone-ground meals; breakfast samp; red and white speckled Jacob's cattle beans, perfect for the bean pot; and a wealth of penny candy from red-hot Atomic balls to long strips of white paper paved with colored candy dots.

Next door is a restaurant called the Bryant House, the only restaurant we know that offers the most basic Vermont meal of all, crackers and milk.

CRACKERS AND MILK

Easy enough—as long as you have the right kind of cracker. "Not just *any* cracker," according to a broadside written on the subject by Country Store owner Vrest Orton. "*Crackers and milk* means Vermont crackers, and if you think you can dislodge this long-relished supper or snack *pièce de résistance* by suggesting that some other kind of crackers, sweet, salty, or in any other form, are better, you will soon discover that nothing is so firmly established as this inseparable and natural combination."

Country Store Common Crackers are available in specialty stores, or can be ordered from:

> The Vermont Country Store
> Mail Order Office
> P.O. Box 3000
> Manchester Ctr., VT 05255
> (802) 362-2400

1 cup cold milk   2 ounces Cheddar cheese
4–6 Common Crackers

Serve milk in wide bowl. Crumble crackers into milk. Eat with spoon, gnawing on Cheddar between spoonfuls.

Serves 1.

To taste a Common Cracker is to stare culinary history hard in the eye. They were first made in Montpelier in 1828 by Timothy and Charles Cross, who began distributing them throughout New England by one-horse wagon. Families (and country stores) bought them by the barrel and devised a whole cuisine around them, from crackers and milk to cracker pudding.

Each cracker is a startlingly arid biscuit, smaller than a golf ball, disk shaped. No true Yankee eats them whole. First, they must be split, an acquired one-hand technique that calls for the cracker to be held in the palm so that a thumbnail can be inserted in the center, prying it in two like a clamshell. Once opened, they can be eaten plain (or along with chowder), or buttered and toasted, or soaked in ice water then buttered and baked (they puff up). They even make a mean mock apple pie.

Or they can be crumbled and used to enhance other tastes, as in this Vermont Country Store recipe for chicken:

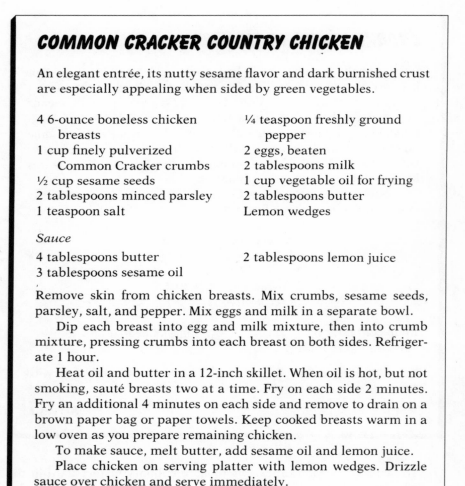

COMMON CRACKER COUNTRY CHICKEN

An elegant entrée, its nutty sesame flavor and dark burnished crust are especially appealing when sided by green vegetables.

4 6-ounce boneless chicken breasts
1 cup finely pulverized Common Cracker crumbs
½ cup sesame seeds
2 tablespoons minced parsley
1 teaspoon salt

¼ teaspoon freshly ground pepper
2 eggs, beaten
2 tablespoons milk
1 cup vegetable oil for frying
2 tablespoons butter
Lemon wedges

Sauce

4 tablespoons butter
3 tablespoons sesame oil

2 tablespoons lemon juice

Remove skin from chicken breasts. Mix crumbs, sesame seeds, parsley, salt, and pepper. Mix eggs and milk in a separate bowl.

Dip each breast into egg and milk mixture, then into crumb mixture, pressing crumbs into each breast on both sides. Refrigerate 1 hour.

Heat oil and butter in a 12-inch skillet. When oil is hot, but not smoking, sauté breasts two at a time. Fry on each side 2 minutes. Fry an additional 4 minutes on each side and remove to drain on a brown paper bag or paper towels. Keep cooked breasts warm in a low oven as you prepare remaining chicken.

To make sauce, melt butter, add sesame oil and lemon juice.

Place chicken on serving platter with lemon wedges. Drizzle sauce over chicken and serve immediately.

Serves 4.

BUTTERNUT BISQUE

Butternut squash is the beige one with a figure that resembles Casper the Friendly Ghost. It is a staple of New England cookery, especially in the fall, when it is harvested and can be stored for weeks in a cool place. At the Bryant House, they make it into a mild luscious soup that goes well with the autumn's crop of fresh-pressed apple cider—and perhaps a few Common Crackers on the side.

2 tablespoons butter	4 cups chicken stock
1 cup chopped onion	½ teaspoon white pepper
1 6–6½-inch butternut squash,	Salt to taste
peeled, seeded, and diced	1 cup milk
into 1-inch pieces (about	1 cup cream
1½ pounds)	Chopped parsley as garnish

Melt butter in a large soup pot. Add onion and sauté until onion softens. Add squash and chicken stock. Cover and bring to a boil. Simmer 20–25 minutes, until squash is tender. Cool, uncovered, 20 minutes. Purée in a blender or food processor until very smooth. (Soup may be refrigerated at this point and finished the next day.)

    Return soup to pot. Add pepper, salt, milk, and cream. Heat gently, but do not boil. Garnish with chopped parsley.

Serves 8.

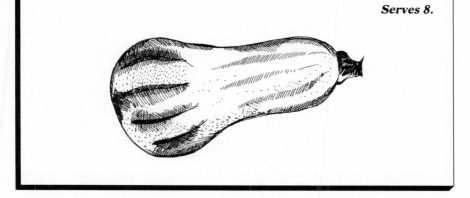

With the notable exception of banana pudding's reign throughout the South, it is the Northeast that is the great treasure-house of American pudding. Every common roadside diner holds the pudding banner high with rice, bread, and tapioca. North of Connecticut that elementary repertoire is augmented with Indian pudding and Grape-Nut pudding, and with old favorites butterscotch, chocolate, and vanilla.

CRACKER PUDDING

The most wonderfully old-fashioned of all puddings is made with Common Crackers. *Secrets of New England Cooking* (1947) gives a recipe with no sugar at all, suggesting a sweet sherry syrup (following recipe). It is pretty good plain, without syrup, too. The raisins are sweet enough; we enjoy the primitive variation of textures, from moist bottom to leathery-crusted top. If you are serving it for dessert, without sauce, you might want to add some sugar to the milk and eggs.

16 Common Crackers
4–5 tablespoons butter
1 cup raisins
2 cups milk

2 eggs, beaten
½ cup sugar (optional)
½ teaspoon salt

Split crackers in half. Butter halves and place 1 layer butter side up in bottom of a well-buttered 10 x 10-inch baking dish. Sprinkle with ⅔ cup of the raisins. Cover with another layer of crackers butter side down, then remaining ⅓ cup of raisins. Mix milk, eggs, optional sugar, and salt and pour over crackers. Let stand in a cool place 2 to 4 hours. Preheat oven to 425°. Bake 20 minutes, or until crackers are brown.

Serves 4–6.

CRACKER PUDDING SHERRY SYRUP

8 tablespoons butter
1 cup brown sugar
2 egg yolks

¼ cup sherry
¼ teaspoon nutmeg

Cream butter and sugar together and melt in top of a double boiler over hot water. Stir in yolks vigorously and continue stirring 3 minutes as mixture thickens. Stir in sherry and nutmeg. Serve warm, drizzled over individual servings of pudding.

A dear old Yankee friend chided us when *Square Meals* was published for not including the squarest meal of all: baked beans. On Saturday night. With brown bread. It was inconceivable to this man that everybody in America didn't know and love the comfort combination on which he was raised. He recalled with glee how after Saturday night, when there were beans left over, he could then enjoy his favorite sandwich: cold baked beans on toast.

Beans are New England's signal starch, the chubby pot in which they are cooked an emblem of the Yankee kitchen. Originally, they were brick oven food, flavored with salt pork and sweetened with maple syrup (only later with molasses), cooked all day long in the oven by the hearth. A New England baked bean is firm, faintly sweetened, and even more faintly spiced, coddled in a thick, not too juicy medium.

Of course beans must be made in a bean pot; to do it right, they should be made with dried pea beans—soldier beans or Jacob's cattle beans (named because their tan mottled skin resembles cows). Start a day and a half ahead, as the beans must be soaked overnight. This recipe comes from the Vermont Country Store.

BEAN POT BAKED BEANS

At the Bryant House, baked beans are always served with brown bread on the side. Although many natives of New England consider that a meal in and of itself, you may want to be heretical and serve hot dogs too.

2 pounds soldier beans, rinsed
   and soaked overnight in
   chilled water
½ pound salt pork, cut into ¼-
   inch pieces
2 medium onions, cut in
   eighths

¼ cup dark brown sugar
½ cup molasses
2 tablespoons Dijon mustard
1 tablespoon salt
1 teaspoon freshly ground
   black pepper
½ teaspoon powdered ginger

Cover beans with water in a stockpot. Bring to a boil. Boil 10 minutes. Drain, reserving liquid.

Place half the salt pork and half the onion in bottom of a 4-quart bean pot or casserole with cover. Add half the beans, then remaining onion, then remaining beans. Top with remaining salt pork.

Preheat oven to 325°. Mix brown sugar, molasses, mustard, salt, pepper, and ginger with as much reserved bean liquid as needed to cover beans. Pour over beans. Cover and bake 6 hours, stirring occasionally. Add more *hot* bean liquid if needed to keep beans moist. Uncover bean pot for final 30 minutes of baking time.

Serve with brown bread (see following recipe) and butter.

Serves 10–12.

SATURDAY NIGHT BOSTON BROWN BREAD

Brown bread goes back three centuries, to when it was a brick oven recipe cooked on a bed of oak leaves and called "ryaninjun"—a contraction of rye (flour) and Indian (cornmeal). Graham (whole wheat) flour was a later addition that became an essential element in the dark, moist loaf that everybody now knows as *Boston* brown bread. This pregraham folk recipe for brown bread was rhymed:

Three cups of corn meal,
One of rye flour;
Three cups of sweet milk,
One cup of sour;
A cup of molasses
To render it sweet,
Two teaspoons of soda
Will make it complete.

The non–brick oven method requires a pudding mold. And please remember that brown bread is *never* cut with a knife. A string held taut between two hands should be used to separate slices from the loaf.

1 cup cornmeal
1 cup medium rye flour
1 cup whole wheat flour
1½ teaspoons salt
1 teaspoon baking soda

¾ cup molasses
1½–2 cups buttermilk or sour milk
1 cup raisins, tossed with 1 tablespoon flour (optional)

Mix meal, flours, salt, and baking soda. Stir in molasses, then enough milk to make a thick batter. Add floured raisins, if desired.

Pour into 2 well-greased 4-cup pudding molds (or 1 8-cup mold), filling molds a little over half-full. Close mold covers securely.

Steam by setting molds on a trivet in a kettle of boiling water —the water should reach halfway up the mold. Boil 2½ hours, adding boiling water as needed to keep water level up.

Preheat oven to 275°. Uncover molds and set in oven 10 minutes so bread will shrink and be removed easily. Remove bread from molds and leave on oven shelf another 5 minutes so a crust can form.

THE SOUTH

PIT BARBECUE

ON THE HAM HOUSE TRAIL

OYSTER BARS AND CREOLE SOUL

MEAT AND THREES

ne hundred degrees, plus. Humidity melts the starch out of your collar and erodes the talcum powder from your back. On even the "scultriest of scultry days" (as an old Mississippi grillman once described August to us), Southerners take time to eat plate lunch.

"Meat and threes" is the common term for this ritual, referring to a piece of smothered chicken or a slab of ham or a country steak, sided by a trio of vegetables, usually long-cooked and sweetened vegetables: broccoli casserole built upon a pallet of soaked and softened white bread, sweet potato soufflés oozing butter, stewed raisins as opulent as Christmas dinner.

Meat and threes is customarily served in humble lunchrooms, designed to look as cool as possible. Walls are lettuce green, with high ceilings and revolving fans to assist the droning air conditioners. Formica tables are set with paper place mats, and silverware comes wrapped in a paper napkin. Instead of bud vases, the table is decorated with empty sauce containers holding toothpicks.

Meat and threes always means lunch served on a plate. Not between bread slices or in a bun, not in a soup or salad bowl. Partitioned plates are best, because they keep the pork chop gravy from mixing with the glaze on the candied yams. Most partitioned plates are made of dense unbreakable plastic that comes in many colors. But all the colors seem like nothing, sort of grayish pinkish greenish blue.

Drippy vegetables, like collard greens soaking in their pot likker, come in little no-color bowls all their own.

This is a balanced meal (unless you choose yams, macaroni, and whipped potatoes as your three vegetables). Like a miniaturized Sunday dinner, it is all labor-intensive food—steamed, fried, broiled, or boiled, never merely slapped together, always *cooked*. And yet, despite the variety of ingredients and the choice of three, sometimes four vegetables, there is never quite enough to stuff you. Unlike Sunday dinner, plate lunch is a short meal, designed to get working people back to the cubicle, the showroom, or the beauty salon.

The right beverage to accompany meat and threes is ice tea—considerably different from dainty afternoon tea service. Ice tea means a cloudy-surfaced plastic tumbler three-quarters full of crushed ice, and a separate pitcher filled with tea—usually presweetened tea.

Many of the finest cafes offer immense tumblers as symbols of their generosity. At Melear's in Fayetteville, Georgia, each twelve-inch-tall, six-inch-wide glass holds one full quart. At Bobby Q's in Cookeville, Tennessee, the tea is served in Mason jars, like a jug of moonshine whiskey, and the menu assures, "We make it fresh every few hours."

BOBBY Q'S LEMON ICE TEA

Margaret Wilburn gave us the Bobby Q recipe for presweetened tea with a citrus tang. Since it should be served over ice (preferably shaved ice), she recommends the tea be brewed extra strong.

1 gallon strong brewed tea
¾ cup sugar
1½ cups unsweetened
    lemonade concentrate

Combine all ingredients; mix to blend. Serve in large tumblers filled with crushed ice.

Makes 1 gallon.

To prove that plate lunch is always hot lunch, we offer an exception to the rule of meat and threes: the lunchtime sandwich known as a hot brown. Baked under a mantle of gooey sauce and cheese, a hot brown *must* be eaten with utensils, just like any serious meal.

Named for Louisville's Brown Hotel (where it was invented), the hot brown sandwich is popular throughout Kentucky. According to a 1949 cookbook called *Out of Kentucky Kitchens* by Marion Flexner, it should be made with bacon and a choice of either chicken or turkey, but we have eaten hot browns in Harrodsburg made with tomato and hard-boiled egg, and in Carrollton augmented with a slice of country ham. Whatever its specs, the culinary point of a hot brown is the detrivialization of lunchtime sandwichery.

KENTUCKY HOT BROWN

"Visitors to the Brown Hotel," Ms. Flexner wrote, "will often order this without consulting the menu."

2 tablespoons butter
2 tablespoons flour
1 cup chicken broth
Salt and pepper to taste
¼ cup grated American cheese
4 slices white toast

4 slices baked chicken or turkey, ¼ inch thick (about ¾ pound)
8 slices bacon, fried crisp
4 tablespoons grated Parmesan cheese

Make a white sauce by melting butter in a small saucepan, stirring in flour, and cooking over low heat, stirring 3–5 minutes. Continue stirring and add chicken broth slowly. Bring to a simmer and continue to stir as mixture thickens. Cook 1–2 minutes. Add salt and pepper.

Add grated American cheese to sauce, stirring until it is melted and blended in.

Place toast on 4 ovenproof plates, topping each with a piece of chicken or turkey. Cover each piece with ¼ cup of the sauce, then 2 slices of the cooked bacon, then 1 tablespoon of the Parmesan cheese.

Place sandwiches under broiler until Parmesan begins to brown.

Serve immediately, on plates straight from the oven.

Makes 4 sandwiches.

Meat and threes is eaten at a table (not standing up at a counter or sitting in a car). On that table you will find an assortment of vinegar peppers and hot sauces to sprinkle on the greens; and if it is a good plate lunch, there will be a basket (handsome canelike woven plastic) full of warm breads: corn sticks or muffins, yeast rolls, buttermilk biscuits—swaddled in a paper napkin.

THE PLATE LUNCH BREAD BASKET

These breads are from the Satsuma Tea Room, an august Nashville lunchroom. At the Satsuma, each customer writes his or her own order on a little pad set on the table. It's a system well suited to plate lunch, used at Mary Mac's in Atlanta and at the late great Mrs. Forde's Coffee Shop in

Laurinburg, North Carolina (which was so local that it had no sign out front saying it was Mrs. Forde's; everybody just kinda knew). Writing one's own ticket is a discreet way of not disclosing one's gluttony to eavesdroppers.

The Satsuma was begun in 1918 by two ladies whose idea, according to *Fun for the Cook* (the Satsuma recipe book), was to serve "excellent food in attractive surroundings at a reasonable cost." The founders were Home Ec teachers, and you can still hear their voices in the introduction to the recipes, which states, "Remember that carelessness does not produce a good dish. All measurements must be level, and in spite of care in seasoning, each dish must be tasted and tested for flavor."

SATSUMA BACON MUFFINS

6 slices bacon	2 tablespoons sugar
2 cups flour	2 eggs, beaten
4 teaspoons baking powder	1 cup milk
½ teaspoon salt	

Fry bacon crisp, then crumble; reserve fat. Preheat oven to 425°. Grease a muffin tin (12 muffins' worth). Sift dry ingredients together. Mix egg and milk and stir into dry ingredients. Do not overmix. Stir in melted bacon fat and chopped bacon. Fill 12 muffin cups nearly full. Bake 20 minutes, until browned.

Makes 12 muffins.

SOUR CREAM RIZ. BISCUITS

"Riz.," in the language of the Southern biscuit maker, means these biscuits have yeast and are thereby riz'd. No serious bread basket is complete without at least one type of biscuit.

1 package dry yeast	½ teaspoon baking soda
½ cup tepid water (110°)	3 tablespoons vegetable
1 teaspoon sugar	shortening
3 cups flour	½ cup milk
1 tablespoon sugar	¼ cup sour cream
1½ teaspoons salt	1 tablespoon butter, melted
1 teaspoon baking powder	

Dissolve yeast in tepid water with teaspoon of sugar. Mix dry ingredients. Cut in shortening until mealy. Stir milk and sour cream into mixture, then add yeast mixture to form a sticky dough. With floured hands pat dough onto a well-floured board. Roll out ½ inch thick and cut with floured rim of a 2-inch glass. Place on a lightly greased baking sheet. Brush biscuit tops with melted butter. Cover lightly with cloth or plastic wrap and let rise 1 hour. Preheat oven to 375°. Bake 12–15 minutes, until pale brown.

Makes 18–20 biscuits.

LUSCIOUS LEMON BREAD

At the front of the Satsuma Tea Room, in a vestibule where customers wait for tables, the day's baked goods are displayed: pumpkin bread, prune cake, strawberry nut bread, biscuits, chess pie, and this tender lemon bread, which belongs in the lunchtime bread basket only after it has seasoned a few days and can be sliced easily. Before that, when the bread is fresh, it makes a tremblingly delicate teatime (afternoon) snack.

¾ cup butter or margarine	¼ teaspoon baking soda
1¼ cups granulated sugar	¾ cup buttermilk
3 eggs	Grated rind of 1 lemon
2¼ cups flour	¾ cup chopped nuts
¼ teaspoon salt	

Glaze

½ cup lemon juice	¾ cup confectioners' sugar

Preheat oven to 300°. Cream butter and granulated sugar. Beat in eggs. Combine dry ingredients and add to mixture alternately with buttermilk. Mix well and stir in lemon rind and nuts. Pour into a greased and floured 9 x 5 x 3-inch bread pan. Bake 80 minutes. Cool 15 minutes in pan. Remove from pan to a cooling rack.

Combine lemon juice and confectioners' sugar. When sugar dissolves, pierce top of loaf in a number of places with a toothpick and spoon glaze over the top.

Makes 1 loaf.

The Satsuma is a downtown place for shoppers and businesspeople. Most plate lunchrooms close on weekends. But there is another group that opens up for after-church supper, selling meat and threes that verge on serious Sunday dinner.

Ma Groover's Pig and Plate, the pride of Valdosta, Georgia, was such a restaurant, frequented not only by town families but by homesick military men from the nearby Air Force base. Dinner at Ma's, seven days a week, was always accompanied by her cracklin corn bread.

PIG AND PLATE
CRACKLIN CORN BREAD MUFFINS

For authentic cracklin corn bread, you need cracklins—bits of roasted pigskin, available in many Southern barbecues. It is possible to use skin from the outside of a pork roast (but you will need to cook a few roasts to get enough). Or—this is heresy!—we have, on occasion, substituted well-cooked and drained thick-sliced bacon.

1½ cups yellow cornmeal
½ cup flour
1 tablespoon baking powder
½ teaspoon salt
3 eggs

1 cup milk
4 tablespoons butter, melted
½ pound cracklins, chopped
    into small bits

Preheat oven to 400°. Grease 12–16 muffin-tin cups generously and put tins in oven to heat. Combine cornmeal, flour, baking powder, and salt in a large mixing bowl. In another bowl blend eggs and milk. Make a well in center of dry ingredients. Add milk mixture and blend about 10 strokes. Add melted butter and cracklins and blend 10 more strokes, just until moistened. Divide among muffin tins. Bake 15–20 minutes until golden brown. Turn onto a rack. Serve warm.

Makes 12–16 muffins.

Vegetables are the soul of meat and threes. After all, consider the numbers: three to one. Such vegetables are no mere side dish, to pretty up the plate. Nor, heaven forbid, are they the idiotic "baby vegetables" that accompany overdressed fashion-plate meals. And of course we don't mean raw or barely cooked *al dente* health food–style veggies.

Meat and threes vegetables, Southern style, are a food group unto themselves, sometimes even served in fours, without any entrée at all. The truth is that entrées in most plate lunch restaurants are boring at best: smothered steak, no-account barbecue, bloodless roast beef. If you are lucky, you will get a decent piece of fried chicken; but we contend that entrées are peripheral to the plate lunch experience, and we refuse to waste ink on them while there are important vegetables to discuss.

Dewy-eyed idealists who define American cuisine as lightly cooked ingredients, served inventively, have never eaten vegetables in the South. Southern vegetables eclipse the meat because they are seriously *cooked*, usually to the point that even if they did begin as fresh, you would never know it. They are cooked, sweetened, sopped in pork-enriched likker or cheese sauce. The result is substantial foodstuff, strong rebuttal to the notion that simple and natural are good.

In the best cafes, the day's list, either mimeographed or handwritten, is clipped inside an otherwise prefab plastic menu. Nobody orders from the plastic part.

At the Acorn in Durham, North Carolina—where the menu touts "vegetables cooked daily . . . and seasoned country style!"—the daily roster is fifteen items long, including turnip greens, butter beans, steamed cabbage, fried okra, pickled beets, and candied yams. They are all terrific—except for one baked potato that we thought we'd try, just for fun. From the frightening appearance of the potato, we guessed we were the only people to have ordered a potato since the previous spring. It was one old spud.

THE GOVERNOR'S POTATO CASSEROLE

That lonely potato at the Acorn was the exception to prove the rule that vegetables in the South are never served without adornment. This slurpy potato casserole, suggested by a recipe from the Mississippi governor's mansion in *A Cook's Tour of Mississippi*, is more like it.

1½ cups large curd cottage
   cheese
1 cup sour cream
1 cup scallions, cut into ½-inch
   segments
1 clove garlic, minced
1 teaspoon salt

5 cups potatoes, peeled, diced,
   and boiled until tender,
   then cooled
½ cup shredded American
   cheese
Paprika

Preheat oven to 350°. Combine cottage cheese, sour cream, scallions, garlic, and salt. Fold in potatoes. Pour into a buttered 8 x 8-inch baking dish. Top with cheese and a sprinkle of paprika. Bake 40 minutes. If you don't like crusty cheese, cover casserole for the first 20 minutes of baking.

Serves 6–8.

There was no way of predicting the pitiful plain potato we got at the Acorn, but it is often the case that certain "vegetables" are obvious ringers. The item listed simply as "salad" on many lunchtime rosters, for instance, will likely turn out to be nothing more than a block of clear Jell-O. At Stub's Restaurant in Yazoo City, Mississippi, our estimable chicken pie plate lunch came with superb candied sweets and turnip greens—and a "salad" that turned out to be a minimalist tableau of half a canned pear with a dab of Miracle Whip on top. "Tossed salad," when listed as one of the vegetable choices, is another sure loser. And do we really have to warn you about "fruit cocktail"?

On the other hand, you can never lose if you order greens (collard, turnip, mustard, spinach) . . . or yams . . . or any kind of cheesy casserole . . . or peas or beans or okra.

Most cafes serve their okra fried, but in South Carolina an order of okra might be mixed with bacon and rice and called "Limping Susan," or the rice might be mixed with black-eyed peas and called "Hoppin John." In Alabama, however, hoppin john will likely arrive without rice at all— merely black-eyed peas cooked with salt pork.

Confused? So are we. In the category of garden pea alone, we have seen at least a dozen different names on local menus, including cowpeas, field peas, lady peas, English peas, crowder peas, polecat peas, and speckled peas. The taxonomy of Southern vegetables is hopelessly obscure. All the colorful names and fanciful combinations, we figure, show just how much attention Southerners lavish on their crops, from farm to kitchen to table.

HOPPIN JOHN

Some culinary histories say that hoppin john got its name from a custom that required children to hop in circles around the table before sitting down to eat. (What a cruel custom!) In *Rice and Beans*, the definitive pamphlet on the subject, John Thorne suggests that the name might be an etymological pejoration of the Caribbean *pois à pigeon* (pigeon peas), a bean brought from Africa to America. Variations of hoppin john are made with black-eyed peas.

1 cup dried red cowpeas	2 tablespoons butter
5 cups water	Tabasco sauce and pepper to
½ pound salt pork	taste
1 cup rice	

Soak peas overnight in just enough water to cover. Drain and add fresh water to cover. Simmer gently until peas are tender, 45–60 minutes.

As peas cook, dice salt pork and fry until fat is rendered and pieces are crisp. Reserve fat.

When beans are soft but not mushy, make sure the water level is about half of what it was (add water if necessary). Add rice, butter, and reserved fat. Stir carefully so as to keep peas whole and simmer, partially covered, 25–30 minutes, until rice is tender.

Remove from heat and let stand, adding Tabasco sauce and pepper to taste. Serve garnished with crisp pieces of salt pork.

Serves 4–6.

Hoppin john, with a wedge of corn bread, is a pleasing all-vegetable meal—especially if its starchy pinguidity is balanced by a little relish. This green tomato chowchow recipe comes from Mary Mac's in Atlanta.

MARY MAC'S GREEN TOMATO CHOWCHOW

1 small hot red pepper, washed and trimmed but not seeded
2 cups washed and cored green tomatoes (about 4)
2 cups washed and seeded green bell peppers (about 2)
2 cups washed and seeded red bell peppers (about 2)

2 cups chopped white onion (about 4)
2 cups chopped green cabbage
2 cups cider vinegar
¾ cup sugar
2 tablespoons salt
½ tablespoon celery seed
½ tablespoon mustard seed

Coarsely chop hot pepper, tomatoes, bell peppers, onion, and cabbage.

In a heavy nonaluminum gallon pot bring cider vinegar to a boil with sugar, salt, and celery and mustard seeds. Add chopped vegetables. Simmer 10 minutes.

Cool quickly by immersing pot in sink of cold water.

Makes 2 quarts chowchow.

Note: Chowchow can be stored in the refrigerator, but it does lose its smack after a few days.

The plate lunch beacon of north Florida is a sunstruck bunker across from the police station in Gainesville: Mama Lo's, a soul food restaurant whose fame has gone far beyond the color barrier. Mama Lo aficionados are a gallimaufry of neighborhood blacks, students from the University of Florida, and road travelers who know about her roster of vegetables, hand-written every day, that is never less than twenty items long. The menu du jour is inscribed in ball-point pen on a page of blue-lined notebook paper, passed among the tables until by the end of the day it is as limp as a steamed leaf.

Some of the choices are plain, like fresh corn on the cob, string beans, and white rice; but most bear the mark of Mama's magic hands—like hoppin john, or her soulful seasoned mashed potatoes, or this broccoli casserole that we made at home from her recipe, then made again the next day because we couldn't get enough.

MAMA LO'S BROCCOLI CASSEROLE

What do you do with day-old white supermarket bread? (Would you ever admit to having such bread in the house?) Do you throw it to the birds? Not if you are a casserole cook in Dixie. Southern casseroles positively thrive on—or should we more accurately say *wallow in*—stale white bread. At the bottom of the Pyrex dish, the spongy white stuff sops up all the good juices and butter and spice, transforming itself from unwanted leftovers into a happy cushion for any number of savory vegetable dishes. One of the most aggressively flavored is Mama Lo's broccoli.

5 slices day-old white bread, torn into bite-size pieces	4 tablespoons butter, melted
1 bunch broccoli	1 cup grated Cheddar cheese
3 eggs	1 teaspoon salt
¼ cup milk	3 tablespoons sugar

Preheat oven to 350°. Butter an 8-inch square Pyrex baking dish. Cover bottom of dish generously with torn bread. Cut broccoli (head and tops of stems) into bite-size pieces and lay broccoli on top of bread. Mix together all remaining ingredients. Pour over broccoli and bread. Cover with aluminum foil. Bake 35 minutes.

Serves 6.

The essence—literally—of the South's special way with vegetables is pot likker. This oily green soup is what chefs in other parts of the country throw down the drain: the liquid left in the pot after leafy things are cooked.

Considering the way vegetables are cooked in other parts of the country, such dregs usually do deserve the drain. But if you start with strong, zestful leaves, and if you flavor the water with a chunk of fatback or a ham bone or a well-smoked hog jowl, and then boil the hell out of everything (a technique necessary in order to soften the leaves to an edible state), then the pot likker that results is nothing less than the ultimate ode to the savor of a well-cooked vegetable.

Pot likker is such a focused food that Mary Mac's, the premier plate lunchroom in Atlanta, offers it as a meal, served by the bowl, corn bread on the side. It doesn't look like a lot, but the viscous broth is intense enough to make a head swim; by the time you get down to the dregs, you are warmed and invigorated, or possibly bowled over by its Popeye-like punch. This is Mary Mac's own recipe:

POT LIKKER TO MAKE YOU STRONG

3 pounds crisp turnip greens	1 teaspoon white pepper
4 cups water	½ pound salt pork
2 teaspoons salt	2–3 cups chicken stock

Wash and pick over greens, removing heavy stems. Wash three or four times, until water is clear and free of grit. Bring water, salt, and pepper to a boil. (Make a note of how high the liquid is in the pot.) Cut *half* of the salt pork into thin slices. Add it to boiling water. Add greens, stirring them down as they wilt. Cover and simmer briskly 1 hour.

As greens simmer, cube remaining salt pork and fry until fat is rendered. (Do not burn drippings.)

Remove greens, chop, and return 1 cup of the chopped greens to broth in which they were cooked. (Serve removed greens as side dish.) Add cubed salt pork and drippings. Add enough chicken stock to bring liquid up to original level. Bring to boil and simmer 5 minutes.

Serve with corn bread, to be crumbled into the likker as it is spooned up.

Makes 5–6 cups.

There needn't be a conspicuously large selection to provide the fulsome spiritual nourishment that marks a meat and threes meal. Even in an *intime* place like Hap Townes in Nashville, there is something downright inspirational about the ritual of sharing the small cafeteria line with townsfolk, getting advice from those who graze here five days a week, picking and choosing, then carrying one's own plate to a table shared by friends and strangers. Few restaurant experiences make the hungry traveler feel so much a part of the daily life in an unfamiliar town.

Until last year, Hap himself manned the steam table (as he had done for forty years), dishing out the meat and threes, providing running commentary about the goodness of the food. He is tall and lean ("When he stands up, it's six o'clock," our tablemate remarked); and his attitude about the plates of food he put together was that of an artist toward a work in progress.

HAP TOWNES'S TENNESSEE STEWED RAISINS

"Soft, sweet raisins," Hap fairly crooned with his low Tennessee voice as he spooned out heaps of these black beauties, which are more like a condiment than a vegetable. Great with ham!

1 15-ounce box dark raisins (2½ cups)	2 tablespoons flour
2 tablespoons butter	3 tablespoons sugar
	2 tablespoons lemon juice

Place raisins in a heavy saucepan. Barely cover with water and bring to a boil over high heat. Turn heat down to medium and cook until water is below first row of raisins. Add butter, stirring until melted. Mix flour and sugar and add to raisins. Cook 2 minutes more, stirring. (If watery, bring back to a boil; if stiff, add water.) Add lemon juice and serve hot.

Serves 6–8.

SHOCKINGLY SWEET STEWED TOMATOES

What a surprise it was to taste tomatoes this sugary, a vivid reminder that they are in fact berries, not vegetables. Drenched with butter, starched up with bread, these are the sweetest, swooniest 'maters you will ever taste. Although it might be possible to make a similar stew with fresh tomatoes, Hap Townes's version depends on the fall-apart pulpiness of the canned variety.

1 28-ounce can whole tomatoes, including juice	8 tablespoons butter
8 slices white bread, well toasted	1 cup sugar

Place tomatoes in a large saucepan. Tear toast into about 4 pieces per slice; add to tomatoes. Add butter and sugar. Simmer, uncovered, 20 minutes, stirring occasionally. Serve warm.

Serves 6–8.

Our *Visitor's Guide* to Tennessee says that Memphis is a "city renowned for its cosmopolitan culture." Maybe. But what we like most is its very uncosmopolitan Southern cooking—and the honored place that cooking holds in the city's daily life.

Memphians are too smart to shuffle away the less-than-glamorous meat and threes tradition in favor of whatever cuisine the gastronomic journals proclaim to be the latest thing. What a delicious irony it is that regional American food and good old-fashioned home cooking—both of which Memphians have enjoyed, nonstop, for years—have suddenly been discovered in cities that abandoned them long ago!

Of all the lunchrooms in Memphis, the most devastating is a two-room cafe across from the railroad tracks called the Buntyn Restaurant. Buntyn is—to put it gently—inconspicuous, sharing its tin awning with

an attached feed store. Like any decent plate lunch joint, it is cheap, fast, and brusque. "Enjoy old fashioned goodness in a home-like atmosphere," says the calling card of owners Milt and Betty Wiggins. But few people would mistake this pea green–walled cafe for home.

No home we know offers the consistent, jaw-dropping culinary miracles of Buntyn, or the variety (a dozen fabulous vegetables every day), or the brimming good cheer of a noisy lunch crowd five days a week, or the dizzying mingled smells of steamy corn bread and yeast rolls, hot fried chicken, baked apples, and warm banana pudding.

Mrs. Wiggins, Buntyn's owner, told us that her kitchen uses no written recipes. "You know how it is," she explained. "A handful of this, a pinch of that. And then you taste it." Doesn't that sound easy? After our last trip to Memphis, with the glow of Buntyn's still fresh on our tongues, we went home and tried to replicate a few favorite items from the menu.

NOT NECESSARILY WALDORF SALAD

Oscar of the Waldorf might come back from the grave, an incensed epicurean zombie, if he ever knew what happened to his high-tone salad in Buntyn's kitchens. The walnuts are gone, and crisp celery is reduced to a minor supporting role behind spongy miniature marshmallows and sweet raisins: dour city swank upstaged by saccharine country charm.

3 crisp apples, cored and cubed
1 tablespoon lemon juice
½ cup sliced celery
¾ cup raisins
½ cup miniature
    marshmallows (white only)

½ cup Miracle Whip salad
    dressing
Iceberg lettuce leaves

Combine all ingredients except lettuce and toss. Place each serving on a lettuce leaf.

Serves 4.

HIGH NOON SWEET POTATO CASSEROLE

Buntyn augments its sweet potatoes with the Dixie cook's favorite mix-ins—raisins and marshmallows. The raisins, cooked with the mashed yams, bloat into tender nuggets of moist sucrosity; the marshmallows vanish, leaving only sweet shadows throughout the mush.

3 large sweet potatoes (2–2½ pounds)
4 tablespoons butter
½ cup evaporated milk
⅓ cup sugar
½ teaspoon vanilla extract
½ teaspoon powdered ginger
½ teaspoon salt
½ cup dark raisins
½ cup miniature marshmallows

Peel and wash potatoes. Put in a pot of cold water and bring to a boil. Cook until tender, about 30 minutes. Drain.

Preheat oven to 375°. Mash potatoes with butter. Add evaporated milk, sugar, vanilla, ginger, salt, raisins, and marshmallows. Put into a buttered 8 x 8-inch baking dish. Bake 30 minutes, until top begins to brown.

Serves 6–8.

HIGH RISE COCONUT CREAM PIE

No dessert is as Memphian in character as coconut cream pie. At Buntyn, the thick cream base is counterpointed by foamy meringue, and the meringue is festooned with browned shreds of coconut. For a slightly less imposing stratum of coconut cream, use whole milk instead of evaporated.

½ cup sifted cake flour
4 tablespoons sugar
⅛ teaspoon salt
½ cup cold whole milk
1½ cups scalded evaporated milk
4 egg yolks, slightly beaten
1 cup shredded coconut
½ teaspoon vanilla extract
1 baked 9-inch pie shell (following recipe)

Meringue
6 egg whites
Pinch of salt
8 tablespoons sugar
½ cup shredded coconut

Combine flour, sugar, and salt; add whole milk and mix well until all lumps are gone. Add evaporated milk gradually. Place in a double boiler and cook until thickened, stirring constantly. Mix a small amount of this heated mixture into egg yolks; return yolks to double boiler. Add coconut and vanilla extract and cook 3 minutes longer, continuing to stir constantly. Remove from heat and allow to cool. Spread cooled filling into baked pie shell.

To make meringue, combine egg whites, salt, and sugar in bowl of electric mixer over pan of simmering water. When whites are lukewarm, beat at high speed until meringue stands in peaks.

Spread over pie, touching entire circumference of crust with meringue. Using back of a spoon, form meringue into festive swirls and sprinkle top with coconut.

Place pie under broiler for a few seconds, until meringue is lightly browned.

BASIC PIECRUST

Work fast with a chilled pastry blender and don't handle the dough any more than necessary once you cut in the shortening. The flakiest piecrusts are made with top-quality home-rendered lard. If that's too much work, Crisco works well. In either case, be sure the water is ice cold.

1½ cups flour
¼ teaspoon salt
½ cup vegetable shortening
    or lard

2–3 tablespoons ice-cold water

Mix flour and salt. Cut in shortening until the mixture is coarse and crumbly. Add water, 1 tablespoon at a time, mixing lightly until dough begins to hold together. Roll out on a lightly floured board to approximately ⅛ inch thick.

Lay dough onto a pie pan, letting it settle gently down to the bottom rim. Pinch over edge, trim any excess, and serrate edge with prongs of a fork, or crimp it with your fingers.

For recipes that call for an unbaked piecrust, it is ready to go. For recipes that call for a prebaked crust, such as the High Rise Coconut Cream Pie (preceding recipe), preheat the oven to 425°, prick bottom of crust with prongs of a fork in about a dozen places, then press aluminum foil (or use pie weights) onto bottom of crust. Bake 5 minutes, remove foil, and bake 5–8 minutes more, until crust is light brown. Remove from oven and cool completely before filling.

Makes 1 9-inch single-crusted pie shell.

Note: To make enough dough for a double-crusted pie, use 2¼ cups flour, ½ teaspoon salt, ¾ cup lard, and 4–6 tablespoons water.

The definitive Deep South dessert—at plate lunch, Sunday dinner, or Saturday night barbecue—is sweet tater pie. And there is nobody who makes it better than Mrs. Bonner. Mrs. Bonner is a wisp of a lady, proprietor and chef at her small cafe in Crawfordville, Georgia, since 1926.

Sixty years ago, she went to Augusta, fresh from the country with all her mother's recipes in her head. She enrolled in a cooking school, but didn't like it one bit. "All they teach in cooking school is how to measure," Mrs. Bonner told us. "I didn't go to Augusta to learn to measure. I never measure when I cook."

So she dropped out of school and opened her cafe. It has thrived ever since. Mrs. Bonner still never measures and never uses written recipes. But the eighty-two-year-old Wonder Woman continues to serve some of the best cafe meals in Georgia, six days a week. "You get on your roller skates and go" is how she expresses her philosophy of work.

Her pie's mellowness explains why almost every unaffected Southerner says "tater" rather than "potato" pie. "Potato" is sophisticated sounding, a three-syllable word. "Tater" is infantile, appropriate for pie that is as yummy as one's best-remembered high-chair food.

MRS. BONNER'S SWEET TATER PIE

Mrs. Bonner uses no spice other than salt—a plain and pure approach we have used in our adaptation of her unwritten recipe. We like the lush flavor of sweet potatoes accented only by vanilla. For an extra kick, you may want to doll the pie up with an additional ½ teaspoon each of cinnamon and nutmeg, or a tablespoon of grated lemon rind and 2 tablespoons of lemon juice.

8 tablespoons butter
1 cup sugar
2 eggs, beaten
2 cups mashed sweet potatoes
　(if using canned potatoes,
　do not use the ones packed
　in syrup)

½ cup evaporated milk
1 teaspoon vanilla extract
¼ teaspoon salt
1 unbaked 9-inch pie shell
　(preceding recipe)

Preheat oven to 375°. Cream butter and sugar together. Add eggs and mix. Add potatoes and mix. Add milk, vanilla extract, and salt. Mix well.

Pour into pie shell and bake 40 minutes.

One of Memphis's most famous cooks is a caterer named Mamie Gammon, who is also proprietor of a plate lunch restaurant named Mamie's. Her noontime customers are a loyal contingent of downtown businesspeople who frequent her place for a familiar mid-Southern repertoire: fried chicken and giblet gravy, corn bread and biscuits, and always lots of buttery, sweetened vegetables. One thing is constant on the menu: fried sweet tater pie, a Tennessee and Arkansas specialty that Mamie does better than anybody else.

FRIED SWEET TATER PIE

Most sweet tater pies are full size, one per customer. But we like to make these wieldy little versions and serve a couple at a time.

Crust

2 cups sifted flour   ½ cup shortening
1 teaspoon salt   ⅓ cup ice-cold water

Filling

2 cups mashed sweet potatoes   ¼ cup evaporated milk
2 egg yolks   3 tablespoons orange juice
⅓ cup corn syrup   Dash salt

Oil for deep frying

Sift flour and salt together. Cut in shortening. Add water and roll out on a floured board to ⅛ inch thick. Cut into circles 4½–5 inches in diameter.

Mix all filling ingredients thoroughly.

Place 1½ tablespoons of filling on each round. Moisten edge of dough and fold over, pressing together with a fork to seal.

Heat oil to 370° and deep-fry pies 4–5 minutes, until golden brown. Drain on paper towels and serve warm or keep in warming oven until ready to serve.

Makes 16 pies, enough to serve 6–8.

Other than the flavors of the food, what amazed us most about Mamie's and Buntyn, and their lunchroom kin throughout the South, is the democracy of the meat and threes plate lunch dining room. White people, black people, white collars, blue collars, prim secretaries in tan pantyhose, workmen in overalls—all classes consider this type of food their own. It is true soul food, but this culinary soul knows no bounds of race or class.

BOARDINGHOUSE MEALS

Dinner in a boardinghouse in the South transforms the act of eating into a party, a social event at which roomers, townspeople, traveling families, local and cosmopolitan folks gather together over what is always an extravagant communal spread. The table is piled high, everyone is free to help themselves, and when any serving dish starts looking empty, it is filled.

Because the meal is shared, with eaters passing platters back and forth, it is a less private experience than dinner in a booth or at a table in an ordinary restaurant. Some of the people at the table know each other already; newcomers are always the subject of curiosity. If you are a stranger, you will be talked to, and you will be expected to talk back. We don't mean the mindless greetings exchanged at the window of a fast food franchise; we are talking about what was once known as polite conversation. The weather, the route you took to get to town, where you're headed, how you like the South, and most especially, how you like Southern food —all are favorite topics.

Most boardinghouses, even those that don't continue to take in boarders, are still somebody's home, decorated with personal artifacts, family pictures, heirloom samplers. No restaurant supply house could ever match the exquisite collection of souvenir plates from all over America that festoons the walls of the Mendenhall Hotel in Mississippi. The antique furniture at the Nu-Wray Inn in Burnsville, North Carolina, could not be purchased at any price from an antiques dealer; it has been collected by the inn, slowly, as needed, since it opened for business in 1850.

One of the truths about a boardinghouse meal is that it is always dispatched with utmost speed. No time is wasted looking at a menu, because every table is set with the same food. No cocktails are served, because boardinghouses are respectable. There is no lingering between courses, because all the courses are on the table at one time.

Furthermore, you get the feeling that boardinghouse proprietors feel there is something slovenly about taking two hours to eat a meal. Only an epicure would draw things out by sipping and tasting and evaluating every little thing. Decent people down their food with gusto and enthusiasm, talking with their mouths full, grabbing biscuits on the fly, *enjoying* every high-spirited moment of the meal. That gives them plenty of time for the important things in life—like sitting in a rocking chair on the front porch after eating.

Even the most gigantic Thanksgiving dinner we have ever seen—at least thirty different platters of food at the Mendenhall Hotel—took no longer than an hour, start to finish. We loved the breakneck pace. Instead of feeling woozy, as we inevitably do after a drawn-out banquet, we felt close to nature, ready for a nap, just like a happy dog who has wolfed down his evening meal.

Mississippi has a style of boardinghouse meal all its own—round-table dining, invented seventy years ago at the Mendenhall Hotel in the town of Mendenhall, halfway between Jackson and Hattiesburg. The hotel's motto, inscribed in needlepoint on a wall of the dining room, is "Eat 'til it ouches."

In the center of huge circular oak tables is a lazy Susan, where the meal is laid out. Around each table sit ten to twenty people. Whenever you want something from the lazy Susan, you simply spin it and grab.

Easy? Sure, but then you are faced with the problem of finding an empty space on the spinning lazy Susan to replace the serving dish—a little bit like pulling into the fast lane on the expressway. One Sunday, when the spinning tables were especially full, and when the citizens of Mendenhall seemed even more than usually energetic in their whirling of the table, we found ourselves holding a dish of candied yams, with no place to put it.

"If you get stuck like that," advised the eager eater to our left, "just pass the plate to your right." And so we did, and the fellow to the right was left to deal with the yams. Such are the strategies of round-table dining.

REVOLVING TABLE
CHICKEN AND DUMPLINGS

Unlike the apple dumplings of Arkansas or meat-filled ethnic dumplings like kreplach, wonton, or ravioli, the dumplings that traditionally come with chicken and dumplings are nothing more than dough, offering weight and texture rather than another flavor to the casserole.

¼ cup plus 2 tablespoons solid vegetable shortening
3½-pound frying chicken, cut into 8 pieces
¼ cup plus 2 tablespoons flour
1 large onion, sliced
2 cloves garlic, crushed

½ pound mushrooms, cut into ¼-inch slices
4 carrots, sliced
1 rib celery, cut into 4 pieces
1 bay leaf
Salt and pepper to taste
1 cup water

Dumplings
1½ cups flour
2 teaspoons baking powder
½ teaspoon salt
⅛ teaspoon pepper
8 tablespoons solid vegetable shortening

5–6 tablespoons cold water
1 egg yolk, beaten with 1 tablespoon water

In a heavy, ovenproof 12-inch skillet heat ¼ cup of the shortening over medium heat. Dust chicken with ¼ cup of the flour, shaking off excess. Add chicken to skillet and cook about 5 minutes, until lightly browned on both sides. Remove chicken to a plate. Add onion, garlic, and mushrooms and cook, stirring constantly, until onion softens. Add carrots, celery, bay leaf, salt, and pepper. Stir to mix. Return chicken to skillet, pour in water, cover, and simmer 30 minutes.

In a small bowl, combine remaining 2 tablespoons of shortening and remaining 2 tablespoons of flour to form a paste. Stir into skillet until dissolved. Remove and discard bay leaf.

To make dumplings, combine flour, baking powder, salt, and pepper. Cut in shortening until mixture resembles coarse crumbs.

Add cold water slowly to form a ball of dough. Place dough on a pastry board dusted with flour. Roll out dough ⅛ inch thick. Cut into 12 x 1½-inch strips. Place over chicken in lattice fashion. Brush with egg mixture. Cover tightly and cook over low heat 25 minutes until dumpling lattice puffs.

Place skillet under broiler 4 inches from heat source 2 minutes, until dumpling browns. Let stand 10 minutes before serving.

Serves 4–6.

McComb, Mississippi, is a town perfumed with azalea blossoms in the spring. At the Dinner Bell, they have their own set of revolving tables, laden every evening with saucy antebellum meals—two or three entrées on the lazy Susan, often including owner John Lopinto's recipe for Creole Rabbit.

JOHN'S CREOLE RABBIT

1 large or 2 small rabbits,
   disjointed
½ cup flour
½ teaspoon salt
Oil for frying
3 large onions, sliced in rings
1 cup diced celery (2 large ribs)
1 cup diced scallions (2

   bunches), including about
   1 inch of green portion
6 cloves garlic, diced fine
4 bay leaves
3 lemons, quartered
¼ teaspoon basil
¾ cup chicken broth
Salt and pepper to taste

Wash and pat dry rabbit parts. Combine flour and salt and dredge rabbit parts in it. Heat oil to 360° and fry rabbit 3–4 minutes per side, until crisp. Remove, drain on paper towels, and place in a large (5–6 quart) covered casserole.

Preheat oven to 350°. Spread all remaining ingredients on top of rabbit, squeezing each lemon quarter, then including rind. Cover and bake 1 hour.

Remove cover of casserole, stir ingredients gently, then return to oven, *uncovered*. Turn heat up to 500°. Bake 15 minutes, or until rabbit is well browned. Discard lemons and bay leaves. Add salt and pepper to taste. Serve over rice.

Serves 6–8.

Prowling through the kitchen of the Mendenhall Hotel was a fascinating education in culinary relativity. On the one hand, owner Fred Morgan vigilantly picked over a bushel of fresh tomatoes carried to the door by a local farmer, finally rejecting them because they had not been allowed to ripen fully on the vine.

On the other hand, Fred bears full allegiance to canned mushroom soup. Purists might scoff, and decry such convenience cooking as laziness, untrue to tradition. But of course, it all depends on what tradition you are talking about. The way we see it, casseroles built around canned mushroom soup are as much an American tradition as green tomato pie or surf 'n' turf.

Even we confess we were dubious about canned soups—until we sampled the rice casserole on Mendenhall's revolving table. A few gooey spoonfuls, and we joined Fred, foursquare for Campbell's.

EAT 'TIL IT OUCHES RICE CASSEROLE

3 scallions, chopped (¼ cup)
2 tablespoons butter
1 can cream of mushroom soup
1 2-ounce can mushrooms
2 cups cooked rice
4–6 ounces sharp cheese, grated (about 1 cup)
½ cup toasted almonds

Preheat oven to 350°. Sauté scallions in butter until butter turns light brown, about 5 minutes. Do not allow butter to burn. Add mushroom soup and juice from can of mushrooms. Mix well. Pour over rice in a shallow 2-quart baking dish; stir to blend. Top with grated cheese, drained mushrooms, and almonds. Bake 15–20 minutes, or until casserole is heated through.

Serves 6.

Like the Mendenhall's rice casserole, asparagus supreme—a regular offering on the round tables of the Dinner Bell—is best when prepared in a broad Pyrex dish. Not that we have anything against the deep, opaque Corning Ware dishes (for a proper tuna noodle casserole, nothing else will do); but we suggest that Corning Ware is more emblematic of Midwestern cookery. In the South, vegetable casseroles are customarily cooked in the clear glass dishes. The reason is that such a wide and stubby configuration allows the chef to sprinkle on a maximum amount of toasted almonds, marshmallows, canned onion rings, chow mein noodles, or, as on this "supreme" concoction (also based on mushroom soup), buttered bread crumbs. And, let's face facts, it's the baubles on top that give these Southern side dishes their Dixie charm.

BOARDINGHOUSE REACH ASPARAGUS SUPREME

2 cans cream of mushroom
   soup
¼ cup chopped onion
¼ cup milk
2 tablespoons butter or
   margarine

6 ounces cream cheese
2 cans cut asparagus, drained
4 hard-boiled eggs, sliced
½ cup buttered bread crumbs

Preheat oven to 350°. Mix soup, onion, milk, butter, and cream cheese. Heat slowly until completely blended.

Place half of drained asparagus in bottom of a Pyrex casserole dish, cover with 2 sliced eggs and half the soup mixture. Make another layer of asparagus, eggs, and soup mixture. Top with buttered bread crumbs. Bake 30 minutes.

Serves 6–8.

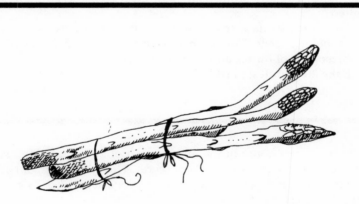

When we stopped at Mary Bobo's boardinghouse in Lynchburg, Tennessee, in 1977, Mrs. Bobo was ninety-five years old; she had been serving family-style dinners since 1908, and her once-public boardinghouse meals had become a special treat available only to visitors of the Jack Daniel's distillery in town. Each day, twenty morning tourists were selected, apparently based on who looked hungry, to have a meal in Mary's brick-walled dining room.

Mary died in 1983, and the boardinghouse was closed. Recently, Lynchburg native Lynne Tolley opened it again, offering dishes based on "Miss Mary's hundred-year-old recipes." Mary Bobo specialties include this Ritz cracker–topped carrot casserole.

MARY BOBO'S CARROT CASSEROLE

We have added more butter and cracker crumbs to Mary Bobo's recipe, so there are plenty to spread over a wide Pyrex dish.

2 pounds carrots, peeled and
    sliced
1 large onion, chopped
6 tablespoons butter
2 tablespoons flour
2 cups milk

1 teaspoon dry mustard
½ teaspoon celery salt
1½ cups grated sharp Cheddar
    cheese
1 cup crumbled Ritz crackers

Cook carrots in lightly salted boiling water 5–7 minutes, until just tender. Drain and set aside.

Preheat oven to 350°. Sauté onion in 2 tablespoons of the butter until tender, about 4 minutes. Add flour and stir constantly over medium-low heat until smooth, about 2 minutes. Add milk and seasonings and cook over medium heat until thickened, about 3 minutes. Remove from heat. Add grated cheese and stir until melted.

Combine carrots with cheese sauce. Pour into a greased 2-quart Pyrex baking dish. Top with cracker crumbs. Melt remaining 4 tablespoons of butter and drizzle over crumbs.

Bake 20 minutes, until bubbly.

Serves 6–8.

A red brick row house in the historic part of Savannah, Mrs. Wilkes's boardinghouse is the city's worst-kept secret. There is no sign outside, and Mrs. Wilkes has never advertised. But everyone who likes to eat knows this remarkable establishment.

Arrive any day after 11:00 a.m., and you know you have found the right place—because you will see a long line of Savannahians waiting for a seat at one of her oval tables. At 11:30 a.m. she says grace, and everyone helps himself to shared platters of chicken and corn bread dressing, okra gumbo, black-eyed peas, and the centerpiece of all traditional Georgia low-country dinner tables, Savannah red rice.

SAVANNAH RED RICE

With shrimp or sausage added, red rice is a one-dish meal. Without them, serve it as a side dish.

4 slices bacon
2 green bell peppers, chopped
2 medium onions, chopped
2 cups cooked rice
1 16-ounce can stewed
     tomatoes
1 cup tomato sauce

1 teaspoon Tabasco sauce
¼ teaspoon black pepper, or to
     taste
1 tablespoon grated Parmesan
     cheese
1 pound cooked shrimp or
     sausage (optional)

Preheat oven to 325°. In a large skillet fry bacon crisp, then drain on paper towels, reserving fat. Crumble bacon. Brown green peppers and onions in bacon drippings. Add rice, tomatoes, tomato sauce, Tabasco, black pepper, and crumbled bacon. Pour into a greased 2-quart casserole and sprinkle top with Parmesan cheese. Shrimp and/or sausage may be added to turn red rice into a main-course casserole. Bake 30 minutes, or until rice is dry enough to separate.

With sausage or shrimp added, serves 4 as a main course.

Bread is not as much a glamour dish as casseroles; but no Southern boardinghouse meal is complete without it. The crucial breadstuffs on the table—on *any* table, at a boardinghouse or at home—are biscuits. And the sorry fact of life for those of us who live outside the South is that genuine biscuits are impossible to make with the supermarket flour we can buy.

In Southern markets you will find bags of White Lily and Martha White brand flour: low-gluten flour, made from soft winter wheat. It is the best way to get the miraculous high-rise fluff that characterizes a true Southern biscuit.

Savannah chef Sarah Gaede says that "the secret of good biscuits is in the flour and the handling. You must handle the dough as gently and as little as possible." So if you're a Yankee who wants to make authentic Southern biscuits, first send away for the flour ($2.50 per five-pound bag, including shipping) to:

White Lily Flour Company
Box 871
Knoxville, TN 37901

PERFECT BUTTERMILK BISCUITS

3 cups White Lily self-rising
   flour

5 tablespoons Crisco (or lard)
1 cup buttermilk

Preheat oven to 425°. Sift flour into a bowl. Mix in Crisco until crumbly. Make a well in center of flour. Pour in buttermilk, mixing gently with fingers until a soft dough is formed. (There will be extra flour left in bowl.) Coat ball of dough with flour, turn out onto a floured board, and knead ten times. Roll out ½ inch thick, cut with 2-inch cutter (or water glass with floured rim), and place on a greased baking sheet. (For crusty sides, place ½ inch apart; for soft sides, put on sheet with sides touching.) Bake 10 minutes, or until light brown.

Makes 20–24 biscuits.

If you don't have the patience to send away for White Lily flour, decent not-as-fluffy biscuits *can* be made with the all-purpose variety. One of the easiest recipes we found is this one, from the Smith House Hotel in Dahlonega, Georgia, an all-you-can-eat oasis of Dixie delights that has been serving family-style dinners since 1922, when a room and three meals a day cost $1.50.

THELMA'S ANGEL BISCUITS

"Thelma" is Thelma Welch, who came to the Smith House in 1946, and has been overseeing the biscuits and fried chicken ever since. These chewy rounds make a swell companion to breakfast, lunch, or dinner. They are very plain, with just a bit of buttermilk savor. We serve them with honey or fruit preserves.

1 package dry yeast
2 tablespoons tepid water
   (110°)
4 tablespoons plus 1 teaspoon
   sugar
5 cups flour

1 teaspoon baking soda
1 tablespoon baking powder
1 teaspoon salt
1 cup butter or margarine
2 cups buttermilk

Dissolve yeast in tepid water with 1 teaspoon of the sugar. Combine flour, remaining 4 tablespoons of sugar, baking soda, baking powder, and salt. Cut in butter or margarine. Add buttermilk, then yeast mixture. Mix thoroughly. Knead a few minutes on a floured surface until smooth, then put in a covered buttered bowl and let stand 1 hour. Punch down dough and roll out about ½ inch thick. Cut into biscuits with floured rim of a small glass. Place on an ungreased cookie sheet and cover as oven preheats to 400°. Bake 10–12 minutes, until light brown.

Makes 40–48 2-inch biscuits.

Note: Unused dough can be frozen or stored in a tightly covered container in refrigerator for 2 weeks. Let it come to room temperature before cutting biscuits.

A hundred years ago, cowboys called Clarendon, Texas, the Saints' Roost, because they knew that if they came in off the range, they had to be on their best behavior. The ladies of the town would have it no other way. The men were expected to take a bath, put on clean clothes, and refrain from cussing. But when the come-and-get-it bell clanged, they did come, because the ladies of Clarendon were famous for their cooking.

And that is still why many travelers through the Southwest have detoured for a meal at the Victorian boardinghouse on Carhart Street once known as Mrs. Bromley's Dining Room. It is closed now; but all who had the pleasure of a Mrs. Bromley meal remember two things: her bread selection (at least six different kinds of rolls and biscuits) and dessert—strawberry shortcake, all you could eat, set up as a do-it-yourself affair on the sideboard. Mrs. Bromley, who learned to cook on a wood-burning stove, often included this moist apricot nut bread at Sunday dinner:

MRS. BROMLEY'S APRICOT NUT BREAD

2½ cups sifted flour
1 cup sugar
¼ teaspoon salt
¼ teaspoon baking powder
¼ teaspoon baking soda
1 cup chopped dried apricots

1 tablespoon hot water
2 eggs
1 cup buttermilk
¼ cup apricot nectar
3 tablespoons butter, melted
1 cup chopped walnuts

Preheat oven to 350°. Sift flour, sugar, salt, baking powder, and soda into the large bowl of an electric mixer. Soak apricots in hot water. Mix eggs, buttermilk, apricot nectar, and melted butter; add to dry ingredients and mix. Add apricots and nuts. Pour into a greased 9 x 5-inch bread pan. Bake 60–75 minutes, or until a cake tester comes out clean.

Makes 1 loaf.

GROCERY STORE DINING

few years back, while attending a convention in Lexington, Kentucky, we played hooky and lit out into the bluegrass countryside early one morning in search of something good to eat. Eager to have a taste of regional food in its natural habitat, we found ourselves detoured into every antiques garage for miles around. Our car's trunk filled up fast with faded WPA posters, hand-turned Bybee pottery, and an N.R.F.B. (Never Removed From Box) Barbie doll—but we were still hungry at noon. We hadn't yet found the country restaurant of our dreams.

So we cruised into the small town of Paint Lick, determined to find something wonderful—if for no reason other than the opportunity it

would provide us to say the town's name the next time anybody asked us where we'd eaten lately.

But there were no restaurants to be seen along the narrow road that functions as Paint Lick's main street. Into the grocery store we tromped, to inquire where the population eats hereabouts, and before our eyes was the fulfillment of all our rural fantasies. We had stumbled into the Paint Lick Rest. and Gro. (sign painter's shorthand for Restaurant and Grocery), a place that functioned not only as a grocery store and town cafe but as a commons in which townsfolk hung around and shot the breeze.

Counter and shelves stocked with merchandise occupied the front of the store. Among the fixtures were BarcaLounger easy chairs for relaxing and a stove for keeping warm.

In back were the cafe tables, covered with vinyl cloths and silverware wrapped in paper napkins. From over a partitioned Melmac plate heaped with mashed potatoes and fried rabbit, a patron called out to us, "If you aren't country folks, we'll make country folks out of you."

We took a seat and feasted on $2.50 plate lunches of fried rabbit and fried chicken accompanied by ham-dotted pinto beans and buttery corn cakes, ice tea on the side. For dessert there was strawberry shortcake, made with fresh berries and cake that was obviously homemade. You don't burn store-bought cake.

PAINT LICK COUNTRY FRIED RABBIT AND GRAVY

2 young rabbits	1 teaspoon salt
2 egg yolks, slightly beaten	½ cup lard
1 cup buttermilk	2½ cups milk
1 cup flour	1 teaspoon pepper
¼ cup yellow cornmeal	Salt to taste

Wash rabbit thoroughly and disjoint.

Combine yolks and buttermilk, gradually add ¾ cup of the flour, cornmeal, and salt. Beat until smooth.

Heat lard in a frying pan to 360°.

Dip rabbit in batter and fry in lard, 7 minutes on each side. Reduce heat to 275° and cook, turning frequently, until rabbit is tender, about 30 more minutes.

Remove rabbit and drain on brown paper. Pour off all but 2 teaspoons of lard in pan. Over medium heat slowly stir remaining ¼ cup of flour into lard, scraping up pieces of crust from bottom of pan. When smooth, gradually stir in milk. Bring to a boil and cook, stirring constantly, until gravy is smooth and thickened, about 3 minutes. Add a little more milk if gravy seems too thick. Remove from heat, add pepper, then salt to taste. Pour into a pitcher and serve with rabbit.

Serves 6–8.

Although the fare is basic plate lunch with a strong rustic accent, the experience of dining in a Southern grocery store is induplicable in any ordinary cafe. As you enjoy your meal, other people shop around you. Or they come to buy bait or ammo or get gas at the pumps out front. Rather than isolating customers as do most ordinary restaurant booths, the tables in a grocery store put you smack in the midst of the important activity in town.

We contend that it is a characteristically Southern phenomenon to combine gastronomy with everything else people do in the course of an ordinary day. Drive along a country road in the Mississippi Delta and you will come across Upholstery Repair–Catfish Parlors, Flats Fixed–Barbecues, and Seamstress–Tamale Stands. One reason these combination places make sense is that they provide the Southerner with ample cause to linger and gossip.

One of our favorite places for catfish was a store in northeastern Arkansas called Porkey's Bar-B-Q and Catfish House, which also happened to be a pawnshop. The catfish served at Porkey's may or may not have been the same ones Porkey went out to catch each afternoon (he was cagey about that issue, because government red tape says he has to buy a license to serve the fish he catches), but there is no question that Porkey was the master of his barbecue, supervising everything from the hog feeding to the slaughter to the twelve-hour roast over an open pit.

To show off his week's barbecue production, he took us back into the pawnshop part of the store to a phalanx of Frigidaires, one of which contained his hickory-cooked Boston butts. And later, as we ate a couple of catfish dinners, we couldn't help but eavesdrop on Porkey's afternoon customer, a local resident temporarily down on his luck, as he explained to Porkey why he had come in to pawn his shotgun. Talk about a taste of local color!

PORKEY SELLER'S PAWNSHOP CATFISH

Porkey sent us this recipe along with news that he had left his pawnshop behind and moved to a nice new location on Bull Shoals Lake: "75 foot dining room, indoor kitchen and rest rooms—sure is nice; come on up." The recipe is simplicity itself; Porkey clued us in to an old-time catfish cook's trick: "Never turn fish over until done." The same basic technique can be used to cook catfish fillets, but somehow it seems more manly to work one's way through the whole fish, right down to the skeleton. Although some recipe writers will tell you it is possible to substitute other fish for the cat, don't you believe them. In fact, old-timers contend that only river catfish, prowling on the bottom, grow the muscles to taste right; pond-raised ones, who lead a pampered life of luxury, are wan.

6 pounds catfish, cleaned but
   whole
Oil for frying
1 cup yellow cornmeal
2 tablespoons flour

1 teaspoon salt
1 teaspoon black pepper
⅛ teaspoon garlic salt
2 cups buttermilk, beaten with
   1 egg

Remove skin from fish by slitting skin just below head and pulling it off. Cut off head and tail and throw them to the cats.

Heat ½ inch of oil to 375° in a large, heavy skillet. Mix dry ingredients. Soak fish in buttermilk and egg, then roll thoroughly in meal mixture. Fry until it is a rich golden brown, 5 minutes per side.

Serves 6.

One of the great grocery stores of the South is located west of Tupelo (where Elvis was born) and south of Oxford (William Faulkner's home) in Mississippi. In the map speck known as Taylor you will find four tin-awning buildings lined up on a skinny country road. One of them is the Taylor Gro.

Although it has an esteemed reputation among catfish cognoscenti, the Taylor Gro. is a functioning store, stocked with White Lily Flour and Lady Beverly One-Size-Fits-All Panty Hose.

Two rooms are partitioned opposite the shelves for dining clientele. The view from the tables in these rooms is lumpy plaster walls covered with graffiti: scribblings about Yoknapatawpha County and names of Faulkner's characters intertwined with proclamations of love and fidelity written by Ole Miss students, who have made a ritual of coming for catfish on the night before a big football game.

The specialty of the Taylor Gro. is whole country catfish, sweet and luscious in its golden crust. On the side: hush puppies, fries, and slaw, and a basket of saltines. Table service is a single fork, wrapped in a paper napkin.

You want atmosphere to go with dinner? Observe the broken-down gas pumps out front, the torn screen door, the naked bulbs hanging above Formica tables and their vinyl-seated kitchen chairs.

YOKNAPATAWPHA HUSH PUPPIES

Sandy crusted, with a sweet onion flavor, these little balls of cornmeal are an *essential* counterpoint to catfish.

2 cups yellow cornmeal	1 egg, beaten
1 tablespoon flour	½ cup milk
2 teaspoons baking powder	½ cup buttermilk
1 tablespoon sugar	6 tablespoons chopped onion
1 teaspoon salt	Oil for deep frying

Sift dry ingredients together. Mix egg with milk, buttermilk, and onion. Stir dry and liquid ingredients together. Heat oil to 375°. Drop batter by tablespoonfuls into hot oil along with (or immediately after) frying catfish. Drain on paper towels.

Makes 24 hush puppies, enough to serve 4–6.

DELTA FRIED DILL PICKLES

We're cheating here, because fried dill pickles are not really grocery store cuisine. But ever since they were invented at the Hollywood Cafe in Hollywood, Mississippi (now moved to Robinsonville), fried dill pickles have grown in popularity to become a favorite catfish companion on plates throughout the Mississippi Delta. Some of the old-time catfishermen scoff at them as novelty food. But see if you don't agree that their sharp, sour tang makes a foil for the sweet luxury of catfish meat. Fry them up along with the catfish and hush puppies.

4 large, crisp sour dill pickles, chilled	1 cup flour
1 egg	1 teaspoon baking powder
1 cup buttermilk	½ teaspoon salt
	Oil for deep frying

Pat pickles dry and slice into ¾-inch slices.

Combine egg and buttermilk. Combine flour, baking powder, and salt and stir into buttermilk mixture just until smooth.

Heat oil to 375°. Dip pickle slices in batter and fry a few at a time until golden brown, about 3 minutes. Drain on paper towels. Serve warm.

Makes 24 slices, enough to serve 4–6.

North of Taylor, near the Tallahatchie River in the town of Abbeville, is a grocery called Ruth 'N' Jimmie's. Buckets of live bait are located on the front porch, and the grocery selection inside is augmented by hardware and dry goods. Toward the back of the wood-slat store there is a long counter and stools, like a soda fountain in a drugstore. But there is nothing pharmaceutical about the menu. The blackboard of daily specials is a lineup of earnest eats like ham or fried steak served with greens and black-eyed peas and corn bread, followed by dark-as-mud fudge pie.

GENERAL STORE FUDGE PIE

An austere, intensely sweet confection, more like candy than pie. We serve it topped with unsweetened whipped cream.

1 unbaked 9-inch pie shell (see p. 123)
6 tablespoons butter
3 ounces unsweetened chocolate

3 eggs
1 cup sugar
½ cup sweetened condensed milk
1 teaspoon vanilla extract

Preheat oven to 400°. Place pie dough in a pan and prick bottom with fork. Flatten a layer of aluminum foil across the crust and bake pie 6 minutes. Remove foil; bake 3 minutes more, until just faintly brown. Remove and turn oven down to 350°. Let piecrust cool.

Melt butter and chocolate together over hot water in top of a double boiler. Stir to mix thoroughly. Cool.

Beat eggs vigorously. Add sugar, sweetened condensed milk, and vanilla extract, beating well. Mix in chocolate. Pour into prepared pie shell. Bake 45 minutes.

Remove pie from oven and let it cool. (It will deflate considerably.) Serve at room temperature or even slightly chilled.

The quintessential grocery store meal in Mississippi is catfish or short order plate lunch: country vittles. New Orleans has a grocery meal with a completely different character. Muffuletta sandwiches—dished out from delis, pool halls, and corner groceries—are low-down, raunchy grub, *city food*, to be eaten with two fists, on the street, or maybe on a bench. The place that claims to have invented the muffuletta sandwich is the Central Grocery on Decatur Street.

The Grocery, like the French Quarter that surrounds it, seems a million miles from the down-home drawls you hear at Ruth 'N' Jimmie's or Porkey Seller's catfish pawnshop. The chatter is Italian or the French-sounding New Orleans patois. The neighborhood store is stocked with pasta, oil, and tomato paste imported from Italy; its walls are decorated with fading travel posters. It pulses with the upbeat rhythms of a neighborhood hangout.

The only food they prepare at the Central Grocery is sandwiches. (Watch them being made at the butcher block table behind the counter.) And there is no place to eat them. But that doesn't stop Orleanians from lining up out into the street for the Grocery's muffulettas, deemed by experts to be the city's best.

A muffuletta is distinguished in two ways from what Northerners call a grinder, hero, or hoagie. First, it is made on a *round* loaf of Italian bread. Loaves are baked in three sizes, but even the smallest, once stuffed, is a giant meal for one. A large muffuletta, cut in quarters, will feed four.

The second unique feature of a muffuletta is the one that makes it taste good. And this one you can do at home even if you cannot get your hands on a round loaf of Italian bread. It is the olive salad that is sprinkled on the cold cuts: pickly, broken-up, pungent olives, perfumed with oil, dripping juice.

A muffuletta, by the way, must always be served at room temperature, never toasted. Hot muffulettas, according to New Orleans food oracle Richard Collins, are "blasphemy . . . introduced by a chain of pizza places to amortize their ovens between the making of wretched pizzas."

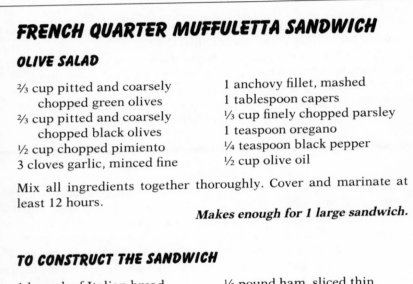

FRENCH QUARTER MUFFULETTA SANDWICH

OLIVE SALAD

⅔ cup pitted and coarsely chopped green olives
⅔ cup pitted and coarsely chopped black olives
½ cup chopped pimiento
3 cloves garlic, minced fine

1 anchovy fillet, mashed
1 tablespoon capers
⅓ cup finely chopped parsley
1 teaspoon oregano
¼ teaspoon black pepper
½ cup olive oil

Mix all ingredients together thoroughly. Cover and marinate at least 12 hours.

Makes enough for 1 large sandwich.

TO CONSTRUCT THE SANDWICH

1 large loaf Italian bread (round loaf preferred)
⅓ pound hard salami, sliced thin

⅓ pound ham, sliced thin
⅓ pound provolone cheese, sliced thin

Slice bread horizontally and scoop out about half of the soft dough from top and bottom.

Brush bottom of loaf with olive oil or juice from olive salad marinade. Layer on cold cuts. Top with as much olive salad as will fit without spilling out. Replace top of loaf.

Slice in quarters. Serve with root beer.

Serves 4.

Not every Southern grocery store restaurant specializes in low-class grub. While utter informality is the rule, there is one place, in Greenville, Mississippi, that takes the aesthetic of the grocery store to a plane of paradoxical luxury. Epicures from all over America make pilgrimages to Doe's Eat Place to feast on the best food money can buy in a dilapidated cinder-block grocery store.

There are no groceries left at Doe's, as the front room has been turned into the steak-broiling area, and the back-room kitchen is also the dining room. But there is a grocery store feel about it nonetheless—especially if you come during the day to chat with the gents who man the front room selling hot tamales by the coffee-canful.

Nobody looks at a menu when they eat at Doe's, because nearly everybody comes to Doe's for steak or shrimp. Doe's recipe for shrimp is a party meal, for sharing on a butcher-paper tablecloth.

DOE'S EAT PLACE BARBECUE SHRIMP

¼ cup olive oil
2½ pounds jumbo shrimp,
   washed but not peeled
1¼ pounds fresh tomatoes,
   peeled and chopped coarse
   (about 4)
1 clove garlic, crushed

1 sprig mint
6 drops Tabasco sauce
4 drops Worcestershire sauce
¼ cup lemon juice
1 teaspoon olive oil
Salt to taste

Heat olive oil in a very large skillet. Add shrimp and fry until golden, about 4 minutes, tossing constantly. Mix all other ingredients, add to shrimp, and simmer 10–15 minutes. Taste; add Tabasco sauce if spicier shrimp are desired.

Serve shrimp in sauce, letting diners peel them with forks or fingers. Provide plenty of napkins.

Serves 4–6.

The only meal Doe's serves is dinner, but the front room of the old grocery store is open for tamale business all day long.

With a geogastronomic logic we have yet to discern to our satisfaction, hot tamales are a specialty throughout the Delta, sold from the windows of home kitchens, at corner stands, and in grocery stores. Doe's packs their tamales in coffee cans, to take home, but we like to think of tamales more as *street food*, to be peeled and eaten while walking or driving. They're a mess, not nearly as self-contained as a hot dog or soft pretzel, but their informality encourages a finger-licking, wipe-your-hands-on-your-jeans style of eating.

STREET-CORNER HOT TAMALES

Tamales in Mississippi are notable for the minimal amount of meat, if any, laced into the steamy corn. The dominant seasoning is chili powder, plenty of it—the best you can find.

3 dozen corn husks
½ pound ground meat
1 clove garlic, minced
1 tablespoon bacon fat
½ cup beef broth
3–4 tablespoons chili powder

2 teaspoons salt
1½ cups warm water
3 cups finely ground yellow
   cornmeal
1 cup lard

Soak corn husks in hot water until pliable, about 1 hour.

Brown meat with garlic in bacon fat. Add broth, chili powder, and 1 teaspoon of the salt. Simmer, uncovered, adding more broth if necessary to make a thick, moist sauce (about 1 cup).

Combine warm water with cornmeal. Let stand.

Cream lard with remaining teaspoon of salt until fluffy. Add cornmeal mixture and beat well.

Combine cornmeal mixture and meat. Spread in husks, leaving a 1-inch edge untouched by filling. Roll husk to form a tight wrapper around filling. Tie each end with a string (or twist tie).

Stand tamales upright on a rack above 1 inch of water in a pot tall and narrow enough to keep them from tipping over. Cover loosely and steam 45 minutes.

Makes 3 dozen.

Note: If corn husks are not available, tamales may be wrapped in Saran Wrap or parchment paper cut into 8 x 5-inch rectangles.

PIT BARBECUE

ith the exception of chili, no food in America gets more mystified than barbecue. The word evokes images of obscure shacks enveloped in a smoky haze; gallon jugs filled with magic sauce; sphinxlike pit masters whose techniques contain wisdom of the ages.

Regional and even neighborhood variations are infinite. In the hills of Tennessee, the secret is the sauce; along the Carolina coast, sauce is insignificant. In Knoxville, it's probably sliced; in Memphis, most like it chopped. When you say barbecue in Owensboro, Kentucky, you are talking about mutton; in south Georgia, goat. In Richmond it is pork butt (where the pork shoulder *butts up* against the torso), coarsely chopped.

To people with an allegiance to barbecue, the pig is a sacred cow. No food is more affectionately associated with the animal from which it was cut than barbecued pork. Pig iconography is ubiquitous. From Piggly Wiggly grocery stores to tiny roadside cafes with names like Dancing Pigs, or Happy Porkers, or Hawg 'n' Hash, images of plump, happy pigs beckon us to come on inside and eat them. "It's Guar-an-teed!" oinks the talking porker on a sign outside the Smokey Pig of Bowling Green, Kentucky.

The cult of the pig is easy to understand when you know that *barbecue* is not only a noun that refers to the product, but also a verb (the cooking process), a specific place, and—most important—an event. It is a social event, whether a family's Sunday dinner or a town's Saturday night celebration. Barbecue signifies home, or hometown, or home state; to eat it again is to taste where you came from.

America's first pit-cooked barbecues were weekend parties that began with the slaughtering of the hog and the digging of a pit. To this day, the premier barbecues in South Carolina maintain weekend-only hours. At Moree's in Andrews, the hogs are put over oak coals each Wednesday at two o'clock in the morning. By Thursday they have become succulent, roasted pork. Now the butt and ham and shoulders are carved, the skin stripped and fried, and the rest of the hog cut into pork hash (two kinds—one blended with hot sauce, the other with a mild vinegar-pepper sauce) and "pork gravy" to be poured over rice. Nothing goes to waste; the pig is used "beard to tail," or in French—*barbe à queue*. By Friday night, Moree's is ready to serve a feast.

As at all the weekend pig pickins, Moree's service is buffet style—all you can pile on a tray for a fixed price. Carolina classicists contend that this is the only way to dish out barbecue. Printed menus, waitresses, and

platters portioned out by the kitchen don't have the hands-on thrill that make pig pickin such a revered culinary ritual.

And yet, the other appropriate place to enjoy barbecue is a drive-in, symbol of a somewhat newer (but every bit as precious) country tradition: car culture. At Maurice's Piggy Park, in Columbia, South Carolina, each parking space's intercom not only displays Mr. Maurice Bessinger's personal pit credo (nothing but fresh pork cooked over hickory logs) and an advertisement for his heirloom recipe million-dollar secret sauce, but it also includes a guarantee: three-minute service! Sure enough, out runs a Piggy Park girl, dressed in red, white, and blue (to match one of the largest American flags in South Carolina, flying overhead); and three minutes later, you are tearing into superior barbecue.

There is one more fact about barbecues, and it is a delicate point that we don't quite know how to make without sounding mean. But the truth of the matter is that at Craig's in DeValls Bluff, Arkansas, and at Mrs. Proffitt's place in the hills of eastern Tennessee, all the employees and a lot of the regular customers resemble the food that comes out of the pit, as if they have been smoked too.

Like giant roasted hams with legs and heavy Southern accents, denizens of the barbecue pit tend to be formidable, plump, robust people. At Mrs. Proffitt's, each of the good old mountain gals who waits on tables wears a clean uniform, white as butcher paper. At Craig's, the porcine image is epitomized by men who arrive in pickup trucks at noon to eat their lunch. Dressed in overalls that look like the canvas sacks in which hams are packed, the big pink boys grab three or four prewrapped sandwiches, extra hot, to go. And inside, the tables are occupied by queen-size local ladies in doubleknit pantsuits, their hair piled high and flawlessly into swirled buns.

Sublime barbecue is a paradox—the most primitive cooking technique imaginable, refined and perfected through generations of practice. The food is direct, but complex. Pit masters' recipes are family treasures, seldom written down, almost never shared. According to Ed Powers of the GA Pig, a pit outside Brunswick, Georgia, "To ask a barbecue man to tell you his sauce recipe is like asking to borrow his wife."

All that said, we must add that an awful lot of the mystery of the pit is hot air. The glory of barbecue comes as much from the expectations of the beholder as from logs that happen to be stacked in a special patented pattern. In other words, with a little bit of effort, it is possible to make some pretty fair barbecue in one's own backyard. Here is how we do it:

BACKYARD BARBECUED PORK

It is possible to dig a pit in your yard, build a rack for the meat, burn hickory wood until it becomes coals, and pit-roast any or all of a pig. For this recipe, a mere covered cook kettle will suffice.

1 Boston butt (6–8 pounds)   Barbecue sauce (following
Hickory chips   recipes)

Trim most of the fat off the outside of the meat. In a large, covered barbecue kettle fire up a pile of charcoal. Meanwhile, soak a couple of handfuls of hickory chips in water.

When coals are white hot, push them to one side of kettle and put a triple layer of heavy-duty aluminum foil on other side (to catch dripping fat and keep kettle clean). Throw a handful of moistened hickory chips on top of coals, put meat above foil (*not* over coals), and cover. Adjust holes in top of kettle to keep heat low (200–250°).

Every 30 minutes, throw another handful of moistened hickory chips on top of coals. At same time, baste meat with barbecue sauce, turn, and baste again.

About an hour into the process, start another, separate charcoal fire somewhere else, to provide you with white hot coals to replenish the fire in your cooker. Do not add cold charcoal to fire!

After about 6–8 hours, meat will be done. A meat thermometer should read 165°. Remove from fire and slice or chop coarse with a cleaver.

Serves 6–8.

Note: Barbecued ribs—spare ribs or baby backs—are prepared in the same manner as the Boston butt, although they will require less time, closer to 4 hours in the covered smoke kettle. Of course, they can be cooked faster, over higher heat, but they will be tougher, drier, and less smoky. When they are done, put them directly over the coals a few minutes on each side to crisp them.

The crust of the cooked Boston butt, which has absorbed a maximum amount of sauce and smoke flavors, is known as *outside meat,* "burnt ends" or "brownies." *Inside meat,* referred to by the experts at Couch's Pit in Jonesboro, Arkansas, as "white meat," should be tender, pale, sweet, and subtly flavored.

At the Ridgewood Restaurant, in Bluff City, Tennessee, the meat is heaped in a pile on a hot griddle after it is sliced, so that some pieces turn crisp, while others, not directly on the grill, remain floppy.

Chopped meat can be coarsely hacked into small cubes (as they do at Pierce's Pitt in Williamsburg, Virginia) or pulverized to the consistency of slaw (as at the Blue Mist in Asheboro, North Carolina).

However it is carved, sliced, or chopped, the barbecue should be served on a soft white bun in sandwiches or on a plate with the appropriate side dishes, which can include slaw, beans, boiled potatoes, french fries, pork hash, pork skin, hush puppies, pickles, corn bread, white bread, and—of course—ice tea. Extra barbecue sauce is optional as a condiment.

You know our recipe for barbecue left out the hard part: the sauce. Therein lies an encyclopedia's worth of controversy—not only over what kind of sauce but over its relative importance to the flavor of the barbecue. Not counting Texas, where barbecue is a separate subject all its own, a roster of significant *Southern* barbecue sauces would include at least these major categories:

1. SMOKY MOUNTAIN TOMATO-BASED SAUCE

The predominant variety, found on barbecue in the hills of Arkansas and through all of Tennessee, down into Alabama, Mississippi, and Georgia. As a general rule, the sauce is sweeter in the cities and in high mountain locations. The home recipe we like best was sent to us by *Roadfood* reader Eleanor Taylor:

8 tablespoons butter
6 cloves garlic
1 lemon, sliced
1 red onion, roughly chopped
4 cups tomato juice
1 8-ounce can crushed
    pineapple
1 cup cider vinegar
1 tablespoon dry mustard

1 cup water
2 beef bouillon cubes
2 whole cloves
2 bay leaves
6 whole allspice
2 pods hot pepper
3 tablespoons paprika
½ cup honey

Melt butter in a large saucepan. Smash garlic and sauté with lemon slices in butter for about 5 minutes. Add all other ingredients and simmer, uncovered, 1 hour. If thicker sauce is desired, continue simmering up to 2 hours.

    Strain into a stainless steel pan or Corning Ware pot. Store in refrigerator.

Makes 4–6 cups, depending on thickness.

2. PIGGY PARK–STYLE MUSTARD-BASED SAUCE

A tart yellow variety unique to central South Carolina, in the area around Columbia. The best-known purveyor of this type of sauce is Maurice's Piggy Park, which describes it as "meat's best friend." The Bessinger recipe is referred to as "the million dollar heirloom" and is top secret. This is our re-creation thereof.

8 tablespoons French's yellow mustard
6 tablespoons sugar
1 cup cider vinegar
2 teaspoons chili powder

1 teaspoon black pepper
1 teaspoon white pepper
½ teaspoon soy sauce
2 tablespoons butter

Combine all ingredients except soy sauce and butter in a saucepan and simmer 10 minutes. Remove from heat. Stir in soy sauce and butter.

Makes 1 cup.

3. TARHEEL VINEGAR SAUCE

Piquant, peppery, and either clear or just faintly tomato-red, vinegar sauce is the standard in North Carolina, toward the shore. Fanciers of North Carolina barbecue claim that this is the only type of sauce that doesn't completely smother the delicate flavors of smoked pork.

8 tablespoons butter
1 cup cider vinegar
1 large sour pickle, chopped fine
2 tablespoons finely chopped onion

2 tablespoons Worcestershire sauce
1 tablespoon lemon juice
1 teaspoon molasses

Combine all ingredients in a saucepan over low heat, cooking until butter melts, stirring frequently.

Makes 2 cups.

We cannot tell a lie. We hardly ever make our own barbecue sauce. We don't even want to know what goes into sauce. For us, it is *the mystery*, the unattainable secrets that make great the barbecues of the South so much more than the sum of their ingredients.

That is why our *real* technique for getting good sauce for home barbecue is to go out and buy it, preferably while traveling.

If that is your plan, we recommend carrying several clean plastic gallon jugs. Some of the best barbecues don't have bottles for carry-out business, but will be happy to fill a jug and charge you accordingly.

In many of the finest smokehouses, it is *essential* that you supply your own bottle. We recall one sensational but now defunct joint not far from Enigma, Georgia, where the pit man said he'd be happy to fill a bottle with his sauce for us, then went outside into the high grass and foraged until he found a cloudy old Jack Daniel's bottle to hold it. As good as the sauce was, we never dared use the stuff out of that bottle. From then on, we vowed to carry our own.

If there is no on-the-road booty in your cupboard, you can send away for sauce. Many of the great and famous barbecues are set up for mail-order business. We recommend:

> Stubby's Hik-Ry Pit (for sweet tomato-based sauce)
> 1000 Park Avenue
> Hot Springs, AR 71901
> (501) 624-9323

> Maurice's Piggy Park (for mustard-based sauce)
> P.O. Box 6847
> West Columbia, SC 29171
> (803) 791-5887

Once you have chosen your sauce and made your barbecue, you must decide how to serve it. The simplest way is on a sandwich, but even barbecue sandwiches vary from region to region. At the Beacon Drive-In in Spartanburg, South Carolina, the sandwich menu lists "slice," "outside," "pork-a-plenty,"and barbecued "ham-a-plenty." At Maurice's Piggy Park in Columbia, if you choose the Big Joe Q Pork sandwich, you have the option, for 20¢ more, of including crackling pork skin among the meat. Throughout the mid-South, barbecue sandwiches automatically come heaped with coleslaw in the bun.

The bun is the one constant. Buns for barbecue are always spongy white bread, with enough body to stay whole when sopped with sauce, but insipid enough to be no more than a sponge for other flavors. Even bread fanatics, for whom a warm, fresh, hard-crusted loaf is heaven, are quick to admit that top-quality bread short-circuits the texture and flavor of good barbecue.

Beyond always-boring bread, companions to barbecue on a plate or platter range from perfunctory starch, like the plain boiled potatoes served around Rocky Mount, North Carolina, to pit beans, the traditional side dish for barbecue in the mountains of Tennessee and Arkansas.

There are no pit beans better than those at Stubby's Hik-Ry Pit in Hot Springs, Arkansas. These are genuine Ozark vittles, made with small cubes of cooked country ham and—as near as we can replicate it at home —molasses as a sweetener.

OZARK HAM AND BEANS, STUBBY STYLE

Stubby's ham and beans are dished out in individual stoneware crocks that are kept warm in the pit until they are served. As the beans sit and stew, they develop a profound lusciousness and an almost crusty texture.

4 cups pea beans	or make your own—see
1½ teaspoons salt	p. 151)
⅓ cup molasses	1 teaspoon dry mustard
⅓ cup brown sugar	1 pound cured country ham
1 cup tomato-based barbecue	(still fatty), diced
sauce (available by mail	1 large onion, studded with
from Stubby's—see p. 153;	4 cloves

Cover beans completely with water and soak overnight. Drain, fill pot with water again, and bring to a boil with salt. Simmer until beans are tender but not mushy, 1–2 hours. Drain. Mixing gently, combine beans with molasses, brown sugar, barbecue sauce, and mustard. Stir in ham.

Preheat oven to 275°. Place onion in bottom of a bean pot. Pour beans in. Cover and bake 6 hours, adding more barbecue sauce if necessary to keep beans moist.

Serves 8.

To make Ozark ham and beans into a full mountain meal, serve them with a pile of scalded mush balls.

SCALDED MUSH BALLS

In America's folk cookery, thrift is the mother of invention. If, for instance, there was cornmeal mush left over after breakfast, it was saved until supper, when the cooled mush was sliced and fried and served with sorghum syrup or a pot of beans. Corn balls, which must be formed while the mush is still warm, are a variation of the fried slices. They are brittle-crisp on the outside, cracking at first bite to reveal a cushiony cake of aromatic cornmeal.

1 teaspoon salt	4 cups boiling water
1¼ cups cornmeal	Oil for frying

Mix salt with meal and stir gradually into boiling water in top of a double boiler. Over direct, moderate heat cook until it thickens, stirring constantly. Place over hot water in a double boiler and cook 1 hour, stirring occasionally. Let cool to tepid.

Form mush into walnut-size balls. Heat 1 inch of oil to 350° in a heavy skillet. Fry balls until crusty golden brown, 4–5 minutes. Turn over once. Drain on paper towels. Serve immediately with sorghum syrup or honey for dipping.

Makes 20 balls.

In Georgia, the inevitable companion to barbecue is Brunswick stew. It comes with all pork platters, either in a small bowl on the side or in one of the sections on a compartmentalized plate.

To serve it as a main course, accompany the stew with corn bread (see p. 266) and section the rabbit or chicken; as a side dish, it should have only half as much meat, and the cooked meat should be removed from its bones and hacked into shreds.

DOMESTICATED BRUNSWICK STEW

The original Brunswick stew, according to culinary lore, was a slave's make-do meal of stale bread, onions, and a brace of fresh-killed squirrels. It has since been fancied up with garden vegetables.

2 pounds cut-up squirrel,
    rabbit, or chicken (1 pound
    if using as a side dish)
¼ cup cooking oil
2 onions, sliced
1 28-ounce can crushed
    tomatoes
½ tablespoon salt

½ tablespoon pepper
1 teaspoon chopped parsley
1 bay leaf
Pinch of thyme
1 cup water
2 cups frozen corn kernels
1 cup frozen lima beans

Brown meat in oil in a large skillet. Remove meat and brown onions in remaining oil. Return meat to pan. Add tomatoes, salt, pepper, parsley, bay leaf, thyme, and water. When bubbling, cover and reduce heat. Simmer 1 hour. If using as a side dish, bone and hack up meat. Add corn and lima beans and, if stew is too thick, up to a cup of water. Simmer 30 minutes more. Add more salt and pepper to taste. Remove bay leaf before serving.

Serves 4–6.

Although a stranger traveling through the South might never know exactly what to expect when ordering a platter of barbecue, it is a good bet there will be slaw. At the Lexington Barbecue #1 in North Carolina, a platter is nothing but meat and finely chopped slaw, arranged half-and-half in a cardboard boat. We think the best North Carolina variation is the mustard slaw served in Rocky Mount, at the venerable Melton's, where it comes as an appetizer before meat, Brunswick stew, and boiled potatoes.

TOBACCO COUNTRY MUSTARD SLAW

Very spicy slaw, matched to the subtleties of barbecued pork.

½ head cabbage (1–1½
    pounds)

¼ cup mayonnaise
1 tablespoon sour cream

1 tablespoon dry mustard
1 tablespoon prepared mustard
¼ teaspoon salt

2 teaspoons sugar
⅓ cup chopped sweet pickles
1 tablespoon sweet pickle juice

Chill cabbage. Shred very fine.

Combine all other ingredients and mix well with 4 cups of shredded cabbage. Chill several hours before serving.

Serves 4 (recipe can be doubled).

"If it fits the pit," reads a sign at the Shady Rest in Owensboro, Kentucky, "we will barbecue it." Meat, fish, fowl—almost anything tastes good after half a day enveloped in hickory smoke.

But are you ready for barbecued salad? It's on the menu throughout Arkansas and western Tennessee; and it's got to be one of the oddest combinations in creation. The salad itself—greens, carrots, bell peppers, etc.—is not actually smoked, but what happens is that once the cool leafy stuff is put together, it is topped with slices of room-temperature smoked beef or pork, which in turn are heaped with *either* tepid barbecue sauce *or* chilly salad dressing (Thousand Island, bleu cheese, French). You might think of it as a Southern-style chef's salad.

ARKANSAS BARBECUED SALAD

Be true to smokehouse tradition and use iceberg lettuce (the only kind crisp enough to hold up under all the weight); if you choose salad dressing rather than barbecue sauce as a topping, use a gloppy, off-the-shelf variety—up to half a bottle per serving.

½ head iceberg lettuce, washed
    and torn into pieces
1 large tomato, cut in eighths
½ red onion, sliced thin
½ green pepper, diced
10 slices cucumber
Radish slices to taste

¼ pound barbecued beef or
    pork, cut in strips, at room
    temperature
Tomato-based barbecue sauce,
    at room temperature, or
    salad dressing to taste

Arrange bed of lettuce on each plate with other vegetables on top. Top with barbecued meat. Ladle sauce or salad dressing over salad.

Makes 2 salads.

Even stranger than barbecue salad is the smoke pit specialty of Coletta's pizzeria in Memphis, Tennessee. Yes, that's right—barbecue pizza. Weird? Sure. But why not? It looks just like Italian pizza, but it has the sass of barbecue sauce instead of Italian-seasoned tomatoes. Our favorite is the minced pork pizza; the succulent, smoky meat is blended with just enough sauce to moisten it (too much sauce makes for a soggy crust).

We've never seen barbecue pizza anywhere outside Memphis; in fact, we've never seen it anywhere other than at Coletta's. But since our initiation there, it's become a regular feature of our weekly Sunday homemade pizza pig-outs.

MEMPHIS-STYLE BARBECUE PIZZA

The True and Pure way to do this is to make barbecue from scratch to spread across this crust. Pork shoulder, hacked and shredded, works best. But if you want to cut corners, we recommend mixing a pound of cooked ground chuck or a pound of cooked pork sausage with a thick and spicy off-the-shelf barbecue sauce (regular or hickory flavor). In Memphis, the barbecue goes on top of the cheese. We prefer it the other way around. This pepper-tweaked crust has a Southern accent thanks to rendered salt pork.

4 ounces salt pork, cut into small cubes	Cornmeal
1 package dry yeast	¾ pound ground chuck or pork sausage, cooked and drained
1 teaspoon sugar	
1 cup tepid water (110°)	¾ cup barbecue sauce
3 cups flour	½–1 pound mozzarella cheese (to taste), shredded
1 teaspoon salt	
1 teaspoon black pepper	

Cook salt pork until all fat is rendered. You should have about 3 tablespoons. (Save bits of salt pork and chop very fine to add to beef or pork, if a very salty topping is desired.)

Combine yeast and sugar with water. When yeast starts to foam, stir it into 2¾ cups of the flour. Add salt, pepper, and 3 tablespoons of rendered fat. Stir vigorously to mix.

Turn dough out onto a floured board. Let rest while you clean and oil bowl.

Knead dough 8–10 minutes, until smooth and elastic, adding flour if needed. Return to bowl, cover with plastic wrap, and let rise in a warm place until double in bulk, 1–2 hours.

Preheat oven to 450°.

Punch down dough, return it to floured board, and flatten it out. Lay it on a 16-inch pizza pan sprinkled with cornmeal.

Combine meat with sauce and spread over pizza crust. Top with mozzarella.

Bake 15–20 minutes, until crust is golden brown.

Serves 4.

Dessert is seldom even an afterthought at most pits, simply because the intensity of great barbecue completely exhausts taste buds. Sweet-sauced meat is, for most Q-hounds, complete, needing no denouement.

We discovered a jim-dandy exception to this rule while motoring across Tennessee, at a shopping center cafe called Bobby Q's in Cookeville. As the name suggests, barbecue was the specialty of the house, served with Pool Room Slaw (from a top-secret eighty-year-old recipe given Bobby by a retired pit master from Nashville), and followed by a different extra-special homemade dessert each day. A newspaper article pinned on the wall raved about Better Than Sex Lemon Pie. The day we stopped in, it was banana pudding—from another closely guarded recipe. With the promise that we would give due credit to Sarah, its inventor, we managed to get them to tell us how they make it:

SARAH'S BANANA PUDDING

What makes Bobby Q pudding special is the brown sugar streaks. When mixing the brown sugar into the custard, do not stir vigorously. Simply *fold* it in, creating a marbleized effect.

⅓ cup granulated sugar
Pinch of salt
3 tablespoons cornstarch
1 12-ounce can evaporated
    milk
1½ cups whole milk
4 egg yolks

1 teaspoon vanilla extract
16–20 vanilla wafers
2 large bananas, sliced
⅔ cup dark brown sugar
4–5 teaspoons hot water
1 cup cream

Mix granulated sugar, salt, and cornstarch. Add evaporated milk and whole milk. Cook in a double boiler, stirring frequently, until it coats the back of a spoon.

Beat egg yolks and add about ½ cup of hot pudding, stirring,

☞

then return yolks to pudding, and cook 3 minutes longer, stirring. Add vanilla. Cool to room temperature, stirring occasionally.

Layer vanilla wafers and bananas in an 8-inch square baking dish.

Melt brown sugar in hot water, creating a thick paste. Stir paste into pudding, just enough to create streaks. Pour over wafers and bananas. Chill.

When pudding is well chilled, whip cream and spread gently across top.

Serves 6–8.

One other place you will likely get dessert after eating Southern barbecue is in Kentucky's mutton belt, in the northwest part of the state. At the Shady Rest in Owensboro, mutton plates are followed by what the menu calls Kentucky Fried Apple Pie. Unlike the deep-fried pies of the Memphis area, these are griddle-cooked in butter, yielding a fragile crescent crust pocketing apples fragrant with spice. They are best served warm, two at a time, straddled by a single scoop of vanilla ice cream.

OWENSBORO GRIDDLE-FRIED APPLE PIE

3 cups crisp apples, peeled and diced (about 3 apples, or 1¼ pounds)	2 cups flour
	1 teaspoon salt
	⅓ cup lard
⅔ cup sugar	4–5 tablespoons cold milk
1 teaspoon cinnamon	4 tablespoons butter

In a covered saucepan simmer apples in just enough water to cover, until apples are tender. Drain, then mix with sugar and cinnamon.

Mix flour and salt. Cut in lard. Add just enough cold milk to create a moist, workable dough.

Roll out dough on a floured board to ⅛ inch thick. Cut into 4½–5-inch-diameter rounds (roll and cut trimmings too) and place 2 tablespoons of stewed apples in center of each round. Fold pastry to form a semicircle and crimp edges with a fork, making sure pie is completely sealed.

In batches, fry in butter over medium heat until nicely browned on both sides, about 3 minutes per side.

Makes 8–10 pies.

ON THE
HAM HOUSE TRAIL

ike a moonshine still smashed by revenuers, the vacant backyard ham house has become an icon of savaged tradition. The dirty deed was done in 1967, when the United States Congress passed the Wholesome Meat Act, and ham houses fell under the jurisdiction of the Department of Agriculture.

The quaint charm of the small, independent ham house has given way to efficient barns where a thousand hams, rather than a mere couple of dozen, can hang for their year-long cure. That kind of government-approved, squeaky-clean supply line isn't much fun. A devotee of country hams wants to stroll around back before breakfast to clear his nostrils with the fine, fetid aroma of hams on the hook, hanging in the ham barn annex of the restaurant.

Despite the feds, ham house restaurants manage to retain a delicious eccentricity. The lowest-level are nothing more than annexes of other businesses—hardware stores or gas stations—where they get hams from a nearby smokehouse, slice them thin, sandwich the sheaves between prefab biscuits, and heat the ham biscuits in a microwave. The result is disconcerting: great wine-red ham buried inside an icky biscuit.

One of the most intriguing such places used to be in Danville, Kentucky—Anderson Country Hams, a corner storefront that shared space with Sim's Garage, a heavy vehicle repair business. The cafe was semicircular, like a tugboat's prow, its large wraparound windows hung with neatly spaced country hams. It always reminded us of the Hall of Fame in the Bronx, the view outside framed by hanging hams.

Anderson's ham was good, but the biscuits were not, so we always got our ham sliced and fried, accompanied by a companion as common as biscuits—griddle-fried corn cakes.

CORN BATTER CAKES TO GO WITH HAM

Throughout the mid-South, from Virginia to western Kentucky, corn cakes (referred to by locals simply as corn bread) are an immensely popular breadstuff, served in lieu of rolls with lunch, at breakfast, or next to bowls of Brunswick stew at dinner. Serve each cake with a pat of butter melting on top.

2 eggs, beaten until lemon
    colored
1 cup buttermilk
1 cup water
1 cup white cornmeal

1 cup flour
½ teaspoon baking soda
½ teaspoon salt
Butter for frying

Combine ingredients in order. Pour 4-inch cakes into a buttered skillet (nonstick preferred). Fry over medium heat until golden brown. Turn and fry other side.

Makes 12–15 corn cakes.

One step up the line from the ham house annex are restaurants that actually have menus, but focus on ham, usually for breakfast. Here the ham is sliced about a quarter inch thick and fried on a griddle or in a cast-iron skillet, resulting in a slab of meat on which the soft pink areas are mottled with sand-textured blotches from the pan, and the rim of fat has turned translucent amber.

Then there are top-of-the-line ham houses—not really ham houses anymore, but full-service restaurants (usually grown up from small ham house cafes). Here a large ham steak is the *pièce de résistance*, and the menu offers entrées featuring, but not limited to, ham. Our favorite such place is the Surrey House in Virginia, which offers eleven varieties of Virginia ham dinner, including ham steak with fried apples, ham croquettes, and ham and oysters.

Even the tackiest roadside stores—the ones that specialize in fireworks and towels-by-the-pound—give a prominent place to "genuine" country hams. And it makes sense. A ham, like a chenille bedspread, is something travelers want to take home with them as a reminder of their trip south.

The fuss might seem overwrought if you think of ham as the blubbery pink oval sold in cans at the supermarket. Country ham is nothing like that. A true country ham is the result of a year-long process, beginning with a hog (preferably peanut fed) slaughtered during the first frosty week in November (preferably by the light of a full moon, according to hoglore).

The hams (and maybe the bacon and the jowls too) are hung up to dry, packed with salt. During the long winter months, the hams "drink in" the curing mixture and drip odoriferous brine onto the floor of the curing house.

As the months pass, the hams ripen, become firm, and lose their moisture. Then—in some parts of the South, such as Smithfield, Virginia, and central Kentucky—they are smoked over hickory, applewood, or pecan boughs until the meat turns brick red.

Whatever the fine points of the cure, smoked or no, the result is an ugly thing, gnarled and moldy. A country ham connoisseur will have it no other way. It's great fun to send away for a country ham in its grungy burlap sack, tear it open, and smell the delicious barnyard stink.

Among the preferred places for mail-order ham are Ballance (for smoked Kentucky hams), Durham's (for unsmoked Virginia highland hams), and the Loveless Motel (for Tennessee hams and country ham slices, if an entire one is too much).

Ballance Country Hams
Route #1, Box 15
Oakland, KY 42159
(502) 563-3956

Durham's Restaurant
E. Main Street
Wytheville, VA 24382
(703) 228-5241

Loveless Motel
Route 100
Nashville, TN 37221
(615) 646-9700

HOW TO COOK A COUNTRY HAM

Once the ham arrives, here's what to do with it. First, unwrap it. Soak it overnight in a sink or large basin, covered with water, changing the water twice. The next day, wash and scrub the ham with a wire brush, removing all the leftover pepper, mold, etc.

Simmer the ham, fully covered with water, 18 minutes per pound, or until the shank bone pulls loose easily. Remove from the water, let cool, and cut off the skin and most fat, leaving a thin layer of fat. Preheat the oven to 350°.

Score the remaining fat in a diamond pattern and place the ham fat side up in a baking pan. Spread generously with a half-and-half mixture of brown sugar and prepared mustard and pour a quart of Coca-Cola into the bottom of the roasting pan. Bake 1 hour, basting two or three times with Coke.

Cool to room temperature. Slice parchment thin.

HELEN DICKERSON'S HAM BISCUITS

One of the best ways to enjoy country ham is sandwiched inside a biscuit. These nice fluffy rounds have just the right pasty blandness to balance the vigor of the ham. At the Chalfonte Hotel in Cape May (the southernmost tip of New Jersey), Helen Dickerson grinds country ham with enough mayonnaise to moisten it, then spreads it on these biscuits.

2 cups flour	4 tablespoons Crisco
2 teaspoons baking powder	Up to 1 cup milk
½ teaspoon salt	

Filling

½ pound country ham	¼ cup mayonnaise

Preheat oven to 400°. Mix dry ingredients; cut in Crisco until crumbly. Add milk gradually until dough is manageable (still sticky, but clinging together). Turn onto a floured board and knead five or six times, only until dough holds together, handling as little as possible. You may need to add a sprinkle of flour, but don't add too much. This dough should be messy and moist. Roll out to ½-inch thickness. Using a biscuit cutter or the floured rim of a drinking glass, cut 2-inch biscuits. Place on a lightly greased baking sheet and bake 10 minutes, or until light brown on top.

   To make filling, chop country ham into tiny pieces. Mix with mayonnaise. Gently cut biscuits in half and fill with ham mixture.

Makes 10–12 ham biscuits.

HAM AND RED-EYE GRAVY

"People from other states often suggest that red-eye gravy should be bottled and sold commercially," say the people at the Country Ham Apartments in Bowling Green, Kentucky. "It can't be done, because there's never any left over."

Red-eye gravy is nothing but the drippings of fried ham mixed with a little water or coffee. The way to make a lot of it is to trim fat from many slices of country ham and fry the fat slowly until it is rendered. Throw a few lean pieces of ham (sliced 1/4–3/8 inch thick) into the fat and fry at medium heat until the ham begins to brown. Turn and cook the other side. Remove the ham from the pan and add a few tablespoonfuls of black coffee to the rendered fat. Cook and stir for 3 minutes. Pour the gravy into a serving bowl and use for dunking biscuits or to spoon over grits.

JUST GRITS

No ham breakfast is complete without them. Few people (and fewer restaurants) make grits from scratch. Instant grits are so convenient. But for the from-scratch chef, here's how to do it.

1 cup unprocessed grits   1/2 teaspoon salt
2 cups water

Wash grits well. Soak in water overnight. Bring to a boil, then add salt and cook in top part of a double boiler over gently simmering water 2 hours, stirring occasionally.

Makes 3 cups grits.

FRIED GRITS

If you've gone to all the trouble of making grits from scratch, you may be disappointed to find that all you wind up with is white mush. James Beard, who thought grits "a rather revolting food," suggested livening them up in the frying pan and serving them with wild game.

3 cups cooked grits   1 cup seasoned bread crumbs
2 eggs, beaten   Butter

Pour freshly boiled grits into a buttered square dish and allow to cool. They will harden. Cut into slices. Dip in eggs and coat with bread crumbs. Sauté in butter until crisp at edges.

Serves 4–6.

FANCY DRESS CHEESE GRITS

Ordinary cheese grits are made by simply stirring some grated cheese into the boiled grits. But this baked casserole, suggested by a recipe from Nashville's Satsuma Tea Room, elevates them from humble breakfast grain to near soufflé status, a polite side dish in the finest of ham houses.

2 cups warm cooked grits   2 teaspoons dry mustard
2 eggs, beaten   ½ teaspoon salt
⅔ cup grated sharp Cheddar   1 tablespoon finely minced
   cheese   onion
4 tablespoons butter, melted

Preheat oven to 350°. Mix all ingredients and pour into a well-buttered 4-cup casserole. Bake, uncovered, 50 minutes. Serve immediately, handling carefully so they don't deflate.

Serves 4.

A full ham breakfast will include not only biscuits and grits and red-eye gravy but cream gravy too. This rib-sticking stuff is sometimes speckled with bits of sausage and poured on biscuits as a meal unto itself. But the way we like it best is in a small dish on the side, for an occasional dunk.

SKINHEAD'S CREAM GRAVY

It was more than a decade ago, at Skinhead's restaurant in Paducah, Kentucky, that we first encountered serious cream gravy. Sure, we had eaten cream gravy, from the velvet luxury of Mom's home version on mashed potatoes, to five-and-dime glue gravy on hot turkey sandwiches. But we had no idea of the true terror that real sawmill gravy can instill in the ham house novitiate.

Skinhead's had been recommended for its catfish, but we arrived at 7:00 a.m. and the Friolators were cold. So we grouchily settled for breakfast. What a trough of eats it turned out to be! Coral red country ham, a bowl of steaming grits, a bowl of red-eye gravy, a lone egg, and a pile of biscuits hot out of the oven. The biscuits were accompanied by a great big pitcher of what the waitress called sawmill gravy, pepper-speckled stuff with a specific gravity on the far side of lead.

Skinhead's recipe makes a pint—suitable for biscuit dunking or as the mantle for a plate of chicken fried steak (see p. 262). We imagine this to be the most horrifying foodstuff on earth to compulsive dieters.

3 tablespoons cold bacon grease ⅓ cup flour	1½ cups milk 1 teaspoon black pepper 1 teaspoon salt

Form a paste of bacon grease and flour. Bring milk to a simmer and add flour mixture, mashing with a spoon to blend. As gravy simmers, add pepper and salt. Simmer 5 minutes, stirring.

Makes enough gravy for 4–6 dunkers.

Note: This will keep several days in the refrigerator, but you will need to add milk to thin it out when reheating.

One of the great ham dishes ever conceived is a specialty of southern Virginia, in the Smithfield-Norfolk area, where small pieces of the famous smoked ham—resilient and salty—are combined with sweet, fragile hunks of crabmeat in a combination dinner prepared "Norfolk style," meaning sautéed in liberal amounts of butter. Serve with plain biscuits or a few rounds of pan corn bread on the side.

CRABMEAT AND SMITHFIELD HAM, NORFOLK STYLE

Crab and ham, Norfolk style, is a study in unimprovable simplicity. Please, we implore you, do not do as one "inventive" chef we once encountered did and splash this perfect combo with wine. In fact, the ideal complementary beverage is Classic Coke, served over crushed ice. This is our version of a meal we enjoyed at the Landmark Crab House in Chincoteague Island, Virginia.

½ pound Smithfield ham,
   trimmed of fat
6 tablespoons butter

1 pound lump crabmeat,
   picked clean

Cut ham into ¼-inch nuggets. Sauté in 2 tablespoons of the butter until ham begins to brown. Add remaining butter; when it is melted, add crabmeat. Cook only until crabmeat is warmed through.

Serves 4.

Travel into the heart of Virginia ham country, around Smithfield and Surry, and you notice that all the fields around are filled with peanut vines. The connection is logical: The best hams are cut from nut-fed hogs. It is a relationship that one expects to continue in the kitchens of the best restaurants in the area.

But few Virginia restaurants highlight peanuts with the same regional pride-in-produce that is so prevalent in ham houses. The most popular peanut dish is peanut soup, which some people know as "Tuskegee Soup" (named after the university where George Washington Carver, the peanut's Zeus, taught and experimented).

For our peanut soup recipe, we went to Surry, Virginia, the small town from which the Jamestown Ferry goes to Williamsburg. Here is Helen and Owen Gwaltney's Surrey House, a citadel of Tidewater cookery famous not only for its peanut soup but for garden vegetables garnished with peanuts, nut-and-green salads, and chocolate peanut sundaes.

The soup recipe we got from Helen Gwaltney has a fine creamy texture (thanks to the peanut butter), but it is agreeably light.

SURREY HOUSE CREAM OF PEANUT SOUP

For soup with more avoirdupois, finish it with a cup of cream or condensed milk. Some nineteenth-century versions call for the addition of the liquor from a quart of oysters, then the oysters themselves as a garnish. And on special occasions, Mrs. Gwaltney told us, each serving might be laced with a shot of sherry.

4 tablespoons butter	2 tablespoons flour
1 cup thinly sliced celery	1 cup creamy peanut butter
1 medium onion, diced	8 tablespoons chopped salted
2 quarts chicken stock or broth	peanuts as garnish

Melt butter in a large saucepan over low heat. Add celery and onion. Cook until tender but not brown. Add chicken stock and bring to a boil. Strain. Return to saucepan and cool to room temperature.

Mix flour with enough cool water to form a paste; beat paste into broth. Blend in peanut butter. Simmer 15 minutes, stirring occasionally. Serve piping hot, garnishing each soup bowl with a tablespoon of chopped peanuts.

Serves 8.

"We were peanuts long before anyone ever heard of Jimmy Carter," the waitress at the Virginia Diner in Wakefield boasted. "You all are sitting in the peanut capital of the world."

"You mean Wakefield?" we asked.

"No, not the town," she said, annoyed at our denseness. "This place! The diner."

Sure enough, all around the cash register were nuts and nut artifacts of every variety, and a bowl of water-blanched peanuts for snacking. What fantastic peanuts! Each tan seed had brutal crunch, its skin faintly blistered. The Virginia Diner sells them in bulk—butter toasted, salted or unsalted in the shell, and as peanut brittle—and also turns them into spectacular peanut pie, a sweet celebration of gooberhood that is dense, sticky, a lot like pecan pie, but with more snap. Although any old peanuts will work in this pie, Virginia Diner peanuts send it off the map. They can be ordered from:

Virginia Diner, Inc.
P.O. Box 310
Wakefield, VA 23888
(804) 899-3106

VIRGINIA DINER PEANUT PIE

3 eggs
1½ cups dark corn syrup
4 tablespoons butter, melted
¼ teaspoon salt
½ teaspoon vanilla extract

1 tablespoon flour
1½ cups coarsely chopped
 unsalted roasted peanuts
1 unbaked 9-inch pie shell (see
 p. 123)

Preheat oven to 375°. Beat eggs until foamy. Add corn syrup, butter, salt, vanilla, and flour. Mix thoroughly. Stir in peanuts. Pour into pie shell. Bake 40–45 minutes until set.

Serves 6–8.

OYSTER BARS
AND CREOLE SOUL

The first time we ate our way south, about fifteen years ago, the Gulf Coast seemed barren. Nothing but bars and taverns, roadhouses and late-night supper clubs. Where did all the decent people eat?

Right under our noses. Having lingered inland in the Deep South, where drinking and upstanding dining are separated, we were unprepared for the fact that most good meals along the Gulf—Louisiana in particular—are served in bars and taverns.

There may be many legal or historical reasons for this fact, but the gustatory logic is impeccable: Gulf Coast seafood goes great with beer. Furthermore, it is at its best when eaten in the spirit of insouciance that characterizes bar food and roadhouse service.

In fact, the most interesting aspect of traveling the Gulf, especially through Cajun country, is the impertinent mixture of its culture's subtleties with appalling crudeness. Witness the region's zydeco music, a polyglot Mississippi blues, sung in Acadian patois, to the blare of an accompanying accordion. That's the way Cajun food is too. You can conclude a profound Louisianian-Italian meal at Mosca's with a melted marshmallow dessert known as pineapple fluff—every bit as déclassé as its name suggests. Appreciation of this land demands a fully developed sense of diverse, even contradictory, values.

As we see it, the way to enjoy an oyster bar is to embrace the Cajun spirit of irreverence. Walk in and wet your whistle with a long neck Jax and a dozen on the half shell. Down the hatch. Now a bowl of boiled crawfish would be nice. Then maybe gumbo to warm things up, with a half-dozen raw oysters on the side, for easing into the gumbo just before you dip in a spoon. If it's soft-shell season, get a couple of parchment-crusted sweeties, sautéed in butter.

Or you can be cheerfully monotonous: Find a stool at the counter and order nothing but dozens on the half shell, sliding them down your throat as fast as the shucker can pry them open. The only embroidery you'll want on this feed is crackers and beer and the standard oyster bar folderol of hot sauce, pickles, and peppers.

Eating seafood on the Gulf has a different aroma from eating it on the East or West coasts. Most fish houses in the West are clean and casual; in the East they have a saline-washed clarity. But from Florida to Texas, there is a definite raunch about the best of them. From Port Arthur west, they smell like petroleum. Farther east, they smell like swamps. Even the cleanest, such as Casamento's in New Orleans, seem sultrier and sexier than their coastal brethren.

Oysters are in season year-round on the Gulf; during the "R" months, they're bigger and worth shipping north. At Ouzts' Oyster Bar in a shady grove by the side of U.S. 98 in Newport, Florida, local Apalachicolas sell for $1.75 a dozen. They are fetched from a battered beer cooler behind the five-stool counter, quickly opened, and presented on shells in a pool of oceanic liquor, their glistening meat steel gray and salty.

In addition to raw oysters, Ouzts' minuscule menu lists stone crab claws, the succulent seafood delicacy of south Florida. The best-known place to feast on stone crab is Joe's of Miami Beach. The large, hard-shelled claws are merely boiled and cracked—delectable as is, but what makes them special at Joe's (other than the vintage 1920s Florida atmosphere) is the dipping sauce, which we like with any chilled shellfish.

JOE'S STONE CRAB MUSTARD SAUCE

3½ teaspoons dry mustard
1 cup mayonnaise
2 teaspoons Worcestershire sauce

1 teaspoon A-1 sauce
1½ tablespoons light cream
⅛ teaspoon salt

Beat all ingredients 3 full minutes. Chill and serve.

Makes ⅔ cup.

It was while downing oysters by the dozen in the Mobile Bay town of Theodore that we met a former merchant marine at the bar who claimed to have invented a specialty unique to Mobile—West Indies salad. His name was Mr. Bayley, and he was a big man who liked to eat. When he learned that we were of like mind, he adopted us for the day. As he drove us to his home so we could sample his quince wine and bread-and-butter pickles, he told us how he started in the restaurant business. (He now runs a local steak house.)

"I had a real one-man show," he explained as we strolled around his yard, drinking chilled soda pop from coolers hidden under bushes and in work sheds. "Customers came in, I took their order, ran in back, cooked it, and then I served it to them. In those days, lump crabmeat was sixty-five cents a pound, so I used to make up big batches of it for myself. I had a dentist customer who came in one day and found me in the kitchen, eating lunch. 'I want what you've got there,' he told me. So I fixed him some. The next day he brought his friends in to taste it. I named it West Indies salad. The only secret to the recipe is getting fresh crabmeat."

MOBILE BAY WEST INDIES SALAD

2 pounds lump crabmeat   ¾ cup cider vinegar
1 large white onion, chopped   1 cup crushed ice
½ cup Wesson oil

In a 2-quart jar make alternate layers of crabmeat and onion, each about 1 inch thick. Continue to top of jar. Combine oil and vinegar and pour over layered crab and onion. Top with crushed ice and close jar. Let marinate in refrigerator 24–36 hours. Serve with saltines on the side.

Serves 10–12 as hors d'oeuvres.

Gulf Coast cookery, infused with recipes from the Caribbean, Latin America, and ethnic groups from all over Europe, relies most heavily on contributions of soul food cooks—whether as slaves or chefs (or quite possibly both). That is why some of the best, most authentic eateries in both New Orleans and Mobile are the ones run by blacks, who acknowledge and celebrate that debt.

In the pantheon of these restaurants is one called Mary's Place, which used to occupy a scrubby lot filled with pecking chickens, on the Mobile Bay in Coden. Mary's was a bare-bones establishment, fifteen tables and a Coke machine, with a Gulf Coast soul food menu of gumbo and Creole-seasoned fried fish, served alongside hot corn sticks and followed by sweet potato pie. Mary Branch always said that the essential ingredient of her baked crabs was white bread, soaked in milk. That is the way we re-created her recipe.

DEVIL CRAB À LA MARY'S PLACE

Variations of baked crab abound from the Gulf Coast to the Chesapeake Bay. Most are spicy, which is why menus list them as deviled crabs; or more menacingly, as devil crab. Mary's were moist and luscious, much less devilish than most. If you like them very peppery, double the amount of hot sauce.

6 slices white bread

1 cup milk

1 egg

1 green bell pepper, minced fine

1 white onion, minced fine

1 rib celery, minced fine

1 clove garlic, minced fine

4 tablespoons butter

1 pound crabmeat, picked clean

1 tablespoon prepared mustard

Salt to taste

1 teaspoon Worcestershire sauce

10 drops Tabasco sauce

Tear bread into pieces. Combine milk and egg and soak bread thoroughly in mixture.

Sauté pepper, onion, celery, and garlic in butter until soft, about 4 minutes.

Add crabmeat to milk-soaked bread and mush together with your hands. Add mustard, salt, Worcestershire, and Tabasco. Add sautéed vegetables. Mix well.

Preheat oven to 400°. Pack into empty, well-oiled crab shells or small ovenproof ramekins. Bake 10 minutes, until sizzling.

Serves 6.

The inextricable Creole soul food connection is nowhere more evident or more delicious than at Eddie Baquet's hidden-away restaurant on Law Street in New Orleans. What we wanted most from Eddie was his recipe for gumbo—a head-spinning brew that has no equals anywhere in town. But Eddie sent us a letter saying that it is a recipe impossible to share. "For years I have cooked by feel," he wrote, explaining that no mere recipe could capture its evanescent magic.

However, Eddie concluded his letter with these encouraging words: "I have substituted trout Baquet to ease the pain of No Gumbo."

NO GUMBO TROUT BAQUET

A relatively simple recipe that showcases the sweetness of *fresh* crabmeat. Anything less, and this dish is not worth making.

1 cup butter or margarine

9 cloves garlic, chopped fine

1 large onion, diced

1½ pounds fresh lump crabmeat

12 fillets tenderloin trout (about 5 ounces each)

¼ cup lemon juice

¼ cup Chablis

Salt and pepper to taste

Melt ½ cup of the butter or margarine in a saucepan. Sauté garlic and onion until onion is transparent but not brown. Add remaining ½ cup of butter or margarine. When melted, add crabmeat. Remove from heat.

Butter a broiler pan to accommodate fish fillets. (If fish has skin, slit it to prevent curling.) Broil fish 5 minutes, or until done. Place 2 fillets on each plate.

Stir lemon juice and Chablis into crabmeat mixture, season to taste, and spoon over trout fillets. Serve immediately.

Serves 6.

New Orleans chefs are famous for offering their guests a lagniappe—an extra little unexpected something. So it was with Eddie's letter. Along with Trout Baquet, he sent us his recipe for oyster dressing.

We were flabbergasted. Eddie's oyster dressing is a star ingredient in one of New Orleans's greatest meals—served alongside a pair of soulful pork chops. *Merci encore, monsieur!*

EDDIE'S CREOLE OYSTER DRESSING

Do not *stuff* chops with this dressing. Serve it alongside or on top of them, or with fried chicken—or by itself.

1 pound lean ground beef
1½ pints oysters, drained and
    chopped
4 cloves garlic, minced
1 rib celery, chopped
1 medium onion, chopped
½ green bell pepper, chopped

1½ teaspoons oregano
1 tablespoon thyme
1½ cups crumbled stale French
    bread
1 egg
⅛ cup chopped parsley
Salt and black pepper to taste

Combine all ingredients and mix thoroughly.

Generously grease a 3–4-quart heavy saucepan or skillet (cast iron preferred). Add dressing and cook over medium heat 40 minutes, stirring often and briskly.

Serves 6.

The signature dish of the Creole soul cook is red beans and rice. Traditionally made on Monday from the weekend's leftover ham bone, it is gastronomic transcendence on a plate, mundane ingredients turned into a celestial meal.

We remember not too long ago, when one could go into the French Quarter, find a stool at Buster Holmes's lunch counter at the corner of Burgundy and Orleans, and get oneself a generous plate of red beans and rice for 75¢. The last time we visited, the price had gone up, but Buster's was every bit as colorful as it ever was. A chalked sign outside advertising "turnip green and sofe drink" was obscured by two transvestites in a screeching catfight.

The inside was rude and messy, with fresh waitresses dishing out $2

blue plate specials along with generous helpings of abuse. The air smelled of sweat and garlic. It was a frightening environment for those of us not accustomed to the aggressive manner of French Quarter street people. But that rough edge only added to the authenticity of the incredible Creole soul dish that inspired Louis Armstrong to sign all his letters, "Red beans and ricely yours . . ."

DRUNK RED BEANS AND RICE

Buster Holmes asserts a recipe from red beans and rice *au vin*. Adding wine is fierce iconoclasm, considering how fussy Orleanians are about the Truth and Purity of red beans and rice recipes. ("A foreigner such as myself," Boston gastronome John Thorne once wrote, "risks serious abuse just by having an opinion on the subject.") But no one is more entitled to diddle with the recipe than Buster, who helped define twentieth-century Creole soul food. Besides, like chili in Texas or chowder on Cape Cod, every real Creole chef adds his own flourish to the basic formula. This recipe was inspired by Buster's, with help from John Thorne's pamphlet *Rice and Beans: The Itinerary of a Recipe*—the last word on the subject. Seeing as how the wine is used merely to soak the beans, be sure to use a cheap one. You don't want this dish with even a residue of couth.

2 cups red beans, washed and drained	2 medium onions, chopped fine
3 cups Sauterne wine	1 cup minced scallion (reserve green tops)
1 meaty ham bone, cracked, or 1 pound salt pork, cubed and boiled 15 minutes to reduce saltiness	⅛ teaspoon thyme
	¼ teaspoon Tabasco sauce
	2 bay leaves
	2 cups rice
1 pound smoked sausage, cut into disks	4½ cups water
	2 cloves garlic, crushed
6 cloves garlic, minced	Salt to taste

Soak beans overnight in wine and enough water to cover. Pour off liquid and put beans in a 6-quart stockpot with 2 quarts of water. Add ham bone, sausage, garlic, onions, scallion, and seasonings, stir gently, and bring to a simmer gradually. Partially cover and simmer gently 3 hours, adding a half-and-half mixture of water and wine as needed to keep beans soupy.

After 2½ hours, mash some of the softened beans against side of pot to thicken gravy.

Put rice in 4½ cups water with crushed garlic and salt to taste and bring to a boil. Cover, lower heat, and simmer until water is evaporated and rice is soft, 20–25 minutes.

Discard bay leaves. Serve beans over rice, garnished with scallion tops.

Serves 8–10.

The last time we arrived in Houston, we were hammered, dead on our feet from a fast cross-country trip. So Houstonians Janice Schindeler and Harry Crofton took us to Tony Mandola's Blue Oyster Bar, a Cajun roadhouse with a lit-from-inside glass brick bar that infuses the dining room with a blue hue reminiscent of a primitive outer space movie. They explained that Tony's is the place they fall into whenever they need mothering. And they told us to order "mama's gumbo."

It really is Tony Mandola's mother's recipe, mud-colored, thick, smelling of the sea and spice, crowded with seafood. Although not as soulful-funky in its seasonings, it was an elegant match for Eddie's in New Orleans.

We returned to Connecticut and found the nicest homecoming present: Tony Mandola's mother's recipe for gumbo, sent by Janice.

TONY MANDOLA'S MAMA'S GUMBO

The secret to this gumbo, Tony said, is the roux. "It's simple, as in all good food. But it takes time . . . as in all good things." Our adaptation of Tony's mother's recipe reduces the amount of flour by one-third.

1¼ cups vegetable oil	1 tablespoon minced garlic
1 cup flour	2 cups whole tomatoes, peeled
1½ cups chopped yellow onion	3 quarts chicken stock
¾ cup chopped celery	¼ cup chopped parsley
½ cup chopped green bell pepper	½ teaspoon black pepper
2 tablespoons diced scallion	1 teaspoon salt
	½ teaspoon cayenne pepper

4 bay leaves
1 pound fresh okra, cut into
1½-inch pieces
2 pounds small to medium
shrimp

1 pound crabmeat
1½ dozen oysters and their
liquor

Heat 1 cup of the oil over medium heat and, stirring constantly, pour in flour gradually. Cook slowly 30–45 minutes, until roux is deep brown, the shade of pecan shells.

Sauté onion in remaining ¼ cup of oil in an 8-quart stockpot. When translucent, add celery, green pepper, scallion, and garlic. When vegetables begin to soften, stir in roux and cook 10 minutes. Crush tomatoes in your hand and add, with their juice, to mixture.

Pour in chicken stock, turn heat to high, stir well to dissolve roux, and add parsley and seasonings. Bring to a boil, then lower heat and simmer 45 minutes. Add okra and cook 5 minutes.

Add shrimp and crabmeat and bring to a boil again. Remove from heat and stir in oysters and liquor. Serve on top of rice.

Serves 10–12.

Gumbo is serious cooking; its flip side is all the easy eating that Gulf Coasters—Louisianians especially—enjoy every day: mountains of plain boiled crawfish and shrimp, fried catfish, raw oysters, and "po boy" sandwiches.

Po boys are dished out in oyster bars and pool halls, from grocery stores, and in small cafes. They come stuffed with anything you like, and are similar to the sandwiches that many ordinary American citizens eat for lunch, except four times as large.

The po boy is a second cousin to the Delaware Valley hoagie or hero sandwich. It is at its best when stuffed with oysters (known as an oyster loaf)—the *pièce de résistance* of street grub in both New Orleans and Cajun country.

At the neighborhood New Orleans oyster bar named Casamento's, the mammoth sandwiches are constructed with entire loaves of pan-shaped white bread, sliced lengthwise, buttered, and toasted. Into these yeasty jaws are piled heaps of freshly shucked oysters, beautiful golden morsels with a brittle skin that shatters at the slightest pressure, giving way to a wave of meltingly warm, briny oyster meat across the tongue.

Other than hard-crusted bread, the crucial factor in an oyster loaf is freshly fried oysters. (At Casamento's, each sandwich's batch is fried while you wait.)

PEACEMAKER OYSTER PO BOY

The culinary legend of the oyster po boy is that it was once known as *la médiatrice*, because it was what dallying husbands brought back to assuage their wives. When served in either a French bread or a whole pan loaf, it is customary to scoop out some of the inside of the bread, forming a pocket that keeps the oysters warm.

3 eggs	1 cup yellow cornmeal
¼ cup cream	Oil for frying
2 dozen freshly shucked oysters	1 12–18-inch loaf French bread
¼ teaspoon salt	Tartar sauce, tomatoes, and/or
¼ teaspoon black pepper	lettuce as garnish
¼ teaspoon cayenne pepper	(optional)
1 cup cracker crumbs	

Beat eggs and cream together. Sprinkle oysters with a mixture of salt and black and cayenne peppers. Dip oysters into egg-and-cream mixture, then roll in cracker crumbs. Return to mixture, then coat thoroughly with cornmeal. Set carefully on wax paper and refrigerate as bread is prepared.

Heat oil in a deep fryer to 375°.

As oil heats, preheat oven to 350°. Slice loaf of bread lengthwise, one-third from top, and scoop out inside of bottom to form a trough. Place in oven 10 minutes, or until warm and crisp.

Fry oysters, a few at a time, 2 minutes each, and drain on paper towels.

Fill loaf with oysters, garnish with tartar sauce, tomatoes, and/or lettuce, if desired. (A good alternative condiment is chili sauce doctored up with horseradish and hot sauce to taste.)

New Orleans variations on the mammoth sandwich theme are boundless: muffulettas (see p. 144), ham po boys, hickory-cooked beef po boys, fried potato po boys (at a joint called Clarence and Lefty's on Almonaster Street), the "Joe Don" sandwich (beef, ham, cheese), and the "half-and-half boat" (hollowed-out white bread, buttered and packed with fried shrimp *and* oysters).

Outside the city, at a restaurant called the Cabin in Burnside, they make the most deluxe po boy of them all, known as a "pirogue," after the bayou canoe of the same name. It is a loaf loaded down with oysters, shrimp, and small fillets of fish, all fried. To make your own pirogue, follow the po boy directions, but use only 1 dozen oysters, plus a half-dozen shrimp and a couple of catfish fillets. The traditional escort for this battleship is red beans and rice!

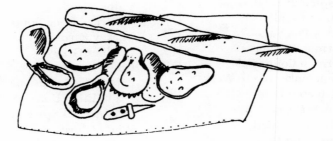

THE MIDWEST

CHICKEN DINNER HALLS

CHICAGO'S DEEP DISH DELIRIUM

UPPER PENINSULA PASTY SHOPS

RUDE FOOD

CAFE SOCIETY

Commentators on the American scene go to the Midwest and seek out small town cafes in hopes of locating the pulse of the nation, the "real America," or some equally profound-sounding perspective about the mental health of the country.

We have never gone to a cafe looking for anything more important than a tenderloin sandwich and a piece of sour cream raisin pie, so our observations about their significance are not of the deep dish variety. But we can tell you what we have learned about American cooking.

We have learned that the "trend-setting" things that happen in the culinary worlds of New York and Los Angeles have little effect on—and are of no interest to—a huge number of happy, healthy eaters.

When the folks pile into the White Way Cafe in Durant, Iowa, for pork chop dinners smothered in canned mushroom soup, do they concern themselves that pesto is now out of fashion but Spanish *tapas* bars are still *au courant?* Who cares! What matters is that the pork is creamy pale, as it always is at the White Way, and that the salad bar is loaded with a dozen composed salads, made with taco chips and miniature marshmallows and mandarin oranges and shredded coconut, and the farm-size pies are hot out of the oven. You don't have to be an Iowan, or a Midwesterner, to appeciate the joys of such a meal. The only thing you cannot be is a snob.

The day starts early in a small town cafe. At Mary's, in Casey, Iowa (pop. 473), the high-back wooden booths were already crowded when we arrived at 7:00 a.m.—even though the cafe was not officially open and the overhead fluorescent lights were not yet on. But the men of Casey were ready for coffee and cinnamon rolls.

Pat Denato of the Des Moines *Sunday Register* once wrote, "You know you're in a genuine Iowa small town cafe when . . . the cinnamon rolls are homemade and are about half the size of your head." Pat said she was "pretty well convinced that Iowa is the cinnamon roll capital of the entire universe."

Dave Berlau, who took over Mary's antique cafe (along with her recipes), would probably agree. Every morning he pops his freshly risen cinnamon rolls into the oven at about 6:30, so if you get there early, like the gents in overalls who crowd the booths, you get them while they're hot.

MARY'S CAFE CINNAMON ROLLS

Give these sweet rolls plenty of time and a nice warm (but not hot) place to rise, and they'll balloon up high, wide, and handsome.

2 packages dry yeast

¼ cup tepid water (110°)

½ cup plus ⅓ cup plus 1 teaspoon granulated sugar

1 cup milk

2 tablespoons lard

1 teaspoon salt

1 egg, beaten

2 teaspoons vanilla extract

3–3½ cups flour

2 tablespoons butter, melted

1½ teaspoons cinnamon

Frosting

2 cups sifted confectioners' sugar

1 tablespoon butter, softened

3–4 tablespoons milk

Dissolve yeast in warm water with 1 teaspoon of the granulated sugar. Let stand.

Scald milk with lard, salt, and ⅓ cup of the granulated sugar. Let cool to tepid. Stir in egg and vanilla.

Measure 3 cups flour into a large bowl. Pour in yeast mixture, then milk mixture, stirring to form a ragged dough.

Turn dough out of bowl onto a floured board. Clean bowl and grease generously with vegetable oil.

Knead dough 8–10 minutes until it is smooth, adding just enough flour so it isn't sticky. Return dough to bowl, roll around to coat thoroughly with oil, and cover with a double layer of plastic wrap (or lid if Tupperware bowl is used).

Let rise until double in bulk, about 1 hour.

Punch down dough and roll out on a lightly floured board to ¼-inch thickness. Brush with melted butter. Mix remaining ½ cup of granulated sugar and cinnamon and sprinkle over buttered dough. Roll from top toward you.

Using a sharp knife and a sure stroke, cut 1-inch-thick slices. Place on a greased baking sheet. Cover with a towel and let rise 30 minutes.

Preheat oven to 325°. Bake 20–25 minutes.

While rolls are baking, beat confectioners' sugar with softened butter and 3 tablespoons of the milk, adding up to a tablespoon more milk to attain a spreadable frosting.

Remove rolls from oven and frost while still warm.

Makes 12 rolls.

Pork is the *sine qua non* of cafe menus. Not barbecued pork, which is more Southern, and not cured country ham, which is too austere, but *pork,* pig meat in the form of tenderloins, chops, and the occasional ham loaf or ham salad.

A few hours south of Chicago, you are in serious pork country. Our favorite time to travel through is May, when farm animals are born. The backroad trip runs through furrowed fields sprouting newly planted corn, past barnyards populated by tiny pink pigs hiding from the sun in triangular pig huts that look like ski chalets for porkers.

Chops are expensive; they are dinner food. At lunchtime all across the heartland, the favored way is tenderloin sandwiches, a rudimentary recipe for which every cafe cook has his or her own subtle secret.

"It's hard to describe the process," said Dave Berlau of Mary's. "We buy the whole loin and cut it ourselves. You've got to pound it out real well. Then once they're dipped in flour, we add a sprinkle of cornmeal, for

the crunch." Tenderloins are customarily served on a bun, unless it is dinnertime, when they come with mashed potatoes.

The most astounding tenderloin we ever ate was served to us in Monmouth, Illinois, at a restaurant called the White Mill. It is not an easy place to find, as it is marked not by its name but by twin black and white signs proclaiming it "Home of Wyatt Earp."

"Is this really Wyatt Earp's home?" we asked the lady behind the counter as we grabbed cafeteria trays and placed an order for two loins.

"I believe it is," she smiled. An enigmatic answer for somebody who must have been asked the question a thousand times.

She was more interested in our tenderloins than in Mr. Earp. "Sandwich or sandy mash?" she asked, and when it was apparent that we didn't know what she was talking about, she explained that sandy mash is mid-Illinois lingo for a halved sandwich served around a mound of mashed potatoes blanketed with gravy.

We chose the straight sandwich, a real showstopper. On a regulation-size bun, the loin extended out six inches in every direction. Fried brittle thin and greaseless, sprinkled liberally with salt, its only problem was that the condiments are only on the inside part, underneath the bun. The rest is nude loin.

That is the point of a good Midwestern tenderloin sandwich: the eccentricity and whopping girth of the cutlet. A uniformly shaped, standard-size tenderloin means that it came from a tenderloin factory. A ragged, jagged, wavy one means that someone in a kitchen has spent time wrestling it into shape.

In a serious tenderloin shop, extension beyond the bun is *de rigueur*. At Flo's, in Marseilles, Illinois, which declares itself "Home of the Jumbo Tenderloin" (and where the motto is, "If I can't eat it, I won't serve it"), you get a sandwich that is impossible to pick up with one hand because no human's thumb and fingers can reach around the cutlet to touch the bun. "That's the fun part," said our waitress at Flo's. "You've got to start on the outside and work your way to the middle."

DINNER PLATE—SIZE TENDERLOIN SANDWICH

1 4–6-inch-long boneless center cut loin of pork	¼ teaspoon pepper
	Yellow cornmeal
1 cup flour	Lard or solid vegetable
1 teaspoon salt	shortening

Cut the loin into slices 1 inch thick. Place each slice between 2 pieces of lightly oiled parchment or wax paper and pound like hell with the side of a cleaver or a wooden mallet until the slice is nearly paper thin.

Combine flour, salt, and pepper. Dip each slice in water, then dredge it in flour mixture. Pat it with yellow cornmeal and refrigerate on wax paper for 1 hour.

Heat ½ inch of lard or shortening in deep skillet to 365°. Slip prepared loins into skillet one at a time and fry until golden brown. Serve on a hamburger bun.

Makes 4–6 tenderloins.

East of tenderloin country, they've got other tricks with pig meat. In Delaware, Ohio, follow the metal arch over Winter Street to a restaurant called Bun's, operated since 1863 by four generations of Hoffman men, all of whom were named George. "This has kept confusion at a minimum," say the paper place mats.

Bun's began as a bakery, and to this day the first thing you see upon entering are glass cases displaying the day's pecan rolls, butterscotch twists, Danish pullaparts, fruit bars, and cocoa cake, iced with fudge. Although Bun's doesn't officially serve breakfast, the people of Delaware make it a habit to come in for a pastry, then serve themselves coffee in the dining room.

Ohio and Pennsylvania are the lands of the loaf, beef or ham, and Bun's is famous for the latter, a heartland specialty seldom found on either coast.

HAM LOAF BY GEORGE

True ham loaf, we are told by Pennsylvania pals, is made with ground *raw* ham. But most butchers are loath to clean their grinder for one measly order. So in its stead we use cooked, sweet, *city* ham (not the salty stuff they eat down South). Even though it is a dish suited to leftovers and is a great way to stretch a little meat to serve a lot of people, this loaf truly honors ham. It is peppery yet sweet, with a wanton porky luxury—what we always hope Spam will taste like when we open up a can. Side it with whipped potatoes.

2 tablespoons minced onion	1 teaspoon pepper
¾ cup bread crumbs	½ teaspoon salt
3 eggs	1 tablespoon prepared yellow
¼ cup milk	mustard
1¼ pounds cooked ham,	1 teaspoon Worcestershire
ground as fine as	sauce
hamburger meat	⅔ cup brown sugar

Preheat oven to 325°. Combine onion, crumbs, eggs, and milk. Mix in ham, pepper, salt, mustard, and Worcestershire. Pat into an 8-inch bread loaf pan. Pat brown sugar on top. Cover pan with foil. Bake 2 hours. After 1 hour and 40 minutes, remove foil, baste top with brown sugar that has melted, and cook uncovered the last 20 minutes. Serve directly from pan.

Serves 5–6.

BUCKEYE FUDGE BUNKER

No sane person leaves Bun's without something from the bakery case, preferably a slice off this monumental brick of Mondo Chocolato. Here's a cake that will *not* remind you of Mom's home cooking. It is definitive *bakery* food, unctuous and cheerfully commercial tasting. It smells sensational as it cooks, and there's nearly as much frosting as cake.

CAKE

1¼ cups flour	1 cup sugar
¾ cup vegetable shortening	1¼ teaspoons baking powder
⅓ cup cocoa	½ teaspoon baking soda

½ teaspoon salt
7 teaspoons powdered milk
½ cup water
¾ teaspoon vanilla extract

½ cup egg whites (about 4
  eggs' worth)
¼ cup water

Preheat oven to 350°. Mix together all ingredients except egg whites and ¼ cup water. Beat with electric mixer at medium speed 5 minutes. Add egg whites and water. Beat another 5 minutes. Pour into a greased and floured 9-inch square cake pan. Bake 25–30 minutes, until a cake tester comes out clean. Cool and remove from pan.

ICING

3½ cups confectioners' sugar
5 ounces unsweetened
  chocolate, melted
1 tablespoon vegetable
  shortening

2 tablespoons corn syrup
¼ teaspoon salt
6 tablespoons water
½ teaspoon vanilla extract

Mix together sugar, chocolate, shortening, syrup, salt, and 3 tablespoons of the water. When well mixed, add remaining 3 tablespoons of water and vanilla. Spread on top and sides of cake.

Makes 1 9-inch square cake.

The seven Amana Colonies, settled by utopians from Germany in the mid-nineteenth century, are no longer pristine small towns. In fact, they are a bona fide tourist attraction. But the colonies maintain a small-town feel, and their restaurants serve genuine heartland food.

Our favorite is the Ronneberg, where the German-American cuisine is served to the accompaniment of a lederhosen-clad host playing an accordion. At the Ronneberg, every meal begins with an array of relishes and appetizers, including a ham dish that smacks of the best pork country farm kitchens. It is an appetizer, but on a warm summer night, served with nothing other than steamed, freshly picked corn on the cob, it is a heartland meal par excellence.

RONNEBERG PICKLED HAM

A ridiculously easy hors d'oeuvre, requiring few ingredients but plenty of time (at least overnight) to blossom. When we are home-bound, wishing we were speeding down a country road through Iowa's contoured farmland, there is nothing that sets our spirits free better than a bowl of pale pickled ham.

1 pound precooked ham, trimmed of all fat and cut into ½-inch cubes
1 medium onion, sliced thin

1½ cups water
1 cup white vinegar
¼ teaspoon black pepper

Combine all ingredients in a bowl, cover, and refrigerate at least 24 hours before serving. This will keep several days in the refrigerator.

Serves 4.

Salad bar: These can be two dirty words to travelers who have reached under too many sneeze guards to pile their plates with wooden crudités and chemically freshened lettuce. But we're not talking about the salad bars in the restaurants of chain motels. We are talking about heartland salad bars, where the small town cafe cook is in her (or his) greatest glory.

In the best cafes, salads are too important to be relegated to a transitional course of mere lettuce and dressing, or a lineup of raw ingredients. To Midwestern cooks, salad bars are an opportunity to show their stuff.

We guess that the Midwestern states buy most of the Jell-O manufactured in the world. And we further guess that 80 percent of all the Midwesterners who buy it own small town cafes, where Jell-O on the salad bar is *essential*. (And we do mean *Jell-O*. Although there are other brands of gelatin, *Jell-O*, like Kleenex or Band-Aids, has become the vernacular term for gelatin—even if it's Knox brand.)

There is one particular shade of Jell-O that is as evocative of an Iowa cafe as a black beret and a glass of wine are of Paris. The color is Herman Munster green, made with lime Jell-O and whipped topping (or, if you are lucky, real cream or cream cheese). In most cases, you will find a few chunks of pineapple in it, plus mini- or micro-mini-marshmallows and maybe nuts. Sometimes it is called pistachio salad; we have seen it listed as "Mountain Dewey Green Salad" and "Cheesey Lime." Its briny hue inspires nautical names, such as "Under the Sea Salad" (especially applied when the Jell-O is layered, and large things such as half-pears are sunk into the bottommost depths). We distinctly remember a phase in the mid-1970s when menus referred to it as "Watergate salad"—the etymology of which evades us.

SEAFOAM LIME MOLD

From Walnut, Iowa, a recipe submitted to the *Centennial Cookbook* by Mrs. August Arp.

1 3-ounce package lime Jell-O
1 cup boiling water
½ cup cold water
1 tablespoon lemon juice
1 8-ounce package cream
   cheese, softened

1½ cups miniature
   marshmallows
1⅔ cups canned crushed
   pineapple (drained, then
   measured); *do not use fresh*
½ cup chopped nuts (optional)

Dissolve Jell-O in boiling water; add cold water and lemon juice. Add gradually to softened cream cheese, beating until well blended. Chill until almost set. Fold in miniature marshmallows, pineapple, and nuts, if desired. Pour into a 5-cup mold and chill until firm.

Serves 6–8.

At Juilleret's, the town cafe of Harbor Springs, Michigan, where the specialty is fresh Lake Superior whitefish, the salad table makes every meal a Sunday picnic. Take your pick from ambrosias, cold macaroni salads, carrot and raisin slaw, and the tastiest spinach and bacon salad anywhere, its jumbo dark green leaves glossy with sweet-and-sour vinaigrette.

MICHIGANDER SUMMER SPINACH SALAD

⅓ cup white vinegar
⅓ cup sugar
1 teaspoon dry mustard
1 teaspoon salt
1 cup light salad oil
2 tablespoons poppy seeds

10 ounces fresh spinach, washed
2 hard-boiled eggs, sliced
6 slices bacon, fried crisp and crumbled

Combine vinegar, sugar, mustard, and salt. Using an electric mixer or whisking vigorously by hand, pour in oil in a thin, slow stream, whisking constantly. Whisk until dressing is smooth and thick, adding poppy seeds last.

Pour dressing over spinach, then garnish individual servings with eggs and bacon.

Serves 4.

PLANKED WHITEFISH

Fish on planks is a Great Lakes presentation that evokes campfires and the great outdoors. It is even better in a restaurant or at home when the fish can be ringed by a phalanx of potatoes, vegetables, or lemon wedges marshaled inside a wall of spuds. Few restaurants go to the trouble; but at Juilleret's it is a summertime tradition. Waitresses carry planks to whole tablefuls of customers, the size of the plank determined by the number of people eating Lake Superior whitefish. To make this dish, you need a clean hardwood plank, well oiled and seasoned.

2–3 pounds whitefish fillets
4 tablespoons butter, melted
1 egg yolk

3 cups freshly made mashed potatoes
Lemon wedges

Preheat oven to 400°. Oil a wood plank and pile fillets in center, no more than 1½ inches high, leaving a 3–4-inch border. Brush fish

☞

with some of the melted butter and bake 20–25 minutes, until fish begins to brown.

Stir egg yolk into mashed potatoes and put mixture into a pastry bag. Working quickly, remove plank from oven. Pipe a wall of potatoes around fish. Drizzle fish with remaining butter and throw on lemon wedges. Place below broiler 5 minutes, or until potatoes begin to brown.

Serves 4–6.

In Iowa, stop in any small-town restaurant where the specialty is tenderloins or T-bone dinners with a plate of haystack (hashed brown) potatoes on the side, and you will likely find a salad bar that showcases a strange and delectable specialty made with peas—Iowa pea salad.

For us, Iowa pea salad is the gastronomic equivalent of a Grant Wood landscape; it is Iowa-in-a-bowl, a heaping helping of innocent American cookery. It is a favorite not only at restaurant salad bars but at church picnics and potluck suppers—whenever spirits and appetites run high. We serve it in the summer, as a cool companion to pork roast and corn cakes, for an old-fashioned Sunday dinner.

Pea salad at the K.C. Cafe in Fairfield, Iowa, is a simple side dish, not much more than cheese-laced, pickle-flavored peas. We enjoyed it alongside a megacaloric K.C. feast of malted milk shakes, pork tenderloins, rhubarb pudding, 5-cup salad (made with whipped topping instead of sour cream), and a cinnamon roll the size of a bulldog's head.

PICKLY PEA SALAD

16 ounces fresh peas (frozen are okay)
4 1-ounce slices yellow American cheese, cut into ½-inch squares
¼ cup sweet pickle juice

2 hard-boiled eggs, chopped fine
½ teaspoon salt
⅓ cup Miracle Whip salad dressing

If using fresh peas, cook until just tender, then cool under running water and drain. If using frozen peas, do not boil; simply soak peas in warm water until defrosted, then drain thoroughly.

Combine peas, cheese, pickle juice, eggs, and salt in a mixing bowl. Gently stir in Miracle Whip. Serve cold.

Serves 4–6.

Iowa is without a doubt the self-publishing cookbook capital of America. We have yet to stop in a bookstore or antiques barn without turning up an irresistible spiral-edged tome by the 4-H mothers or the Petuniaville P.T.A., loaded with every local cook's best recipes.

There is a lot of duplication and subtle variation in these books, as is true of any folk art. One of the most interesting recurring themes is *Herman* recipes. Herman is a yeast starter that grows slowly and is used to make coffee cake, bread, etc., the point being to use only *some* of your Herman so that there is always more, always growing, to keep for yourself or give to a friend. Herman is an edible chain letter.

Where did Herman come from and how did he get named? We have seen explanations that trace the first Herman starter back to Jesus and a certain Mount Herman in Israel; to Hermann, Missouri; and to a little girl in Richmond, Virginia, who simply wanted to give a silly name to her mommy's bubbly sourdough starter. Whatever Herman's origins, he has been traveling across America, via home kitchens, for at least ten years; and judging by the number of Herman recipes we have come across in local cookbooks, he is one popular guy.

HERMAN STARTER

From the *Pella [Iowa] Christian Grade School Mothers' Club Cookbook*. What makes Herman different from ordinary sourdough starters is the inclusion of sugar or honey. Herman's sweetness makes him especially suitable for sweet cakes and rolls.

1 package dry yeast	2 teaspoons honey or sugar
2½ cups tepid water (110°)	2½ cups flour

Dissolve yeast in ½ cup of the water. When foamy, mix with honey, flour, and remaining 2 cups of water. Store in a large crock or glass jar. Cover with a damp cloth and rubber band. Keep at room temperature 24–48 hours; Herman will bubble up. Stir down bubbles, then refrigerate, stirring daily with a wooden spoon. On the fifth day, feed Herman:

1 cup flour	½ cup sugar
1 cup milk	

On the tenth day, remove 2 cups of Herman for baking, then add the same ingredients as on the fifth day to keep the starter going. (After adding these ingredients, you may divide Herman in half,

☞

and give one-half to a friend to feed.) Use the 2 cups of Herman you removed to make this coffee cake, from a recipe contributed by Mary Teachout to the *Pella Christian Grade School Mothers' Club Cookbook*:

HERMAN COFFEE CAKE

2 cups Herman Starter
2 cups flour
½ teaspoon salt
½ teaspoon baking soda
2 teaspoons baking powder
1½ teaspoons cinnamon
1 cup sugar

1 teaspoon nutmeg
1 teaspoon powdered ginger
2 eggs
⅔ cup light salad oil
1 cup walnuts, chopped coarse
1 cup raisins

Mix all ingredients together, pour into a well-oiled 9 x 9 x 2-inch pan. Preheat oven to 350°. As oven heats, mix topping.

TOPPING

1 tablespoon flour
½ teaspoon cinnamon
1 cup brown sugar

4 tablespoons butter or
    margarine, melted

Combine ingredients and sprinkle over top of cake. Put cake in preheated oven and bake 40 minutes. When cake comes out of oven, make glaze.

GLAZE

1½ cups sifted confectioners'
    sugar
1 tablespoon milk

2–3 tablespoons lemon juice
    and/or liqueur of choice

Beat ingredients together until drizzly. Drizzle over still-warm cake. Serve from baking pan.

Serves 8–10.

Our favorite Iowa cookbook is the *Homemaker Cookbook*, published by the *Journal-Herald* of Avoca (available from the *Journal-Herald*, Avoca, IA 51521). It is a compilation of weekly "Homemaker of the Week" newspaper columns, including photographs of each homemaker. Lady after lady is pictured next to her shelf of knickknacks, quilting in a favorite chair, or in front of the decorated Christmas tree. They are flashbulb pictures, shot with a single brutal light, and most of the ladies appear stunned. But their accompanying biographies bring them to life: "Randy and Judy met at barber school" . . . "Mrs. Childers has caught several large fish" . . . "Mr. and Mrs. Beatty look forward to taking a vacation annually every summer" . . .

Mrs. Barbara Syas, who is employed at the Council Bluffs Trailer Repair (and whose husband Richard is employed at the American Beef plant), contributed a distinctively Midwestern layered lettuce salad when she was selected as the *Journal-Herald*'s Homemaker of the Week.

HOMEMAKER OF THE WEEK LAYERED LETTUCE

½ head iceberg lettuce, washed
⅔ cup diced celery
3 hard-boiled eggs, diced
1 small sweet onion, diced
1 10-ounce package frozen
    peas, defrosted
2 green bell peppers, diced
1 cup Miracle Whip salad
    dressing

1 tablespoon sugar
8 slices bacon, fried and diced
4 ounces Cheddar cheese,
    grated
Additional bacon and parsley
    as garnish

Tear cleaned lettuce into bite-size pieces and place in a 9 x 9-inch glass dish, filling it about ⅔ full. Layer rest of ingredients in order given, through peppers. Combine Miracle Whip and sugar and spread over peppers as you would frosting. Top with bacon, then with grated cheese.

Cover with plastic wrap and refrigerate 8–12 hours. At serving time, garnish with additional bacon and parsley. Keeps well in refrigerator several days.

Serves 6–8.

It did not surprise us to learn that one of our favorite items on the salad bar at the White Way Cafe was inspired by a self-published cookbook. When we asked Carroll Marshall for his recipe for tortilla salad, he sent us a dog-eared copy of the *Prairie Cooks Cookbook*, compiled in 1978 by Pat Birkett (Box 886, Jacksonville, IL 62651). In her introduction to the spiral-bound treasury, Pat writes that the book was "the culmination of a long-standing dream." It is a gold mine of heartland recipes that East and West coasts never know, including Pat's own recipe for this south-of-the-border treat on the White Way's salad bar.

PRAIRIE COOKS TORTILLA SALAD

Don't make tortilla salad to serve between courses. It is a meal. Meat, starch, cheese, salad, condiments, and tortilla chips—this hefty hodgepodge has it all.

½ pound ground beef
¼ teaspoon salt
1 16-ounce can pinto beans,
  drained
1 teaspoon crushed cumin
  seeds
1 head iceberg lettuce, torn
  into bits
1 onion, chopped

½ pound Cheddar cheese,
  grated
1 avocado, cubed
1 large tomato, chopped
½ cup Miracle Whip salad
  dressing
¼ cup taco sauce
1 teaspoon chili powder
Taco-flavored Doritos to taste

Brown beef with salt; add beans and cumin. Remove from heat.

In a large bowl combine lettuce, onion, cheese, avocado, and tomato. Add beef and beans (still warm) and toss.

Mix salad dressing, taco sauce, and chili powder. Stir into salad.

Mix in Doritos, broken but not pulverized, just before serving.

Makes 4–6 big salads.

We were tipped off to the Coffee Cup Cafe in the pint-size town of Sully, Iowa, by a *Goodfood* reader (whose letter and name we have since lost—are you out there?). The note recommended rhubarb pie and home-made sausage. Yum! As we hogged down one of the best cafe meals to be had in the Midwest, we noticed a peculiar item on the menu called Dutch salad.

Having just come from the Tulip Time festivities in nearby Pella, we knew we were in Dutch country. The name on nearly every rural mailbox we passed began with "Van." But Dutch salad was new to us, so we ordered some.

Out came a bowl of iceberg lettuce blanketed with heavy yellow dressing. The dressing was laced with bacon and slices of hard-boiled egg, and it was *warm*, fairly smothering the lettuce down below. "People come from towns all around here just to have Dutch lettuce," Coffee Cup owner Linda Zylstra told us. It took a little coaxing to get the recipe, but we promised Linda that she would gain new friends rather than lose customers if we used it. So if you visit the Coffee Cup in Sully, please tell her that the Sterns sent you.

COFFEE CUP DUTCH LETTUCE DRESSING

2 cups Miracle Whip salad
   dressing
3 tablespoons prepared
   mustard

½ cup sugar
Pinch of salt
Pinch of pepper
1 teaspoon celery seed

Combine all ingredients and warm in a microwave or on top of a double boiler. Pour onto chilled lettuce and top with crumbled bacon and sliced hard-boiled eggs to taste.

Makes 2 cups dressing.

Of all the salads on the salad bar or lunch platter, the one easiest to take for granted is coleslaw. There are as many recipes for coleslaw as there are pockets of ethnic culture in this land. We have eaten slaw drowned in cream, in vinegar, and in hot sauce. We have had it inside sandwiches and on the side of fried chicken. In Illinois it will likely be spangled with celery seeds, and farther west with poppy seeds.

It was on a slaw-hunting expedition through the Southwest and lower Midwest that we came upon the most wondrous coleslaw of all, not at a town cafe but at a steak house in Wichita, named Doc's. We had followed the old cattle trail north into Kansas, stopping at Doc's because it had been recommended for its T-bone dinners. The steaks were fine, but what knocked our socks off was Doc's garlic slaw. It was fire-eatin' dynamite: finely chopped green cabbage, bound in cream and mayonnaise, shot through with garlic—gobs of garlic—presented as a single scoop on a bed of lettuce.

GARLIC SLAW À LA DOC'S

1 teaspoon salt
⅔ cup sugar
⅓ cup cider vinegar
1 cup cream
2 tablespoons mayonnaise

2 tablespoons finely minced
   garlic
8 cups finely shredded green
   cabbage

Mix all ingredients except cabbage in a bowl until smooth. Pour over cabbage. Toss well. Chill and serve.

Serves 8–10.

Pies are essential to cafe cuisine. No small-town eatery that cares about its reputation would dare open its doors without a proud selection of slices oozing butterscotch or berries onto thick white plates, and meringues swirling higher than the pie is wide. How the pies are displayed is an important lure into the cafe. For the sake of convenience, most cafes precut their pies. Fine with us, because a freestanding slice provides a good fix on the filling-to-topping ratio. If the pie is good, the cafe doesn't have to worry about the slice drying out, because there won't be any leftovers by the end of lunch hour.

What draws the crowds to the Norske Nook in Osseo, Wisconsin, is Helen Myhre's pie wizardry. There is no doubt, the moment you enter the Norske Nook, that it is a major pie stop. Displayed in the pie case or on the counter, some of them still hot from the oven, is the day's array: broad-beamed sour cream raisin pie, strawberry pie with dribbles of berry breaking through fissures in the golden crust, blueberry pie, apple and apple crumb pies. And there are cakes too: carrot cake, white and choco-late layer cakes, caramel rolls, fruit bars, and about a half-dozen kinds of cookies. Anything you would ever want to accompany that midafternoon cup of coffee.

The Norske Nook was where we first tasted sour cream raisin pie, a dairyland dense pack topped with a swirling meringue.

NORSKE NOOK SOUR CREAM RAISIN PIE

What we like about Helen's recipe is that the raisins are cooked with the other stuff from the beginning. That way, they soften and plump, dappling the ivory-colored sour cream with their sweet-ness. It is an elementary-flavored pie—dairy wealth abetted by the raisins, with no mitigation of their double-whammy sweetness.

2 cups sour cream
2¼ cups sugar
4 teaspoons flour
4 eggs, separated, plus 1 extra
  white

1½ cups raisins
1 baked 9-inch pie shell (see
  p. 123)
¼ teaspoon salt

Combine sour cream, 1¾ cups of the sugar, flour, egg yolks, and raisins in a heavy saucepan or top of a double boiler and cook, stirring constantly, until thick and glossy. Pour into baked pie shell and chill. Put egg whites into a metal mixing bowl over a pan of hot water. Stir in remaining ½ cup of sugar and salt. After a few seconds, when whites are tepid and sugar is dissolved, whip until they stand in peaks. Spread across pie, touching entire rim of crust, and place under broiler until just barely browned (less than a minute).

It wasn't so long ago that margarine was *banned* in Wisconsin, the state that calls itself America's Dairyland, where cream pie makers outdo each other with the loft of their confections. The best of these pastries is what people in Wisconsin call a "torte," a large block of alabaster-colored creamy goodness layered with a bit of pie filling.

Check out the tortes sold in a tiny cafe named Gosse's, where working-men come to eat the famous charcoal-grilled bratwursts of Sheboygan. A factory town surrounded by Wisconsin farmland, Sheboygan has taverns with some of the most wonderfully outmoded glass brick fronts we have ever seen. And those rugged "Sheboygan brat" sandwiches are hot stuff. As we polished off some brat sandwiches one lunch hour, we noticed that although the menu listed pies, all the men at Gosse's tables were eating big square sections of what looked like cheesecake.

SHEBOYGAN BANANAS AND CREAM TORTE

Any old pie filling—homemade or from a can—will suffice. Our personal favorite is bananas and cream, which go so well with the graham cracker crust.

1½ cups crushed graham crackers
10 tablespoons butter, melted
¼ cup granulated sugar
¼ cup flour
¼ cup finely chopped walnuts
8 ounces cream cheese, softened

¾ cup confectioners' sugar
4 cups cream
4 tablespoons butter
3 cups sliced bananas (3 large)
½ cup brown sugar

Preheat oven to 350°. Mix graham crackers, melted butter, granulated sugar, flour, and nuts. Reserve ½ cup of the crust and press the rest evenly into an ungreased 11 x 13-inch baking pan. Bake 10 minutes. Cool.

In a large bowl mix cream cheese, confectioners' sugar, and 2 cups of the cream. Beat at high speed with electric mixer 3 minutes, until thick. Spread on cooled crust.

Melt butter in a skillet and sauté bananas until they begin to soften. Add ½ cup of the cream and brown sugar. Simmer and stir about 5 minutes, until thick. Cool to room temperature.

When cool, spread banana filling on cream layer. Whip remaining 1½ cups of cream. Top bananas with whipped cream. Sprinkle reserved crust on top. Keep refrigerated. Slice and serve in square blocks.

Serves 10–12.

Indiana's indulgence in sugar and dairy gluttony is known as farm pie or sugar cream pie, a paste-thick circle of sweetened and enriched high-butterfat cream. Most old-fashioned Hoosier housewives have their own family recipe. One of the best restaurant versions is served in Indiana's Amish country.

It is the Village Inn in Middlebury, a wonderful pie stop while motorvating along I-80. There are livestock auctions and a weekly flea market up the road in Shipshewanna and a great department store on Main Street —Gohn Brothers, specializing in dry goods for Amish people including black lisle stockings, bonnets, and work clothes with suspender snaps (zippers are too modern for the Amish).

The Village Inn is next to Gohn Brothers. If all the pies and customers were removed, it would look like any old luncheonette. But you know there is something special when you park in the lot next door and notice that alongside the Fords and Chevies are rickety black carriages, their horses tethered at a bar.

This Main Street town cafe is a favorite of the beard-and-suspender crowd—Mennonites whose pie prowess is second to none. They come to the Village Inn for a hearty lunch of chicken and noodles or meat loaf (preceded by appetizers of tapioca pudding!), a breakfast of headcheese and mush, and an outstanding selection of cream and fruit pies.

The inn almost always has an item known as O.F., or old-fashioned cream pie. It is like custard pie, but made with brown sugar and cream instead of white sugar and milk.

O.F. PIE

A delicate-bodied pie with a powerhouse candy flavor, O.F. (which is how it's posted on the blackboard menu) is our choice for a midafternoon pick-me-up after spending the morning plowing through the indoor-outdoor flea market in nearby Shipshewanna.

2 eggs	½ cup milk
5 tablespoons butter	¼ teaspoon salt
1 cup dark brown sugar	1 teaspoon vanilla extract
½ cup granulated sugar	1 unbaked 9-inch pie shell (see
3 tablespoons flour	p. 123)
1 cup cream	

Preheat oven to 425°. Beat eggs until lemon colored. Cream butter with sugars. Alternately add flour, cream, and milk, then salt and vanilla. Add eggs, beating just enough to blend (do not overbeat). Pour into crust and bake 10 minutes. Reduce heat to 300° and bake 40 minutes more. Remove and cool until custard is firm.

Summer in the upper Midwest means a succession of ripening berries, cherries, and fruits, all of which are made into pies featured at small town cafes. One of the most delicious Midwestern pies is made with rhubarb, the long, crunchy stalks that look like rosy celery. Rhubarb pie hits the menu mid-May.

According to the Norske Nook's Helen Myhre, the secret of a great rhubarb pie is "a full stick of butter in every pie." If you like your rhubarb tart, you may want to cut that measurement in half.

DAIRYLAND RHUBARB PIE

Boiling the rhubarb, as this recipe suggests, yields a gentle, nearly homogenized filling, rather than rhubarb *al dente*. Less boiling yields firmer filling, but too little time means stringy rhubarb.

3 cups rhubarb, cut up and boiled until soft	3 eggs
1 cup sugar	2 unbaked 9- or 10-inch pie shells (top and bottom) (see
½ cup flour	p. 123)
Sprinkle of nutmeg	4–8 tablespoons butter

Preheat oven to 400°. Mix together rhubarb, sugar, flour, nutmeg, and eggs. Pour into pie shell and dot top with pinches of butter. Cover with top shell, pinch edges, and prick top crust with a fork. Bake 15 minutes; reduce heat to 350° and bake 20–25 minutes more, until top crust is dark golden brown.

Note: If using a 9-inch pan and/or 8 tablespoons of butter, there will be an abundance of filling. We suggest putting a larger pan in the oven beneath the pie pan to catch any butter or filling that oozes out.

When we visited the Riverside Restaurant in Stockport, Ohio, we were so carried away with the pleasures of their Sunday chicken and mashed potatoes and fabulous elderberry pie that we wrote in *Goodfood* that the berries were picked from the honeysuckle trees in owner Frances Brandon's fields. "We have had many good laughs about that one," Mrs. Brandon later told us. "Honeysuckle grows on honeysuckle trees. And elderberries grow on elderberry bushes along the edges of farm fields."

Now that we've gotten that straight, here is Frances's recipe. If you don't have access to elderberry bushes, any small, sweet summer berries will do. Aunt Ida, by the way, is Frances's Pennsylvania Dutch grandfather's sister, who, according to Frances, "made it to perfection."

AUNT IDA'S ELDERBERRY PIE

1 quart elderberries, cleaned
2 unbaked 9-inch pie shells
   (top and bottom) (see p.
   123)
1 cup sugar

2 tablespoons cornstarch
Pinch of salt
1 teaspoon lemon juice
1 tablespoon butter

Preheat oven to 400°. Put berries into bottom pie shell. Mix sugar, cornstarch, and salt and sprinkle over berries. Sprinkle on lemon juice and dot with butter. Cover with top crust and pinch edges. Prick holes in top crust for steam to escape. Bake 10 minutes. Reduce heat to 350° and bake 30–40 minutes more.

WHERE NICE PEOPLE EAT

e are normal Americans, which means that dinner at our house is served at six o'clock, leaving time for reading and television, then eight hours' sleep. It's always been six, since we were children, unless we were ill, which meant it was at five, in time for early bed.

Somewhere at the geocultural fringes of the country, it has been decreed that it is uncouth to eat so early. Even dinner at eight has begun to seem square. *Soigné* people don't think about eating until nine or ten at night.

That is why we like dinner in the Midwest. The last time we visited the finest eatery in Ohio—Miller's Dining Room—we arrived at six forty-five. The place was packed. By the time we polished off our apple silk cheese pie, about seven-thirty, Miller's was closing up around us.

Although each region of the country has restaurants where nice people eat, Miller's is one of a number of especially moral-seeming dining rooms unique to the Midwest. Their hours imply an upstanding life; and their cuisine is a direct descendant of farm food, including an abundance of unadorned fresh vegetables, a show-off state fair variety of bread and rolls, and desserts laden with butter, cream, and eggs.

Many of them began as tearooms, specializing in lunch for ladies in town to go shopping. Others—like Boder's on the River outside Milwaukee, or Miller's, west of downtown Cleveland—have always been destinations for families, especially on Sunday. In a spirit of politeness and order, their staffs are uniformed, doting, nurselike.

For a sense of their bedrock-righteous self-image, look at the book they sell at Boder's on the River: forty-five pages of family and restaurant history, all intertwined, including snapshots of favorite family autos, the new generation Boders, and pages of heirloom recipes on which the kitchen's reputation is built. Old Boders retire and young Boders take charge, this book says; but corn fritters, and the spirit of family feasting in which they are served, are hallowed institutions that will never change.

ALL IN THE FAMILY CORN FRITTERS

When Boder's first opened, it was deep in the country, with a corn-field just outside the dining room window. When customers ordered sweet corn, Mr. Boder made a show of going out into the field where they could see him picking a few ears, then returning to the kitchen. If you can get it, corn scraped off a newly picked cob gives these fritters dazzling farm flavor. Serve them with roast chicken (following recipe). The Boders' Model A Ford, by the way, was nicknamed "Fritter."

2 cups flour	3 eggs, separated
1 teaspoon salt	1 cup niblet corn (if fresh,
2 tablespoons baking powder	blanch before using)
1 tablespoon corn oil	Vegetable shortening for frying
1½ teaspoons vinegar	Confectioners' sugar
1 cup milk	Maple syrup

Sift dry ingredients together. Add corn oil, vinegar, milk, egg yolks, and corn. Mix well. Beat egg whites stiff and fold into corn mixture. Fill a deep skillet with shortening; heat to 350°. Drop batter by tablespoonfuls into fat. Fry until dark golden brown, 2–3 minutes.

Preheat oven to 325°. Place finished fritters in empty muffin tins and bake 10 minutes. Sprinkle with confectioners' sugar and serve with maple syrup.

Makes 16–20 fritters.

PLAIN ROAST CHICKEN

What could be nicer? You can jazz this chicken up with fresh herbs, or stuff it with stuffing, but whatever you do, nothing can improve upon its simple succulence. Side it with Boder's corn fritters (preceding recipe) or apple fritters (see p. 224).

1 3-pound chicken, washed and patted dry, at room temperature.	Salt and pepper to taste
	5 tablespoons butter, softened
	3 tablespoons butter, melted

Preheat oven to 450°. Season inside of chicken with salt and pepper. Rub 2 tablespoons of the softened butter inside chicken. Rub outside of chicken with remaining 3 tablespoons of butter. Place on a rack in a roasting pan. Roast 15 minutes, then baste with melted butter. Roast 15 minutes more. Baste chicken with juices from roasting pan. Roast 20 minutes more. A meat thermometer inserted in thigh should read 165°. Remove from oven and allow chicken to settle before carving.

Serves 2.

FRIEDA BODER'S OLD-FASHIONED DATE AND NUT TORTE

When the Boders opened their country restaurant in 1929, the menu featured Frieda Boder's date and nut torte, but in the years that followed, the recipe was lost. Mae Lohmann, a former Boder's employee who left to start Lohmann's Steak House, kept her copy (and kept the torte on her steak house menu). So when the Boders put their cookbook together, Mae returned this famous, original recipe. It makes a loaf-shaped cake, faintly chewy, unbelievably luxurious.

⅔ cup flour
5 teaspoons baking powder
¼ teaspoon salt
⅔ cup coarsely chopped
    walnuts
1⅔ cups coarsely chopped
    dates

5 eggs, separated
1 cup sugar
1 teaspoon vanilla extract
⅛ teaspoon cream of tartar

Preheat oven to 325°. Line a well-buttered 9 x 5 x 3-inch bread pan with wax paper, then butter paper generously.

Sift flour, baking powder, and salt into a large bowl. Add nuts and dates. Mix until dates are coated thoroughly.

In a small bowl beat egg yolks and gradually add sugar and vanilla until well blended. Add to date mixture. Stir well.

Beat egg whites with cream of tartar until stiff. Fold into date batter until well blended.

Pour into prepared pan and bake 1 hour, or until edges are dark brown and cake tester comes out clean. (Center will rise and fall during baking.)

Turn pan over to remove cake. Remove wax paper and cut cake in 1-inch-thick slabs.

We found Miller's Dining Room during one of the worst fights of our married life. We had planned a day's itinerary with military precision and were exactly on schedule. The plan was to have pickerel dinner at a restaurant on the Lake Erie shore in Port Clinton, Ohio. Jane was at the wheel.

Bombing along Interstate 80, it was easy to miss the exit. At least that was Jane's excuse as Michael grew apoplectic with rage. Going back meant an hour's detour, in the wrong direction. Jane accused Michael of never being flexible enough to change directions; Michael accused Jane of acting out a secret loathing for pickerel.

There we were, mid-Ohio, with no dinner in sight. How we wound up at Miller's is lost in time, but with ravenous appetites intact and irritable spirits still raw, we stumbled into this restaurant on the west side of Cleveland like strangers into paradise.

We and Miller's were made for each other. The dining room was dusky blue with touches of colonial decor that reminded us of a well-furnished living room à la *Look* magazine, circa 1958. The menu was a rhapsody of white turkey dinners, jiggly Jell-O salads, and hot sticky buns. It was as middle American, red-white-and-blue as anything that Grant Wood ever conceived, corny and square as can be, and thoroughly endearing to our savage hearts. The fight seemed miles behind as we picked hot corn sticks from the battered tray on which they were offered. By the time we sailed into dessert, we were batting eyelashes at each other like turtle doves.

"We strive to maintain a homelike atmosphere and serve quality food at moderate prices for family dining, without liquor," said John Miller, who founded Miller's Dining Room. "On New Year's Eve we served eight hundred persons and closed at nine-thirty p.m." The sign outside reads "A Place for the Family."

Mr. Miller's daughter, Doris Urbansky, took over the restaurant after learning the ropes as a dietitian for Stouffer's. Her mother explained Miller's success: "Patrons like our white tablecloths, waitresses circulating with trays of assorted rolls and salads, and finger bowls at dinner."

BATTERED TRAY CORN STICKS

Throughout a Miller's meal, waitresses patrol the dining room carrying battered metal trays with breadstuffs, hot from the kitchen. These corn sticks, so oven warm and delicate they threaten to break apart when lifted, are always the first to disappear off the tray. Because the texture of cornmeal is cushioned by flour, Miller's sticks are Midwestern bready more than Deep South gritty.

☞

1 cup flour
½ cup cornmeal
3 tablespoons sugar
1 teaspoon salt
1 tablespoon baking powder

½ cup milk
⅓ cup water
2 eggs, beaten
⅓ cup vegetable oil

Mix dry ingredients. Mix liquid ingredients and add to dry. Cover and refrigerate 1 hour.

Grease corn griddle irons generously and put in oven as it preheats to 500°. (Grease will smoke.)

Spoon batter into irons, filling hollows, and bake 8 minutes, until golden brown.

Makes 1 dozen 5-inch sticks.

CHERRY CREAM IMPERIAL

After Miller's bread tray, the next tray that comes around is decked out with salads—a rainbow-hued selection of slaws, molds, fruit cups, and leafy things. The most spectacular are always the shimmering gelatinized ones, some crystal clear, others opaque. The Urbansky family sent us one of their best, Cherry Cream Imperial. The recipe was subtitled, "by a salad cook—Natalie Fedyniak." It is a major production number; Ms. Fedyniak is the Busby Berkeley of Jell-O.

½ cup milk
¼ cup sugar
½ teaspoon vanilla extract
½ tablespoon plus 1 teaspoon
    unflavored gelatin
1 tablespoon plus 2 teaspoons
    cold water
½ cup sour cream
1 16-ounce can pitted dark

sweet cherries in heavy
    syrup
1 3-ounce package cherry
    Jell-O
Dash salt
Juice of ¼ lemon
1 cup boiling water
¼ cup heavy cream

Combine milk, sugar, and vanilla in a saucepan. Place over medium heat and stir until sugar is dissolved, about 3 minutes (do not boil). Soften ½ tablespoon of the unflavored gelatin in 1 tablespoon of the cold water. Add to hot milk mixture, stir well to dissolve gelatin, and cool to lukewarm. Add sour cream and whip until smooth. Pour into a metal bowl or pie tin and chill overnight.

Drain cherries, reserving syrup. Dissolve cherry Jell-O, salt, and lemon juice in boiling water, stirring well. Soften remaining teaspoon of unflavored gelatin in remaining 2 teaspoons of cold water, add to hot cherry Jell-O, and stir to blend. Measure ½ cup reserved cherry syrup (adding water if necessary) and add to cherry Jell-O mixture. Chill.

Whip cream; set aside.

Cut refrigerated vanilla cream into ½-inch cubes.

When cherry Jell-O is as thick as egg whites, combine it with whipped cream and whip until smooth. Add well-drained cherries and vanilla-cream cubes, mixing gently to avoid breaking cubes.

Place in a 4-cup mold and chill until set. Serve on lettuce leaves

Serves 6–8.

Because it was the Pilgrims who first ate Thanksgiving, many people associate turkey with New England. But it is in the Midwest that turkey is in its true glory. No matter how it's fancied up—with cream sauce and sweet peas or on a bed of chow mein noodles—it is still bland turkey, a perfect match for restaurants where *niceness* is valued.

There are none nicer than the Strongbow Turkey Inn of Valparaiso, Indiana. For years we got letters from people telling us about it, but we thought we were too smart for a place where the waitresses wear long skirts and the management hands out dictionaries that explain that "yedl, yedl, yedl" is the sound turkeys make when they are happy. It sounded too hokey for us sophisticates.

We should hang our heads and gobble in shame. Eating at the Strongbow Inn was a revelation. The menu celebrates turkey in every way, from the Platonic ideal of turkey dinner (with stuffing, mashed potatoes, and cranberry relish) to turkey liver pâté and Potawatami roll-ups (turkey chunks and cranberry sauce in a crepe).

The Strongbow Inn began in the 1930s, when Bess Thrun announced to her college professor husband that she didn't like living in downtown Valparaiso, Indiana, and she intended to start a turkey farm. She bought a hundred hens and a dozen toms and began what was to become a turkey dynasty.

Today, the Strongbow Turkey Inn, run by her daughter Chuggie and Chuggie's husband, Charles Adams, can serve a thousand people every day —using a menu centered almost exclusively on Strongbow turkeys. These recipes are all devised by Mrs. Thrun.

VALPARAISO TURKEY BONE SOUP

Here is what to do with a turkey carcass the day after. If you do not serve it as soup, it will come in handy as the "turkey broth" called for in the Strongbow recipes for turkey pie and gravy.

Broken bones and skin from
   turkey carcass
3 stalks celery
2 carrots, quartered

1 onion, quartered
6 peppercorns
1 bay leaf
Salt to taste

Place all ingredients except salt in a large kettle. Cover with water. Bring to a boil and simmer, partially covered, 2 hours. Cool slightly and strain. Add salt to taste. Chill thoroughly and remove hardened layer of turkey fat that congeals on top.

Makes 2–2½ quarts.

TURKEY FARMER'S PIE

4 tablespoons butter
½ cup chopped onion
1 cup sliced celery
3 tablespoons flour
2 cups hot turkey broth (see
   preceding recipe)

½ teaspoon salt
⅛ teaspoon poultry seasoning
3 cups cubed cooked turkey
Enough dough for 3 9-inch pies
   (see p. 123)

Melt butter in a medium-size skillet. Add onion and celery and sauté until onion is transparent but not brown. Add flour and cook and stir until bubbly. Add broth and seasonings, stirring and cooking until thick. Add turkey. Cool completely, then chill 1 hour.

Preheat oven to 400°. Roll out dough and cut 4 6-inch rounds and 4 5-inch rounds.

Place 6-inch round of dough in a small fruit bowl, as a form to shape pie. Place turkey mixture inside and cover with 5-inch round. Moisten edges and bring up edges of lower dough, crimping over top layer. The smaller layer will be the bottom for baking. The 6-inch round will be on top, nice and smooth.

Place pies on a lightly greased cookie sheet, larger round up, and prick tops in a few places. Bake 25 minutes, or until brown. Serve with Gobbler Gravy (following recipe).

Serves 4.

GOBBLER GRAVY

3 tablespoons turkey fat or
   butter
3 tablespoons flour

2 cups turkey broth (see p. 212)
½ teaspoon salt

Melt fat or butter over medium heat. Blend in flour until smooth. Cook and stir about 2 minutes over medium-low heat. Add broth gradually, stirring constantly, to make a thick and bubbly gravy. Add salt.

Makes 2 cups.

When we talk about family restaurants, we cannot get closer to home than the Indian Trail in Winnetka, Illinois. For years, it was where the Stern family gathered for celebration meals. The head of the clan was wealthy Aunt Liz; when she took everybody out, that meant that Michael had the green light to order steak.

Don't get us wrong. The Indian Trail is hardly a steak house. It is the archetypal nice person's restaurant, where the dinner hour ends by 9:00 p.m. and where a large proportion of the clientele arrives with the aid of walkers and canes. But there was always something special about eating at the Indian Trail, and steak, the most expensive item on the menu, seemed the only appropriate meal to eat when taken out by one's richest relative. This steak was a dainty morsel, served on a piece of toast denuded of its crusts.

The older people at the table had the good sense to stick with Indian Trail favorites like Great Lakes whitefish or pork loin. Or the most white glove meal of all: fricassee of turkey breast served on chow mein noodles. Listed on the menu as "guest luncheon," this is turkey at its maximum level of niceness. The noodles, we assure you, do not in any way hint at anything Oriental. They are but a stylish variation of the classic potato nest for holding chicken à la king.

GUEST LUNCHEON

1 large turkey breast (5–6 pounds)
2 onions, quartered
1 teaspoon salt
8 tablespoons butter
1 cup flour

6 cups turkey stock (save from simmering breast)
Poultry seasoning to taste
Salt and white pepper to taste
4 cups chow mein noodles
¾ cup sliced toasted almonds

Simmer turkey breast with onions and 1 teaspoon salt 2–2½ hours, or until tender. Set breast aside to cool. Strain and reserve stock.

Melt butter and blend in flour slowly. Cook over medium-low heat 5 minutes, stirring constantly. Add turkey stock, stirring until sauce thickens and is bubbly. Add seasonings.

Slice cooled breast into ¼-inch slices. Add to gravy. Simmer over low heat until warmed through.

Serve on a bed of chow mein noodles, topped with sliced toasted almonds.

Serves 8–10.

It has become fashionable to disdain iceberg lettuce, known in the heartland as head lettuce, but there is nothing else with its crunch, which is why it is so popular for salads with robust dressing. At the Indian Trail, you can get creamy, pink-hued Gorgonzola or a sweet, translucent celery seed dressing. To make it look authentically Indian Trail, slice the head lettuce into 1-inch-thick slabs, put each slab on a plate, and blanket it.

CELERY SEED DRESSING À LA ETHEL DOLL

Our version of celery seed dressing was suggested by the *Home-maker Cookbook* of Avoca, Iowa, and a recipe contributed by Mrs. Ethel Doll, "who likes to volunteer her talent in playing the piano at many church activities such as ladies aid, etc."

½ cup sugar
1 teaspoon dry mustard
1 teaspoon salt
¼ cup finely grated onion

½ cup vinegar
1 cup salad oil
2 tablespoons celery seeds

Put sugar, mustard, salt, onion, and vinegar in blender. Blend until smooth.

With machine still running, slowly pour in salad oil, blending until thick and smooth. Add celery seeds last. Serve on iceberg lettuce or fresh fruit.

Makes about 2 cups dressing.

INDIAN TRAIL SPICE MUFFINS

Freshly made bread is the first and surest sign of an honest kitchen. These aromatic spice muffins, set upon the Indian Trail table as soon as menus arrive, are usually gone by the time orders are taken. But that's okay. There are always more.

2 cups flour
1 cup sugar
1 teaspoon baking soda
1 teaspoon ground cloves
1 teaspoon cinnamon
1 teaspoon nutmeg

1 cup sour milk or buttermilk
1 egg, beaten
8 tablespoons butter, melted
½ cup chopped pecans
½ cup raisins

Preheat oven to 400°. Combine dry ingredients. Combine milk, egg, and melted butter. Add to dry ingredients, beating only enough to blend. Stir in nuts and raisins. Fill greased muffin tins nearly full. Bake 20 minutes.

Makes 18 muffins.

Now comes the fun part. After a demure meal, even a sensible cook can be a little frivolous. The best way to do that is with gobs of whipped cream.

West of Lake Michigan, the dessert repertoire is especially rich with dairy farm goodness. The Indian Trail is known for the uncompromised purity of its whipped cream specialties.

WHITE GLOVE HAZELNUT RUM WHIPPED CREAM ROLL

This cloudlike roll is at once homespun and the height of elegance; fragile, yet immensely satisfying.

Cake

4 eggs, separated
1 cup granulated sugar
3 tablespoons unflavored bread
    crumbs
½ teaspoon rum
Pinch of salt

⅛ teaspoon cream of tartar
6 ounces hazelnuts, ground
    coarse (about 1 pound
    before shelling)
Confectioners' sugar

Filling

2 cups heavy cream
1 tablespoon sugar

1 tablespoon rum

Preheat oven to 325°. Beat egg yolks and ½ cup of the granulated sugar with electric mixer at high speed until lemon colored. Add bread crumbs, ½ teaspoon rum, and salt. Beat egg whites with cream of tartar until stiff, slowly adding remaining ½ cup of granulated sugar as they stiffen. Fold whites into yolk mixture. Fold in nuts.

Pour batter into a well-greased and floured 11 x 16-inch jelly-roll pan. Spread evenly edge to edge with spatula. Bake 15–20 minutes.

Remove from pan immediately by inverting pan over a clean cloth covered with confectioners' sugar. Cut off crisp edges of cake (if any) and roll while hot, like a jelly roll.

As cake cools, make filling. Whip cream with sugar and rum.

When cake is cool, unroll carefully and spread with flavored whipped cream. Reroll, then gently roll from towel onto a serving dish. Slice to serve.

Serves 6–8.

We were holed up in Milwaukee to visit a favorite used-book store. Five floors of mildewed books—sheer heaven. We spent our mornings shrieking with delight as we unearthed rarities like *Modern Homecraft*, put out by the Electrical League in 1938, and alternately spraying our noses with antihistamines and gasping for air. By noon, we were exhausted and ready for lunch.

We asked the clerk where to eat. He looked us over and launched into a list of restaurants that all sounded the same: "Bennigans, Brautigans, Berrigans, Cardigans." We could tell by the frequent mention of potato skins and nachos that he had pegged us as the type who couldn't get through lunch without a Harvey Wallbanger. But we didn't bite, so he kept going, finally saying what we wanted to hear: "Well, there is a place, but you probably won't like it. It's where all the old ladies go, sort of a knickknack shop with sandwiches." We were off in a flash.

The Watts Tea Shop surpassed all our expectations. On the second floor of a china store, it is a place where brides register and learn about such refined amenities as crystal sconces, Spode teacups, and silver napkin rings. Take the elevator to the second floor and you will find the simple lunchroom. Here ladies dine on shrimp Newburg and chicken salad, sandwiches on homemade bread, fresh-squeezed lemonade, and "Russian chocolate," a blend of coffee and chocolate, topped with whipped cream.

There are only a few desserts, set out on a cart near the entryway. Among them is Filled Sunshine Cake. Until 1976, when a reporter for the Milwaukee *Sentinel* managed to get the recipe from Mr. Watts, it was top secret—a formula, according to the reporter, "that money has never been able to buy from the kitchen staff." It is a complicated recipe, but if you want to compliment a sweet-toothed guest, this bright and springy confection is guaranteed to wow any connoisseur of ladies' cakes.

FILLED SUNSHINE CAKE

CAKE

9 eggs, separated
¼ cup warm water
1 cup sugar
1 cup triple-sifted cake flour

1 teaspoon cream of tartar
¼ teaspoon salt
1 teaspoon vanilla extract

Preheat oven to 350°. Combine egg yolks, water, and ½ cup of the sugar. Beat with electric mixer at medium speed until light and fluffy, 10–15 minutes. Add flour, ¼ cup at a time, mixing only until blended. Whip egg whites with cream of tartar and salt until soft peaks form. Add remaining ½ cup of sugar gradually and beat until stiff peaks form. Add vanilla. Fold into batter. Bake in an ungreased 10-inch angel food cake or tube cake pan 45 minutes. Let cool completely. Remove from pan and use a serrated knife to cut ☞

cake carefully into 3 layers. Fill with French Custard Filling. Frost with Boiled Frosting.

FRENCH CUSTARD FILLING

4 egg yolks, beaten
¾ cup sifted confectioners'
   sugar

¾ cup milk
1 cup butter, softened
1 teaspoon vanilla extract

Cook yolks, sugar, and milk in top of a double boiler over simmering water, stirring often, 15–20 minutes, or until custard coats a spoon. Cool to room temperature. Cream butter thoroughly with vanilla. Add custard slowly. Continue beating until fluffy and smooth. Spread between layers of cake.

BOILED FROSTING

1⅓ cups sugar
½ cup water
3 egg whites

Pinch of salt
1 teaspoon vanilla extract
Grated rind of 1 orange

Combine sugar and water and boil until syrup spins a thread (242°). Beat egg whites and salt to soft peak. Pour hot syrup very slowly into whites, continuing to beat. Beat until frosting stands in stiff peaks and is ready to spread. Add vanilla. Cover top and sides of cake. Sprinkle orange rind on top.

Serves 10–12.

Note: Cake should be served the same day as it is frosted, as boiled frosting tends to become grainy.

We had recently started a newspaper column put out by the Universal Press Syndicate in Kansas City, so when we arrived in K.C., our mission was twofold: to eat a lot of fried chicken and to meet our editors. But between gravy boats and sales projection figures, a third task soon arose.

Alan McDermott, our column's editor, mentioned a place called Leona Yarbrough's, his favorite spot for lunch. "It's been around forever," he said. "It's where the blue hairs eat."

We demanded to go to lunch at Leona's, but as the hour approached, Alan grew more nervous. "Maybe it's not what you have in mind," he sputtered. "I mean, the portions are little, and the food is bland, and the place is sort of fuddy-duddy." It was sounding better all the time.

It was sensational. Leona Yarbrough's is as much a Kansas City institution as Arthur Bryant's or Wolferman's English Muffins (just down the street). If you eat lunch there, you will see Leona, with her blond hair and white apron, peeking into the dining room to make sure that customers are enjoying the egg salad sandwiches on homemade whole wheat.

Alan was still nervous during lunch. "I don't think the egg salad is as good as usual . . . the pie is sweeter than it should be . . . the crust is too thick." His nervousness was unfounded, just the old familiar bringing-guests-to-your-favorite-restaurant panic. We ordered five desserts to share. One of the great ones was rice custard pudding, a layered version of rice pudding:

LEONA YARBROUGH'S RICE CUSTARD PUDDING

2 cups water
½ cup rice
½ teaspoon salt
¼ cup raisins
4 eggs, beaten until frothy

¾ cup sugar
½ teaspoon vanilla extract
2 cups milk
Butter
Nutmeg

Bring water to a boil. Add rice and salt. Cook, uncovered, over very low heat until water is gone, about 45–55 minutes. Take off heat, cover, and let steam 5 minutes. Add raisins.

Preheat oven to 350°. Whisk eggs, sugar, and vanilla until well blended. Whisk in milk. Butter an 8 x 6-inch glass or ceramic baking dish generously. Spread rice and raisins on bottom and pour custard carefully over the top. Sprinkle with grated nutmeg. Set baking dish in a larger pan and pour boiling water around it to half its depth.

Bake 35–40 minutes, until just set. Remove from water bath and let cool. Serve slightly warm or at room temperature.

Serves 6.

CHICKEN DINNER HALLS

Fried chicken might be the most all-American meal of all. It is impossible to be formal or solemn about it; it is *nearly* impossible to eat it with any utensils other than one's greasy fingers. Recipes are simple, but techniques are shrouded in generations of culinary mystification.

Nearly every state in the nation stakes its claim to great fried chicken. But nowhere is chicken dinner as ritualized as it is in the middle of the country, in a wide belt that extends from the Blue Ridge Mountains through small towns in southern Ohio and Kentucky, westward into Oklahoma, with its farthest outpost at Mrs. Allen's Family Style Meals in Sweetwater, Texas. Indianapolis, Kansas City, Oklahoma City—these, and a thousand small towns in between, are where America's fried chicken soul resides.

If you have any doubt about the Midwest's passion for fried chicken, try to get a table on Sunday afternoon at Hollyhock Hill or the Iron Skillet, twin temples of Indianapolis chicken adoration. Impossible. Indianapolitans are there before you, lined up, as they have been for fifty years. Both restaurants offer nearly identical food and surroundings, a taste of what the Hollyhock menu calls "Hoosier Fried Chicken—hand-fried like Mother used to do," served in "one of the very few Family Style restaurant operations still in existence in the U.S.A."

Despite a clearly discernible prehistoric caveman motif in Indianapolis restaurants (including one dinosaur-decorated bar where waitresses wear leopard-skin sarongs and you sit at leather-clothed tables), Indianapolis fried chicken is served in ultracivilized surroundings—restaurants where you want to take a prissy aunt on Sunday.

Sunday is when people *dress* for chicken dinner. And their pastel church clothes blend perfectly with the hollyhocks outside, cake-frosting color scheme inside, and the white wrought-iron latticework that holds the plastic plants. The waitresses wear long dresses, and the really big tables, the ones fixed up with lazy Susans in the center, are rimmed with little boys in chimp-size jackets and girls with bows in their hair, learning from Mom and Dad how to swirl drumsticks in the gravy.

HOOSIER FRIED CHICKEN AND GIBLET GRAVY

According to *America Cooks*, a pioneering regional cookbook published in 1940, "the subject of gravy is a grave one in Indiana, where no ordinary pallid library paste goes into the gravy boat, but a sound meat and giblet sauce that gives meaning to the fried chicken, and is done in lavish country style." The gravy is made in the same pan—always an iron skillet—that is used to fry the chicken.

1 3–4-pound frying chicken,
   cut into pieces
Salt and pepper to taste
3 cups milk
1 tablespoon lemon juice
Giblets from chicken,
   including neck

1½ cups lard
1½ cups vegetable shortening
1½ cups plus 2 tablespoons
   flour
3 teaspoons salt

Wash chicken parts and pat dry. Sprinkle with salt and pepper and immerse in milk and lemon juice in a large bowl. Cover and refrigerate at least 1 hour.

As chicken soaks, boil giblets, including neck, until tender. Chop giblets into small pieces, pick meat from neck, and discard bones. Set aside.

Remove soaking chicken from refrigerator so it warms to room temperature.

Heat lard and shortening to 370° in an iron skillet (there should be ¼–½ inch of fat).

Piece by piece, remove chicken from milk (save milk) and dredge chicken in 1½ cups of the flour mixed with 3 teaspoons salt. Starting with dark meat, place pieces skin side down in hot fat. Fry 5 minutes, turn, and fry 5 minutes more. Reduce heat, cover, and fry about 12 minutes per side, until chicken is dark brown.

Remove from skillet and drain on paper towels.

To make pan gravy, pour off all but a tablespoon or two of fat from skillet, leaving all the bits and pieces of crust that have stuck to pan. Over high heat add remaining 2 tablespoons of flour slowly, stirring, to make a thick roux. Add 2 cups of the reserved milk slowly, continuing to stir. Bring to a boil, add giblets and neck meat, and simmer 2 minutes. Add pepper to taste.

Serves 3–4.

For us, the ultimate Kansas City dining experience is at joints like Boots and Coats or Stroud's, where the customers aren't the least bit bashful about slurping, smacking, and all the other good grubby things one does to amplify the pleasure of great fried chicken.

There is a rollicking roadhouse feel about these places, especially at Stroud's (the old one; they have recently opened an upscale "Stroud's Oak Ridge Manor"), with its worn wooden floors and checked oilcloth-covered tables and the sign outside reading "Home of Pan-Fried Chicken." People crowd into the wide-open dining room to have fun, which they do by ordering mammoth feasts that include cinnamon rolls, butter-dripping mashed potatoes, and vigorously peppered pan gravy.

Boots and Coats serves biscuits instead of cinnamon rolls and cottage fried potatoes instead of mashed, but the chicken is hard to tell apart.

Indeed, the chicken at all of Kansas City's premier chickateria is related, the recipes created by, or at least inspired by, a legendary cook named Chicken Betty. Betty, known as the Pied Piper of Chickendom, learned to catch, kill, pluck, clean, and fry chickens when she was a little girl on her parents' farm in Nebraska. As a grown-up, she was employed by nearly every renowned kitchen in town, setting up the chicken-frying operation, then moving on to other restaurants that needed her skills. Betty's fame was so great that even the *New York Times* took notice a few years ago and printed her recipe.

It is absolutely straightforward, depending on *fresh* chickens and the almighty iron skillet. She recommends plenty of pepper and advises that you really work the chicken through the flour, to make sure it sticks.

CHICKEN BETTY'S FRIED CHICKEN AND GRAVY

Get yourself a couple of brown paper bags before doing this recipe. One is for the flour (shake the chicken in it, piece by piece). The other is for draining the chicken after it cooks. Many chicken aficionados claim that paper-bag draining is crucial. We also believe in *lots* of black pepper for the gravy.

1 3–3½-pound frying chicken	2 tablespoons black pepper
1 egg	1 teaspoon Accent
⅔ cup milk	1 cup lard
2 cups flour	1 cup Crisco
1 tablespoon salt	

Gravy

2 scant tablespoons flour	Salt and pepper to taste
2–3 cups milk, as needed	

Cut chicken into thighs, drumsticks, wings, breasts, and backbone. Wash and pat dry. Let stand until room temperature. Mix egg and milk. Combine flour, salt, pepper, and Accent. Dip chicken, piece by piece, in egg and milk, then dredge in flour mixture.

Heat fat in a skillet to 370°. Fry chicken on each side 5 minutes. Cover, lower heat, and fry 15 minutes on each side until dark brown.

To make gravy, pour off all but 1 tablespoon of fat from pan. Over high heat add flour, stirring to make a roux. Cook until brown. Add milk slowly, continuing to stir. Bring to a boil. Simmer 3 minutes. Add salt and pepper to taste.

Serves 3–4.

KANSAS CITY
COTTAGE FRIED POTATOES

The big difference between Kansas City and Indianapolis chicken is the potatoes. Some chicken halls in Indianapolis actually dish out phony spuds—a petty crime in any context, a felony when next to something as good as their genuine skillet-fried chicken. Kansas City, on the other hand, is a potatoman's town; each place serves the real thing its own special way.

Stroud's gives them to you mashed, suitable for cradling gravy. Granny's serves mashed, American fries (like thick potato chips), and pan fries (available with onions and green peppers strewn among the spuds). Our favorite potatoes were the ones we ate at R.C.'s years ago: cottage fries, a variegated heap of tater textures less pillowy than mashed, but more exciting. The idea behind cottage fries is to cook them so that every disk is a little different, from the few crunchy ones that have to get brutally scraped off the griddle, to the falling-apart circles that are as soft as mashed potatoes, sopped with butter.

5 medium-size thin-skinned potatoes	5 tablespoons butter 1 tablespoon diced onion
1 clove garlic	Salt and pepper to taste

Scrub potatoes clean and boil until cooked but still firm; drain; slice into ¼-inch disks.

Cut garlic clove and rub it all over a large skillet.

Melt 3 tablespoons of the butter in a skillet over medium heat; add onion, then potatoes. Stir to coat all disks. Turn heat up to medium high. Don't stir. When potatoes are well browned, dot top with remaining 2 tablespoons of butter. Add salt and pepper to taste. Turn potatoes over, artistically rearranging and separating disks to attain maximum textural variety.

Serves 4.

PAN FRIES WITH ONIONS AND PEPPERS

4 baking potatoes
2 tablespoons corn oil
2 tablespoons butter

1 onion, chopped
1 green bell pepper, chopped
Salt and pepper to taste

Preheat oven to 400°. Wrap potatoes in foil and bake 1 hour. Turn off oven and let potatoes remain in oven wrapped in foil for another hour. Refrigerate (still in foil) overnight, or until fully chilled.

Remove potatoes from foil, peel and cut into ½-inch cubes.

In a large skillet, melt corn oil with butter. Sauté onion and green pepper until they soften. Pour cubed potatoes into skillet and stir together with onion and pepper. Sprinkle more oil around edge of pan if very crisp potatoes are desired. Fry, tossing occasionally, until potatoes are browned. Season with salt and pepper.

Serves 4.

Biscuits are the expected breadstuff with fried chicken. They're great for dunking in gravy. But in many of America's finest chicken dinner halls, from Rhode Island to Kansas City, biscuits are deemed too plain. Instead, the fried chicken, potatoes, and gravy are accompanied by something a little sweet.

APPLE TREE APPLE FRITTERS

Apple relish, apple butter, apple pie, and apple fritters are the specialties of Stephenson's Apple Tree Inn outside of Kansas City, to which huge populations of chicken-loving pilgrims journey every Sunday. Those who are pure of palate will want to fry these fritters in their own clean oil. That's the upstanding way to do it. But what the heck, we figured; we'll be eating them with the chicken, so why not fry them in the same oil as the chicken? We liked the results, a confluence of sweet and savory.

Oil for deep frying
1 egg, beaten
1 cup milk
1 cup finely chopped unpeeled
    cored apple
¼ cup granulated sugar
¼ teaspoon salt

1 teaspoon grated orange peel
3 tablespoons orange juice
½ teaspoon vanilla extract
2 cups flour
1 tablespoon baking powder
Sifted confectioners' sugar

Preheat oil to 350°. Combine egg, milk, apple, sugar, salt, orange peel, juice, and vanilla. Combine flour and baking powder separately. Stir into egg mixture, only enough to moisten all the flour.

Drop batter by rounded teaspoonfuls into fat. Fry until golden brown, about 3 minutes, turning once. Drain on paper towels. Roll in confectioners' sugar. Serve warm.

Makes about 36 fritters,
enough to serve 8–10.

PAN-STICKER CINNAMON ROLLS FOR CHICKEN DINNER

Like sticky buns, but not quite as sweet, these rolls are great for family-style eating, especially if served directly from the oven, in the baking pan. As they cool, the caramelized gunk at the bottom of the pan gets sticky and begins to harden, so provide a couple of sturdy spatulas for scraping up all the good stuff with the rolls. (They are as good for breakfast as they are with fried chicken.)

1 package dry yeast
¾ cup plus 1 teaspoon
    granulated sugar
¼ cup tepid water (110°)
½ cup warm milk
1 teaspoon salt

7 tablespoons butter, melted
2 eggs
1 teaspoon vanilla extract
2¾–3 cups flour
1½ teaspoons cinnamon

Glaze

6 tablespoons butter, softened
½ cup brown sugar

1 tablespoon dark corn syrup

Dissolve yeast and 1 teaspoon of the granulated sugar in water.

Beat milk, ¼ cup of the granulated sugar, salt, 4 tablespoons of the melted butter, eggs, and vanilla until smooth. Add yeast mixture.

Pour liquid into a bowl with 2¾ cups of the flour. Stir vigorously. Turn onto a floured board and let rest while you clean and butter bowl.

Knead dough 10 minutes, adding enough flour to create a smooth mass.

Return dough to bowl, roll around to coat with butter, and cover. Let rise in a warm place until double in bulk, about 2 hours.

As dough rises, prepare glaze by beating softened butter with brown sugar and corn syrup until smooth. Spread across bottom of a 12-inch iron skillet or cake pan.

Punch down dough and roll out ¼ inch thick. Brush with 2 tablespoons of the melted butter, reserving about 1 tablespoon of butter; then sprinkle with mixture of cinnamon and remaining ½ cup of granulated sugar. Roll from top into a tight tube and cut into 1-inch slices.

Lay pieces into prepared skillet, almost touching. Brush tops with remaining melted butter. Cover and let rise 1 hour.

Preheat oven to 375°. Bake rolls 20–25 minutes, until golden brown. Cool in pan 5 minutes. If not serving immediately, lift rolls out of pan with spatula, scraping up maximum amount of caramel glaze.

Makes 15–18 rolls.

You can have a brownie for dessert at Hollyhock Hill, but if you want to be true to the spirit of these happy meals and to Midwestern eating habits, you will conclude your chicken feast with ice cream.

In Kansas City, you get vanilla or chocolate, with fudge sauce on top. In Indiana, peppermint ice cream is *de rigueur*. Pink and white, sweet as a bowlful of sugar, heavy cream textured, peppermint ice cream is, along with sugar cream pie, one of the two definitive Hoosier desserts. (They even have decent peppermint ice cream at the highway oases off I-80!) For fried chicken picnics, nothing else will do.

AFTER-CHICKEN
PEPPERMINT ICE CREAM

You will need an ice cream maker—electric or hand-cranked. This recipe makes pretty pastel pink ice cream that is *not too sweet*—ideal for hot fudge toppings, or with a piece of chocolate cake. For sweeter ice cream, use 1 cup of corn syrup.

24 Brach's Starlight Mints	⅔ cup light corn syrup
2 cups half-and-half	1 teaspoon peppermint extract
2 cups cream	

Pulverize mints by putting them under a clean, dry cloth and hitting them with a hammer. Leave a few tiny chunks, but mostly you want a fine, pink powder.

Mix half-and-half, cream, corn syrup, and peppermint extract and pour into freezing bowl of ice cream maker.

When cream has thickened, but is not quite completely frozen, add pulverized mints.

Makes 2 pints.

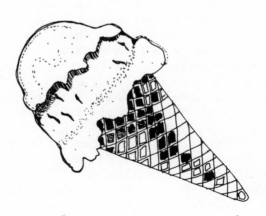

CHICAGO'S
DEEP DISH DELIRIUM

Chicago tries harder. And when Chicago cooks try hard, they outdo everybody else.

Look what happened to pizza. According to legend, it got rooted in Chicago almost accidentally, in 1947. Restaurateurs Ike Sewell and Ric Riccardo were planning to open a Mexican eatery at the corner of Wabash and Ohio. Before opening, so the story goes, Riccardo ate enchiladas prepared by the Mexican bartender they had hired. According to Mr. Sewell, the Mexican food made Riccardo so sick that he ran off to Italy, where he, like many recently returned GI's, discovered pizza. The partners decided to open a pizzeria instead of a Mexican restaurant.

But they wanted to serve a pizza that was more substantial than the peasant food Riccardo had tasted in Sicily. They also did not want to emulate the thin-crusted pizza that had been common in the Italian neighborhoods of America's East Coast since at least the 1920s. They decided to invent their own style of pizza, something unique—hearty, yet with gourmet ingredients. Chicago-style pizza was born.

In the next twenty-five years, deep dish pan pizza became known as Chicago's own. Despite Sewell and Riccardo's intention to elevate it as a gourmet dish, their first restaurant, Uno's, remained a raffish place, literally underground, with graffiti on the walls. It took some time before pan pizza caught on; in 1957, three years after Ric Riccardo's death, Ike Sewell opened a second location (Pizzeria Due); by the late 1970s, the two pizzerias were baking two thousand pies per day.

As the fame of Chicago pizza spread, Sewell was deluged with franchise schemes. For years he resisted, but finally in 1979 Uno'ses began popping up in cities all over the country. No pizza aficionado takes any of the clones seriously, not if they've had a taste of the sorry, soggy things sold elsewhere as Chicago pizza. Alan Kelson of *Chicago* magazine maintained that the secret of Ike Sewell's original deep dish pizza "is the two women who've been working for him for years [Aldean Stoudamire at Uno's and Elnora Russell at Due's]. They make it by feel."

ORIGINAL CHICAGO DEEP DISH PIZZA

True Chicago pizza is a gustable Mount St. Helens bubbling with cheese, tomatoes, and whatever else you've ordered. To make it right, you need a deep dish pizza pan or a large cake pan, 12–15 inches in diameter, about 2 inches deep. Uno's pizza is especially good with wide slabs of Italian sausage.

Crust

1 package dry yeast	½ cup yellow cornmeal
1 teaspoon sugar	1 teaspoon salt
1 cup tepid water (110°)	¼ cup light salad oil
2¾–3 cups flour	

Topping

¾ pound mozzarella cheese, sliced	tomatoes, very well drained and crushed
1 pound Italian sausage, cooked and drained	2 teaspoons oregano
1 28-ounce can whole	4 tablespoons grated Parmesan cheese

Dissolve yeast and sugar in ¼ cup of the water.

Combine 2¾ cups of the flour, cornmeal, salt, oil, and remaining ¾ cup of water in a bowl. When yeast is foamy, add it and stir vigorously.

Turn out onto a floured board and let rest while you clean and oil bowl.

Knead dough 6–8 minutes, adding flour if necessary to create a springy dough. Return to bowl, roll around to cover with oil, cover with a double layer of plastic wrap, and let rise until double in bulk, 1–2 hours.

When ready to make pizza, preheat oven to 500°.

Punch down dough. Oil pizza pan generously and push dough into it with oiled fingers, creating a 1½-inch-high circumference of dough. Let rise in pan while you assemble topping.

Layer mozzarella across surface of dough. Top with sausage, then tomatoes, oregano, and finally Parmesan.

Bake 15 minutes. Lower oven heat to 375° and bake 20–25 minutes more, checking bottom of crust for doneness. You want it light tan, not dark brown.

Serve hot from pan or serving platter.

Serves 4.

Uno's, and its pizza-in-a-pan, are just the beginning of the Chicago pizza saga.

In 1973 Joe and Efren Boglio opened Giordano's, a pizzeria named after their mother, who was famous in the family for her Old Country Easter pizza—deep dish, twin crusted, stuffed with sweet ricotta cheese. Ricotta stuffing was considered too exotic for customers who knew only mozzarella, so the Boglios packed their pan pizza with homemade fennel and garlic sausage, mozzarella, and mushrooms, capped all that with another crust, and frosted the crust with tomato sauce, Parmesan, Romano, and a sprinkle of Italian spice. The stuffed pizza was born, and the Chicago pizza sweepstakes moved into high gear.

MAMA'S STUFFED PIZZA

Stuffed pizza ingredients vary from the traditional (as below) to all-vegetarian stuffings, multi-cheese mixtures, and seafood in cheese sauce. Whatever you stuff between the crusts, be sure that it is cooked (baked, sautéed, whatever) beforehand. The half hour this pie spends in the oven is enough to heat the stuffing and melt the cheese, but it will not cook pork or bacon, or peppers, mushrooms, etc.

Crust

1 package dry yeast
1 teaspoon sugar
1⅓ cups tepid water (110°)
3¾–4 cups flour

½ cup yellow cornmeal
¼ cup olive oil
2 teaspoons salt

Filling

2 cloves garlic, minced
2 tablespoons olive oil
1 pound mozzarella cheese, shredded

1 pound Italian sausage, cooked and drained, crumbled or cut into disks

Topping

1 18-ounce can whole tomatoes, drained and crushed coarse, or ⅔ cup pizza sauce
2 teaspoons oregano

2 tablespoons grated Parmesan cheese
2 tablespoons grated Romano cheese

Dissolve yeast and sugar in ⅓ cup of the water.

Combine 3¾ cups of the flour with cornmeal, olive oil, salt, and remaining 1 cup of water. When yeast is foamy, add it, stirring vigorously. Turn out onto a floured board and let rest while you clean and oil bowl.

Knead dough 6–8 minutes, adding flour if necessary to create a smooth dough. Return to bowl, cover with a double layer of plastic wrap, and let rise until double in bulk, 1–2 hours.

When ready to make pizza, preheat oven to 500°.

Punch down risen dough. Tear off about three-quarters of it, leaving one-quarter in bowl, covered. With oiled fingers, press dough into well-oiled deep dish pizza pan or cake pan, making sure you create an even 2-inch-high circumference.

To make filling, steep garlic in olive oil. Combine mozzarella, sausage, and garlic (including oil in which it has steeped), and empty them into pizza shell.

Roll and carefully stretch remaining ball of dough into a circle large enough to fit over pizza pan. Crimp bottom and top dough together all around and poke holes in top with a toothpick.

Bake 15 minutes. Lower oven temperature to 350°. Bake 10 minutes more.

To make topping, mix crushed tomatoes and oregano and spread across top crust (or use high-quality pizza sauce). Sprinkle with grated cheeses. Return to oven. Bake 10 minutes longer.

Serves 6.

ALTERNATIVE FILLINGS
FOR STUFFED PIZZA

PRIMAVERA FILLING

½ pound fontina cheese, grated coarse
1 large beefsteak tomato, sliced
1 medium-size yellow squash, sliced thin
1 red onion, sliced thin

1 green bell pepper, sliced in strips
1 tablespoon fresh parsley
1 clove garlic, minced fine (optional)

Distribute cheese in bottom of pizza shell and top with vegetables, adding garlic if desired. Eliminate tomato topping. After 20 minutes in oven, brush top with olive oil and sprinkle with Parmesan cheese.

FOUR CHEESE FILLING

½ pound ricotta cheese
½ pound Swiss cheese, cubed
½ pound smoked Gouda
    cheese, cubed

½ pound blue-veined cheese,
    crumbled

Mix all ingredients in a large bowl and put into pizza shell. Eliminate Parmesan and Romano cheeses from topping.

The next great leap in the evolution of Chicago pizza was conceived at Edwardo's: a creamy-centered mile-high pizza soufflé, laced with spinach or fresh basil (for pesto pizza). Giordano's countered with their own stuffed spinach special, listed on the menu under "Where It All Began"—three different cheeses, spinach, and mushrooms sandwiched between the crusts. All over town, Chicago pizzerias began to offer not merely pan pizza but stuffed and overstuffed pizza, pizza pot pie, double-deckers, and health-food crust. The latest wrinkle, at Abati's downtown, is—are you ready?—flaming pizza!

SPINACH SOUFFLÉ PIZZA

At Edwardo's they paint the top crust with tomato sauce, creating an Italian flag color scheme when the pizza is sliced and the spinach revealed. Lovely, but we prefer to frost the top with oil and garlic, a sharp counterpoint to the fluffy stuff down below.

Crust

1 package dry yeast
1 teaspoon sugar
1½ cups tepid water (110°)
3½–4 cups flour

½ cup yellow cornmeal
⅓ cup olive oil
1½ teaspoons salt

Filling

1 pound fresh raw spinach,
    washed, dried, and
    chopped, stems removed
8 ounces low-moisture
    mozzarella cheese,
    shredded

2 cups ricotta cheese

Topping

2 cloves garlic, minced fine
2 tablespoons olive oil
1 teaspoon oregano

5 tablespoons grated Parmesan
   cheese

Dissolve yeast and sugar in ½ cup of the water. Combine 3½ cups of the flour with cornmeal, olive oil, salt, and remaining 1 cup of water. When yeast is foamy, add it, stirring vigorously. Turn out onto a floured board and let rest while you clean and oil bowl.

Knead dough 6–8 minutes, adding flour if necessary to create a smooth dough. Return to bowl, cover with a double layer of plastic wrap, and let rise until double in bulk, 1–2 hours.

When ready to make pizza, preheat oven to 500°.

Punch down risen dough. Tear off about three-quarters of it, leaving one-quarter in bowl, covered. With oiled fingers, press dough into well-oiled deep dish pizza pan or cake pan, making sure you create an even 2-inch-high circumference.

To make filling, mix spinach, mozzarella, and ricotta and put inside pizza dough.

Roll and carefully stretch remaining dough into a circle large enough to cover pie and fit it on top, turning edge under and crimping closed. Prick holes in top crust with a toothpick.

Bake 10 minutes. Lower heat to 400°. Bake 10 minutes more.

To make topping, steep garlic in olive oil. Spread across top of pizza. Sprinkle on oregano and Parmesan cheese. Bake 15 minutes more, until cheese on top begins to brown.

Serves 4–6.

The theme of the Chicago pizza story is one-upmanship, a mania for going one better than the competition. As we see it, the ever-rising pizzas reflect the same zeal that gives Chicago the tallest buildings, the largest urban art works, and the longest list of available toppings for a hot dog. Civic-minded Chicagoans seem to be engaged in a tireless campaign to prove that the Second City is second to none.

The last time we went pizza hunting in Chicago, we had arrived by plane, carless, and felt like lonesome cowboys whose horses had galloped over the mesa. So we found a cabdriver who promised to lead us to mozzarella Mecca. He drove north on Milwaukee Avenue to Father and Son pizza, home of the thinnest crust in town. Milwaukee Avenue, we assure you, is an adventure itself—especially farther north, what our cabbie later called the "lamp neighborhood," where each modest brick-fronted home displays a single, spectacularly ornate lamp in its window.

Father and Son, closer to the heart of the city, serves pizza New York style ("thicker than thin, more sauce, more cheese, more Italian"), Chicago style ("thick dough delight, juicier and more cheese"), and Thin and Crispy ("the kind that made us famous").

Other than the cracker-thinness of its dough, Father and Son is distinguished by its whimsical toppings, including pineapple, sirloin steak, and omelette. The best of the lot, as far as we are concerned, is taco topping, on the thin and crispy crust.

SKINNY SKINNY TACO PIZZA

The secret of a really elegant, crisp-crusted pizza is to develop the gluten in the dough enough so you can *stretch* it without tearing. That means extra kneading time, by hand, and extra rising time. It also means investing in a baker's peel and a pizza stone, an unglazed tile that makes any home oven into a pizza oven. A thin crust is ideal for minimalist pizzas, such as garlic and Parmesan, or olive oil and fresh basil. But it's got enough strength to hold up even under a glut of meat and cheese.

Crust

1 package dry yeast
1 teaspoon sugar
1 cup tepid water (110°)

2¾–3 cups flour
2 tablespoons olive oil
2 teaspoons salt

Taco topping

1 pound hamburger meat,
  ground fine
½ teaspoon salt
½ teaspoon pepper
1 teaspoon ground cumin

1 onion, peeled and chopped
1½ cups taco sauce
¾ pound Monterey Jack
  cheese, shredded

Dissolve yeast and sugar in ¼ cup of the water.

Combine 2¾ cups of the flour with olive oil, salt, and remaining ¾ cup of water. When yeast is foamy, add it and stir vigorously. Turn out onto a floured board and let rest while you clean and oil bowl.

Knead dough a full 15 minutes, adding flour if necessary. Return to bowl, roll around to coat with oil, cover with a double layer of plastic wrap, and let rise 2 hours. Punch down dough and let rise again 1 hour.

When ready to make pizza, sprinkle pizza stone with cornmeal, put it in oven, and preheat oven to 500°.

To prepare topping, cook hamburger meat, salt, pepper, cumin, and onion together. Drain off any fat. Add taco sauce.

Divide dough in half, leaving one-half under plastic wrap in bowl. Flatten other half on a lightly floured board. Use a rolling pin to flatten it evenly.

When dough is stretched thin, ease it onto a baker's peel dusted with cornmeal. Top it with half of meat topping and half of cheese.

Using a quick jerking motion, slide pizza off baker's peel onto heated stone in oven (a technique best learned by watching a pro).

Cook 10–15 minutes, until crust is crisp and brown. Prepare second pizza while first one cooks.

Cook second pizza.

*Makes 2 pizzas,
enough to serve 4.*

UPPER PENINSULA
PASTY SHOPS

here is a lot of debate about what is and what is not true American cuisine, but anyone who has traveled through Michigan's Upper Peninsula can tell you for certain that the Cornish pasty, cooked by Michiganders of Finnish descent, is as American as a planked Lake Superior whitefish.

Pasty shops are everywhere in the U.P., serving the stuffed pastry crescents from Cornwall with the same nonchalant attitude you get toward franchised burgers in lower Michigan and the other forty-nine states.

At the Red Onion, a cinder-block bunker in Negaunee (with a branch in Escanaba), the pasty business is so oriented toward the mobile trade that there is exactly one dining table in the house. Coffee is help-yourself, and there are packs of Twinkies for dessert. The pasties come ready-wrapped in foil, in paper sacks, looking like the most unappealing fast food. But when you peel the foil back on a Red Onion pasty, you see that it is a vision of bakery beauty, the edge of its dark, flaky crust braided to seal in the juices, the inside packed with a peppery blend of beef and pork and potatoes, with little orange squares of carrots or rutabagas thrown in for color.

The point of the pasty is its mobility; it was designed to be handled with impunity. It came to Michigan with the Cornish settlers who arrived in the middle of the nineteenth century to work the iron mines. The perfect self-contained miner's lunch, it slipped neatly into a pocket and was easily reheated on the end of a shovel. Plus you could eat it by hand, without utensils. By the time the Finnish people settled in Superiorland, the Cornish pasty was entrenched, and they adopted (and adapted) it as their own.

Serious gastroethnographers distinguish between a true Upper Peninsula Cornish pasty, made with cubes of steak, and a Finnish-style U.P. pasty, made with ground beef and pork. Further debate swirls around issues such as whether the dough should be made with lard or suet; and the filling—with or without rutabaga; and the crimp of the crust—at the top or along the side edge.

We learned how to make a definitive Finnish pasty from the now-departed Finlandia Restaurant and Bakery in Marquette, where they sold them either frozen or hot and ready to travel or on a lovely blue-speckled plate. The first time we stopped at Finlandia, we sat in a plastic brocade booth and eagerly asked the waitress if she had any pasties (pronouncing them *pay-stees*). *"Paystees* you wear," she cracked. *"Pasties* [*a* as in *hat*] you eat."

Finlandia pasties resembled a Platonic ideal—smooth tan ovals, with the seam underneath, so when they were set upon the plate, they appeared absolutely seamless, identical studies in pastry perfectionism. Each blimp was packed with finely shredded beef and pork, bound with tiny cubes of potato, bits of red onion, and carrot. The crust was thin and sophisticated, at first seeming too delicate to serve its traditional role as the carrying pouch for the heavy load of ingredients.

FINLANDIA PASTIES

Experienced pastry cooks will be able to whip up the crust with nothing more than a bowl and a couple of knives. We find the food processor indispensable for doing the dough right.

Dough

4 cups flour
Dash salt

1½ cups Crisco
1 cup cold water

Filling

½ pound ground beef
¼ pound ground pork
¼ cup finely chopped beef suet
1 large potato, peeled and
    diced fine
2 carrots, peeled and diced fine
1 small red onion, diced fine

½ rutabaga, peeled and diced
    fine
⅛ cup finely chopped fresh
    parsley
1 teaspoon salt
¼ teaspoon pepper
2 tablespoons butter, melted

Combine flour and salt. Cut in shortening. Add water slowly until mixture forms a sticky ball. With floured hands, shape into a ball, wrap with wax paper, and put in refrigerator 1 hour before preparing filling.

Preheat oven to 350°. Combine filling ingredients in a large bowl, tossing until thoroughly mixed.

Divide dough into 4 equal parts. Using a rolling pin on a floured board, roll each into an 8–10-inch circle.

Place 1 cup filling in center of each circle. Fold both sides up and crimp firmly, forming a half-moon shape.

Use a large spatula to lift each pasty from floured board and set it seam side down on a greased cookie sheet. Bake 75 minutes, until light brown.

Makes 4 meal-size pasties.

Who could leave Finlandia without a sample from the bakery case? Here were lined up sticky buns and apple fritters, freshly made doughnuts, and loaves of what were called nisa bread, a fascinating Finnish specialty redolent of cardamom, but barely sweetened. This is how we make cardamom bread at home.

NISA BREAD

1 package dry yeast
½ cup plus 1 teaspoon sugar
½ cup tepid water (110°)
8 tablespoons butter
⅔ cup milk
2 eggs
2 teaspoons salt

1 tablespoon ground
   cardamom
1 cup rye flour
3–4 cups all-purpose flour
1 egg yolk, beaten with 1
   teaspoon water

Dissolve yeast and 1 teaspoon of the sugar in water. Melt butter, move from heat, add milk and remaining ½ cup of sugar, stirring until dissolved. When butter and milk mixture is lukewarm, whisk in eggs, then add yeast mixture.

Combine salt, cardamom, rye flour, and 3 cups of the all-purpose flour. Combine with yeast mixture, stirring until mixture forms a ball and pulls away from sides of bowl. Turn out onto a floured board. Clean and butter bowl.

Knead dough, adding up to a cup of all-purpose flour, as needed, to create a smooth, workable dough. Knead 6–8 minutes until smooth and elastic. Return to bowl, cover, and let rise until double in bulk, about 2 hours.

Punch down dough and divide dough in half. Roll each half into an oblong. Place the oblongs on a buttered baking sheet and brush with egg yolk. Cover loosely with plastic wrap.

Preheat oven to 350° as loaves rise 45 minutes.

Bake 40 minutes, or until loaves sound hollow when tapped. Cool on a rack.

Makes 2 loaves.

For a traditional Cornish pasty there is only one place to go: Lawry's Pasty Shop in Ishpeming. The perfect time is in the fall, when the Upper Peninsula looks like the corniest scene on a gun shop calendar. It is a land of blue skies, cobalt lakes, and a large population of deer and fish. A hunter's paradise; even squeamish humane types cannot help but enjoy the endless elbow room.

Lawry's, on the road west out of Ishpeming, is run seven days a week by Nancy Lawry, who starts every morning from scratch, making 200 to 400 pasties every day (with the single day record being 700, on a recent Fourth of July).

Nancy's pasties are beef only, no pork, with more suet than the Finnish version. They are formed into flat crescents rather than ovoid pillows, and the ratio of crust to stuffing is higher, resulting in a sturdier and more readily portable meal.

It is perfectly right and mannerly to do without utensils when eating one of these fat pockets. It is a hefty load, and it feels good to bite as you cradle it in a napkin, enjoying its warmth.

Although Nancy happily told us everything that goes into one of her renowned pasties, she could not provide exact measurements. "That's a kinda touchy subject up here," she said. "Pasties are our reputation, and I'd be worried if someone else got a hold of just how we do it."

So we fiddled and fussed at home and devised this version of Nancy's Cornish pasties, based on the hints she gave us:

COAL MINER'S TRUE CORNISH PASTIES

A rugged (but deliciously flaky) crust makes these pasties eminently portable.

Crust

4 cups flour	1½ cups finely ground beef
½ teaspoon baking powder	suet
1 teaspoon salt	1 cup ice-cold water

Filling

¾ pound lean beef, cubed or ground coarse	1 red onion, diced
1½ cups peeled and finely diced potatoes	2 teaspoons salt
	½ teaspoon pepper
1½ cups peeled and finely diced turnips	2 tablespoons butter, melted

Combine flour, baking powder, and salt. Add suet, mixing until mealy. Add ice water and mix to form a sticky ball. With floured hands, shape into a ball, wrap with wax paper, and put in refrigerator 1 hour before preparing filling.

Preheat oven to 375°. Combine filling ingredients in a large bowl and mix thoroughly, squishing with your hands so there are no large clods of meat.

Divide dough into 4 equal parts. Using a rolling pin on a floured board, roll each into an 8–10-inch circle. Dough will be tough.

Place 1 heaping cup of filling in center of each dough circle. Fold dough over and crimp firmly, leaving no uncrimped seam.

Lift each pasty carefully from floured board and set it on a greased cookie sheet in such a way that the seam runs along the side, in a flat half-moon shape.

Bake 1 hour, until golden brown.

Makes 4 meal-size pasties.

Although it is a favorite stop for summer tourists, Lawry's is a local kind of place, small and friendly, decorated with a lot of carefully tended plants. One of the great treats of eating here comes after your pasty is polished off: Nancy's sensational desserts. She makes buttercrumb-topped apple pie, brittle sugar cookies, and from a recipe handed down by her grandmother, Eliza Larmour, the best gingersnap cookies we ever ate.

ELIZA LARMOUR'S GINGERSNAPS

Sugar and spice and plenty of Crisco make these plump fissured disks meltingly lush.

1 cup Crisco	1 teaspoon cinnamon
1 cup sugar	1 teaspoon ground cloves
1 egg	½ teaspoon powdered ginger
¼ cup dark molasses	2 cups flour
1 tablespoon baking soda	Additional sugar for rolling
¼ teaspoon salt	dough balls

Preheat oven to 350°. Cream shortening and sugar. Add egg and molasses. Add dry ingredients.

Form into 1-inch balls, roll balls in sugar, and place 1–2 inches apart on ungreased cookie sheets. Bake 12 minutes.

Cool on cookie sheets until firm. Remove carefully with a spatula.

Makes 16 cookies.

RUDE FOOD

The city streets of the Midwest are a majestic hodgepodge of fast food and quickie meals for scarfing down with reckless panache.

We are not talking about the phenomenon of grazing, wherein upwardly mobile, antsy-pants urbanites eat their fill of tarry Italianate gelato and raw-dough chocolate chip cookies. The street food we mean is anything but chic. It is plebeian grub, most of it just a glimmer away from its melting pot roots.

The rude food of the Midwest has been elevated by its partisans—blue and white collar alike—to cult status. Chili, red hots, Italian beef: these are subjects to stir one's soul.

Take chili. You could start another civil war debating which state makes the best. Texans have argued loud enough to have most of the rest of the country convinced that theirs is definitive. But try to find a decent bowl of red the next time you're in Texas. The amazing fact is that only a handful of modern Texas restaurants specialize in chili—and most of them are for the tourists.

That is why we offer the Midwest, Cincinnati in particular, as the chili capital of America. You cannot turn the corner in Cincinnati without passing a cafe sign advertising chili. More than 100 chili parlors, some of them affiliated with the great chili chains (Skyline, Empress, Gold Star), some independent, specialize in variations of a style of chili unique to Cincinnati.

This Midwest melting pot extravaganza would be heresy in the Southwest. It *is* spicy, but it is never very hot; instead of cumin and jalapeño pepper, you taste cinnamon and sage. And if you really want to *épater le Texican*, you will serve it as they often do in Cincinnati, with a garnish of oyster crackers! The top-of-the-line chili, with the works—spaghetti, chili meat, beans, onions, and cheese—is called 5-way.

Cincinnati chili has not only unique ingredients but a language all its own, extensively documented in an article by Timothy Charles Lloyd called "The Cincinnati Chili Culinary Complex" in *Western Folklore* (Vol. 40, No. 1). "The correspondence between the order of additional ingredients and higher-numbered ways follows a strict rule," Mr. Lloyd notes. "Cheese = three, onions = four, beans = five." If you want spaghetti, chili, and onions, but no cheese you *do not* order "three way with onions instead of cheese," or "two way plus onions." You must order "four way no cheese." Dig?

An exception to the rules is the combination of spaghetti, chili, and beans, which "in the interest of economy," according to Mr. Lloyd, is called a "chili bean." Another anomaly, told to us by a Cincinnati chili chef, is spaghetti, chili, and cheese, no beans or onions. That, the man says, is called a "haywagon."

You will get plenty of argument from Cincinnatians about which chili parlor serves the best in town, but we find it hard to imagine a more perfect mix of flavors and textures than that dished out at the Camp Washington Chili Parlor, a chilihead shrine open twenty-four hours a day, every day but Sunday, since 1940. Here the blend is meaty, dark red, seductively aromatic, made in sixty-gallon batches every day from freshly ground lean bull meat.

The chef and owner is John Johnson, who started brewing chili when he came to America as a schoolboy from Greece in 1951. What makes his chili special are his secret spices, which he buys from two different suppliers, so that neither one will be able to figure out his formula. Mr. and Mrs. Johnson blend their spice mixture every two weeks, then lock it inside a vault above the restaurant's kitchen. As the chili is being made, John Johnson slips upstairs, gets two brown bagfuls, and quickly dumps them into the smoky vat. We got a whiff of one bag as he carried it through the kitchen—and nearly passed out.

No chef in Cincinnati divulges chili secrets, but for Cincinnatians suffering hometown food nostalgia, and anyone else who enjoys a roundhouse platter of good eats, here is our own recipe for the real thing, perfected with the advice and guidance of Mr. Johnson:

QUEEN OF CHILIS

Starting with beef, garlic, cumin, cinnamon, and allspice, each chef quickly turns this dish into his own—hot, sweet, thick, however it is preferred.

3 onions
1 pound ground chuck
2 cloves garlic, minced
1 cup barbecue sauce
1 cup water
1 tablespoon chili powder
1 teaspoon ground black
    pepper
½ ounce unsweetened
    chocolate, grated
½ teaspoon ground cumin
½ teaspoon turmeric
½ teaspoon allspice

½ teaspoon cinnamon
¼ teaspoon ground cloves
¼ teaspoon ground coriander
¼ teaspoon ground cardamom
1 teaspoon salt
Tomato juice, as needed
9 ounces spaghetti, cooked and
    buttered
1 16-ounce can kidney beans,
    heated
1 pound Cheddar cheese,
    shredded
Oyster crackers

Chop 2 of the onions and set aside; chop remaining onion fine. Salt a large skillet. Turn heat to medium and add meat, finely chopped onion, and garlic. Break up meat with fork and cook until it is browned. Drain fat.

Add barbecue sauce and water. Bring to a boil. Add remaining seasonings.

Cover and simmer over very low heat 30 minutes, stirring and tasting occasionally, adding tomato juice if mixture is getting too dry to ladle up easily. (We like this chili best when it is reheated after being allowed to "age" overnight in the refrigerator.)

To construct the plate of 5-way, layer spaghetti on a plate (a small oval plate is traditional), top it with hot chili, then with a sparse layer of beans, then reserved chopped onions. Pat on plenty of cheese while chili is still hot and serve immediately, with oyster crackers on the side.

Serves 4.

Cincinnatians like their chili so much that its traditional accompaniment is—chili dogs! Little wieners, three or four inches long, nestled in buns, topped with chili meat: They are known as "Coneys" throughout the eastern half of the Midwest in honor of their New York roots. But the three-bite dogs sold from street-corner Coney shops bear no relation to the large, crackle-skinned franks served at Nathan's in the East. Cincinnati, Cleveland, Detroit—each is a Coney capital.

Coneys belong in the same genre of grub as White Castle hamburgers, meaning that you buy not one or two but a bunch of them, maybe a half dozen, and heft the little fellas, one at a time, in your big fat fist, consuming them like large cocktail franks.

There is a psychological boost to eating miniaturized junk food. Unlike a foot-long wiener, which can present a humbling challenge, a little Coney in the hand makes anyone feel like a giant. Even wimps dispatch the puny things in a few jaw-stretching bites—never more than four.

Coneys topped with chili are still called Coneys—never chili dogs. In Cincinnati, they are almost always served beneath a blanket of chili meat (the same stuff ladled on spaghetti noodles), plus raw onions and shredded Cheddar. In Detroit and Cleveland, and at small-town stands that specialize in Coneys (and may serve chili on the side), the topping is hardly ever referred to as chili. It's "Coney sauce."

Several years ago, a *Roadfood* reader sent us a recipe for Dog 'n' Suds Coney Sauce. But there was no return address on the envelope, and her letter has since vanished, leaving us with only the recipe. And a good one it is!

We aren't certain if this is truly the Coney sauce used at Dog 'n' Suds drive-ins, or simply our anonymous correspondent's interpretation thereof. Whatever, it makes a swell topping for any style of wiener, red or white, all-beef or pork, Coney-size or foot-long.

ANONYMOUS PERSON'S DOG 'N' SUDS CONEY SAUCE

1 pound ground beef
1 small onion, chopped
2 tablespoons prepared
    mustard
2 tablespoons vinegar
2 tablespoons sugar

1 tablespoon water
1 teaspoon Worcestershire
    sauce
¼ teaspoon celery seed
¼ teaspoon Tabasco sauce
Ketchup, as needed

In a salted skillet, brown ground beef with onion over medium heat, breaking up meat with a fork to crumble it fine. Drain off fat.

Add all other ingredients, except ketchup. Mix well, then add enough ketchup to keep mixture loose. Simmer, partially covered, 1 hour, adding ketchup as needed.

Makes enough sauce for 6–8 medium-size wieners.

Chili in Chicago is somewhat peripheral, but no city is mores serious about its wieners. "The hot dog has been developed to its full potential in Chicago," write Rich Bowen and Dick Fay in *Hot Dog Chicago*, a high-spirited guide to more than 100 hot dog stands. The hot dog connoisseur can dine in street-smart style at Happy Dawg, Disco Dog, Poochie's, The Slush Pup, Bowser Dog, or Between the Buns.

They never heard of Coney Islands in the Windy City. The term is "red hots," and they are seldom topped with chili or cheese, as in Detroit and Cincinnati; certainly not with kraut, as in New York. Instead, you get them with the works: pickle spears, mustard, piccalilli, onions, and little firebrand pods known as sport peppers. A garden and a dog in a bun.

It is the toppings that make the red hot sing. There is no limit to the amount and variety of condiments that people in Chicago pile on. Bowser Dog, a stand on Irving Park, actually has an item listed on its menu that is a hot dog garnished with—a hamburger! It is a pliable gray patty, wrapped around a fat wiener, topped with cucumbers, tomato, and lettuce.

RED HOT MUSTARD

Chicago hot dogs, the best of them manufactured by David Berg or the Vienna Sausage Company, are merely grilled or steeped in water: no fancy cooking allowed. Buns come fresh from local bakeries and are served warm from the steam cabinet. We do not recommend you try making either dogs or buns at home. Instead, satisfy your creative urge by making this very hot homemade mustard, with a celery salt Chicago accent. Then mix the mustard with sweet relish, and you're in business.

¼ cup dry mustard
½ cup cider vinegar
2 teaspoons sugar

½ teaspoon salt
1 teaspoon celery salt
2 egg yolks, well beaten

Thoroughly mix mustard, vinegar, sugar, salt, and celery salt in top of a double boiler. Place over simmering water. Beat in egg yolks with wire whisk. Whisk constantly 3–5 minutes over simmering water, until mustard thickens to spreading consistency.

Let cool to room temperature. Store in refrigerator.

Makes ⅔ cup mustard.

Although Chicagoans are crazy for red hots, their street food *pièce de résistance* is an Italian beef sandwich. It's razor-thin roast beef, sopped with aromatic natural juices, unique for the garlicky bite of its gravy. There is nothing truly Italian about it, except that it's served on brawny rolls from Italian bakeries, and many of its top purveyors are of Italian descent.

ITALIAN BEEF

We have never met a Chicagoan who makes Italian beef at home. It is pure street food, enjoyable not only for itself but for the gregarious, social nature of most open-air Italian beef stands (to call them *restaurants* is straining the term). If we lived in Chicago, we'd never bother to make Italian beef at home. We would eat it on the stroll, with a big slushy Italian ice in the other hand.

6 cloves garlic, cut in slivers
3–4-pound boneless chuck
   roast
1 cup water
2 bay leaves
1 tablespoon dry crushed red
   pepper

1 tablespoon oregano
1 tablespoon salt
1 tablespoon coarsely ground
   black pepper

Preheat oven to 250°. With a small knife insert garlic slivers into roast all over. Put water in a deep baking pan not much larger than roast. Add roast and seasonings. Cover tightly and bake 2 hours, basting three or four times.

Remove beef from pan and allow to settle. With an extremely sharp knife slice into razor-thin pieces.

Meanwhile, degrease then taste gravy in pan. It should be highly seasoned, with a pepper bite. Adjust seasonings to taste and ☞

place sliced beef in gravy. Allow it to wallow 15–20 minutes before serving. If desired, you can mix in ½ cup of barbecue sauce (although true aficionados prefer their gravy "clear").

Serves 8.

Like the city's red hots, an Italian beef sandwich is sold with a load of garnishes—either marinated roasted peppers or a hot pepper relish called "giardiniera," consisting of peppers, carrots, capers, and celery in pickly marinade. The deluxe version of an Italian beef sandwich is called a "combo" or a "half-and-half"—heaps of beef accompanied by a length of charcoal-grilled Italian sausage, blanketed with roasted sweet peppers.

ROASTED SWEET PEPPERS

The soft texture and fire-flavored tang of roasted peppers are necessary to round out the garlic bolt of the Italian beef experience. If you have a separate broiler, you can make them while the beef is roasting. Or they can be made in advance and refrigerated (but always serve them at room temperature). They're great not only with Italian beef but with sausage or on homemade pizza.

Red or green bell peppers   Oregano
Olive oil   Salt and pepper to taste

Wash and dry peppers. Place them on a broiling pan beneath broiler. When part nearest heat blackens, turn peppers. Continue turning, until as much skin as possible has been blackened by heat. Remove from broiler and wrap in wet paper towels. When peppers are cool enough to handle, peel off charred skin. Remove stems and seeds. Put peppers in a bowl with a sprinkle of olive oil and a dash of oregano, salt, and pepper.

The secret of an Italian beef sandwich, beyond quality beef and roasted peppers, is the bread: fresh and crusty, tough enough to hold up when sopped with gravy. You need a loaf that invites abuse, so sturdy that no matter what you sandwich inside, it retains its brawn.

TORPEDO LOAVES
FOR STREET SANDWICHES

An all-day job, these rolls induce major feelings of accomplishment in the chef. There is nothing better for a two-fisted sandwich of any kind, from Italian beef to a Philadelphia hoagie.

2 packages dry yeast	1 tablespoon salt
2 teaspoons sugar	3 tablespoons olive oil
2 cups tepid water (110°)	Semolina or yellow cornmeal
5–5½ cups flour	

Combine yeast and sugar with ½ cup of the water. In a large bowl mix 5 cups of the flour, salt, olive oil, and remaining 1½ cups of water. When yeast is foamy, add it, stirring vigorously until dough pulls from sides of bowl. Turn out onto a floured board; clean and oil bowl.

Knead dough 10 full minutes, adding flour if necessary. Dough should be smooth and elastic. Return to bowl, roll dough to cover with oil, and cover bowl with a double layer of plastic wrap. Let rise in a cool place (about 65° is perfect) up to 4 hours, until it nearly triples in size.

Punch down dough, cover, and allow to rise again until double in size, 1–2 hours.

Preheat oven to 400°. Punch down dough. Divide it into quarters; divide each quarter into 2 pieces. Form each piece into a torpedo-shaped cylinder 8 inches long and place it on a baking sheet dusted with semolina or yellow cornmeal (or, even better, on an unglazed tile or pizza stone).

Slash top of each roll with a razor blade.

Using a plant atomizer filled with cold water, spray a mist onto rolls and pop them in oven. Five minutes later, open oven door and spray another mist inside, keeping door open as briefly as possible. Repeat after another 5 minutes.

Bake a total of 22 minutes, until rolls are nicely browned. Remove from baking sheet and cool on wire rack.

Makes 8 rolls.

When it comes to the urban grub of the Midwest, Chicago and Kansas City get all the press for their deep dish pizza, barbecue, red hots, and fried chicken. Good eats, all of it; but we think it is about time someone stood up for the unsung culinary treasures of St. Louis.

We thought we were pretty smart, knowing about toasted ravioli, a specialty of the Italian restaurants in the ethnic neighborhood known as the Hill. But who would have expected St. Louis to be the home of the fried brain sandwich?

Taverns throughout the city specialize in brain sandwiches. They even compete in an annual brain cookoff. Looking through the yellow pages, we zeroed in on one called the Haven, which had a small display ad declaring it "Home of the Old Tyme Brain Sandwich." Not the least bit interested in nouvelle brains, we headed for the Haven.

When we stumbled in, about nine o'clock one night, we were the only people in the house not wearing baseball uniforms. The Haven sponsors a team, and after the game, everyone comes back to drink beer and eat brains. Gordon Beck, who makes them, explained to us that his was an "old tyme" brain sandwich because he serves an intact half brain, not the ground-up brains that lazy chefs around town serve.

OLD TYME BEER BATTER BRAIN SANDWICH

You will understand the trend to newfangled sandwiches when you clean your first set of brains. Membrane abounds, and it takes a lot of work to clean them. But for the genuine St. Louis sandwich, luscious and tender as can be, it's the only way to go.

2–3 calf's brains (both halves)	12 ounces flat beer
1 large onion, stuck with 4 cloves	2 teaspoons salt
1½ cups flour	Oil for frying

Wash brains well and soak in cold water 30 minutes. Carefully pick away any remaining membrane, veins, etc. Drop into boiling water; simmer gently 15 minutes with clove-dotted onion. Remove brains carefully from liquid and pat dry.

Stir 1 cup of the flour gradually into beer until well mixed. Stir in salt.

Heat oil in deep fryer to 375°.

Take each half brain and roll in remaining ½ cup of flour, then dip in beer batter. Fry in hot oil until golden brown, about 5 minutes. Drain well.

Serve each half brain on rye, with pickles, onions, and a squirt of mustard, if desired.

Makes enough brains for 4–6 sandwiches.

It is only a slight exaggeration to say that every block in St. Louis has at least one chop suey shop. Noodle parlors, as they are known locally, began as Chinese-run restaurants catering exclusively to blacks. Many of them still do, and some have a soul food edge to the menu.

The cultural connotations of chop suey are fascinating. We cannot remember the last time we saw it on a Chinese menu, certainly not in any kind of chic Chinese restaurant. No doubt, it has been there on menus, but our attention is usually diverted to the socially approved *arriviste* items from Szechuan or Hunan. Experts in such matters tell us that even they are passé today, which makes chop suey positively antediluvian. Who could resist a taste?

What gruel! And the most amazing thing about it is that in the noodle shops we visited—mere takeout parlors with nothing much more than a man and a wok in back—it is made from scratch, order by order. At China Chop Suey on West Florissant and at Old St. Louis Chop Suey in the Baden Market, we watched the mushrooms and celery and onion sliced and fried and mixed with chunks of tender white meat chicken, then seasoned, stirred, and simmered. Then came the cornstarch, and whammo, it all turned beige, just like out of a can! But it's better than that; and it is authentic.

ST. LOUIS NOODLE PARLOR CHOP SUEY

The only proper way to serve St. Louis chop suey is in a white cardboard box, with a fork. It should be made in a wok. Otherwise, you will have to increase the oil to 2–3 tablespoons.

1 pound raw chicken or cooked pork, cut into small pieces	1 cup sliced mushroom caps
1 tablespoon peanut oil	1 small onion, diced
1 cup bean sprouts	1 rib celery, sliced
½ cup thinly cut bamboo shoots	1½ cups water
	1 tablespoon cornstarch
	Soy sauce to taste

In a wok stir-fry chicken in oil until fully white, 1–2 minutes. Add sprouts and stir. Add bamboo shoots, mushroom caps, onion, and celery. Stir thoroughly. Add 1 cup of the water. Cover and let simmer 5 minutes.

Dissolve cornstarch in remaining ½ cup of water and add to wok, stirring until thick. Season with soy sauce.

Serves 4.

St. Pauls are the unsolved mystery of St. Louis noodle parlors. Every menu lists St. Pauls—pork, ham, chicken, beef, or shrimp; they're a popular item, a sandwich that contains a small patty of egg foo young minus the gravy, served on white bread, dressed with pickles and a slice of onion.

The mystery is that no St. Louisan seems to know how St. Pauls got their name. Why aren't they called St. Louises? No such dish exists in St. Paul, Minnesota. Is St. Paul the patron saint of noodle parlors? Even Howard Wong of the Lotus Room, who grew up with St. Pauls, didn't have a clue. If anyone has an answer, we would love to know. Meanwhile, here is how to make a genuine St. Louis St. Paul:

SHRIMP ST. PAUL

2 eggs
½ cup bean sprouts
1 tablespoon minced scallion
2 mushrooms, diced
1 water chestnut, diced

3 medium shrimp, peeled and
   diced
Salt and pepper to taste
1 tablespoon peanut oil

Beat eggs in a bowl. Add sprouts, scallion, mushrooms, water chestnut, shrimp, salt, and pepper. Heat peanut oil in a wok or small frying pan. Pour in eggs and fry until light brown, about 1 minute. Turn and fry other side about 1 minute. When browned on both sides, scoot patty up to side of wok and squeeze out excess oil with spatula. Cut in half and serve on untoasted white bread.

Makes enough filling for 2 sandwiches.

The cuisine of Siouxland (as Nebraska, South Dakota, and Iowa around Sioux City are called) can be summed up in one word: beef. We like beef as much as anybody, but for people who pride ourselves on an ability to unearth exotic regional dishes, it can get boring.

Along came Sioux City's Marcia Poole to rescue us. "When I moved here," she chuckled, "I thought it sounded kind of obscene, but there is one thing Sioux City has that nobody else does, and that's loosemeats." Loosemeats, Marcia explained, are also known as taverns, Charlie Boys, and Tastees. Furthermore, she suggested, one seldom refers to a singular loosemeat. It is loosemeats, like grits or duxelles.

The original loosemeats sandwich was served in 1934 at Ye Olde Tavern Inn in Sioux City by Abraham and Bertha Kaled. It was called a tavern, and what it was, was loose meat: spiced hamburger, fried not as a patty, but as little burger pebbles on a bun. Like a sloppy joe, but without the slop.

Some Midwesterners know this sandwich as a Maid-Rite, sold in franchised operations throughout eastern Iowa. There were once hundreds of Maid-Rite shops, and we hear that the chain is about to bounce back. If you can't get to Iowa for a Maid-Rite in its natural habitat, here is our own Connecticut-style loosemeats:

LOOSEMEATS

1 clove garlic, minced
2 tablespoons vegetable oil
1 medium onion, chopped fine
1 pound ground chuck
½ cup tomato juice
2 tablespoons brown sugar

½ teaspoon black pepper
½ teaspoon Worcestershire
  sauce
2 teaspoons seasoned salt
½ teaspoon Gravy Master or
  Kitchen Bouquet

In a large skillet over medium heat, sauté garlic in oil until it begins to brown. Add onion and sauté until soft. Add meat, stirring constantly with a fork to keep it crumbly.

When meat is brown, add all remaining ingredients and simmer, uncovered, stirring occasionally, until dry—about 15–20 minutes. Serve on hamburger buns.

Makes enough for 4 sandwiches.

About ten years ago, our friend Julia Welch went to work at the University of Nebraska in Lincoln. For a skinny person, Julia loves to eat; but she was blue in Nebraska after weeks of nothing but beef and corn. Then one day we got a letter with a bulletin. Julia had discovered "Runzas"! Runzas, she explained, are like Michigan pasties, a meat pie in a pastry wrapper. But in the case of Runzas, it is a mixture of beef and cabbage, and the pastry is more like bread than piecrust.

A smart fast-food chain trademarked the name Runza, and now they are sold from a group of restaurants that are as sanitary and boring as McDonald's. They are fast food, but they taste much better than their banal surroundings would suggest. We have never seen Runzas anywhere outside of Nebraska, and yet the one place we found a Runza recipe was in our ever-trusty Oakland, Iowa, *Centennial Cookbook:*

RUNZA-LIKE SANDWICHES

Runza dough

1 package dry yeast	1 egg
¼ cup sugar	3 tablespoons butter, melted
1 cup tepid water (110°)	and cooled to tepid
1 teaspoon salt	3–3½ cups flour

Filling

¾ pound ground beef	1 teaspoon salt
¼ cup minced onion	½ teaspoon pepper
1½ cups shredded cabbage	Dash Tabasco sauce
¼ cup water	

Mix yeast and 1 teaspoon of the sugar in ¼ cup of the water. When foamy, add salt, egg, melted butter, remaining sugar, and remaining ¾ cup of water. Stir in 3 cups of the flour. Turn out onto a floured board; clean and butter bowl.

Knead dough 3–5 minutes, until smooth. Return to bowl, cover, and let rise until double in bulk, about 1½ hours.

As dough rises, brown beef and onion. Drain fat. Add cabbage, water, salt, pepper, and Tabasco. Simmer 15–20 minutes. Cool to room temperature.

Preheat oven to 350°.

Divide dough into 8 equal balls. With a rolling pin on a lightly floured board roll each ball out to a 4–6-inch-diameter circle. Place one-eighth of filling into center of each circle and pull top and bottom of circle up, forming a tube. Press together, moistening slightly. Crimp sides to seal in filling completely and tightly. Place 8 filled Runzas on a greased cookie sheet.

Bake 20 minutes, until light brown. Serve warm.

Makes 8 Runzas.

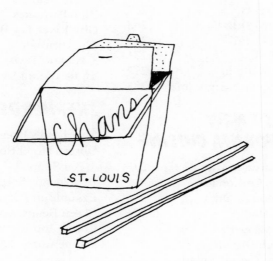

ST. LOUIS

THE WEST

MANLY FOOD

NOT SO NEW CALIFORNIA CUISINE

INDIAN RESERVATIONS

SHEPHERDS' HOTELS

WESTERN BREAKFAST

MANLY FOOD

hen motoring west, there are times we feel like prissy dudes in a vintage Western. You know the stereotype: the Eastern fop on the stagecoach, confronted by whiskey-breath vulgarians and war-whooping Indians. He mops his brow with a monogrammed hankie and clutches dearly his volume of Proust or mother of pearl opera glasses.

Understand that back home we are regarded as a rather gutsy duo. We poke fun at Boston friends who gather for chamber music fetes and New Yorkers who scream when they visit our rural home and see raccoon eyes peering in the bathroom window.

But it is we who feel on the butt end of the laughter when we walk into rough Western cafes and confront a distinct style of frontier gastron-

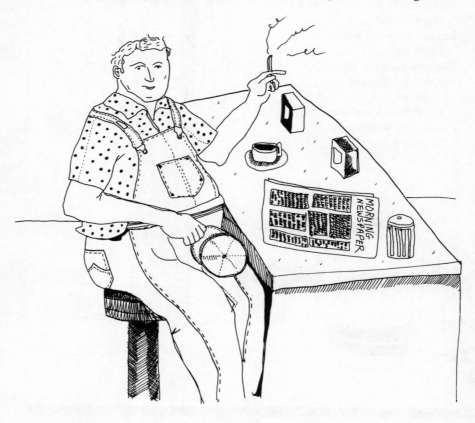

omy that is descended from chuck wagon chow, train gang cookies, and truck stop fry chefs.

Not all the West is raw; certainly not the Coast. The parts we're talking about are the sunbaked strips of west Texas, half-dead towns along the ghost of what once was Route 66, desert oases in Arizona, and high mountain mining camps in Colorado.

This West is man's country, and it is the home of manly food. Feminists have our apologies, but we have sat shoulder to masculine shoulder in one too many barbecues, chili parlors, and truck stops to say it any differently.

Observe Louie Mueller's place in Taylor, Texas. You wouldn't exactly call it a restaurant, not even a cafe. It's a barbecue, fashioned out of an old gymnasium in 1906. The walls and ceiling were once painted green, but after being aged in the smoke of "bull meat and brisket" for three-quarters of a century, they have evolved a resinous patina that looks like tortoise shell. Your hair will smell of it for hours after you leave.

Slices are whomped off the brisket, laid on butcher paper, and presented on a cafeteria tray: carry it yourself to a rough wooden table. On the side, have whole jalapeño peppers and supermarket white bread to use as a dam for the juices of the meat.

Such barbecue is very much an away-from-home cuisine, the work of specialists, prepared at parties on the ranch or by smoke pit annexes to grocery stores (originally established as an outlet for unsold cuts of beef). The pit, the logs, the long hours—all preclude a tradition of home cooking. But with only a small amount of effort (and a long, long time), delicious brisket can be made at home.

TEXAS BARBECUE

1 5-pound beef brisket	¼ cup coarse black pepper
¼ cup salt	¼ cup paprika

Pat brisket all over with an equal mixture of salt, pepper, and paprika.

Build a charcoal fire in an outdoor barbecue kettle (the kind with a top). If true Texas flavor is desired, add damp mesquite chips to the white-hot coals. When coals are white hot, scoot them to side of kettle and place a baking pan in kettle to catch juices.

Lay brisket fat side down on grill above pan, then cover kettle and adjust airholes on top so you have a *very* slow fire. Unlike grilled meat, barbecued meat is cooked by the heat of the smoke, not of the flame. If the fire is flaming, add damp mesquite twigs or

☞

hickory chips, or sprinkle coals with water. If the fire is low enough, one kettleful will smolder all day. If it seems to be dying out, make a separate fire elsewhere so that you can add white-hot charcoal (never raw wood).

Turn meat every hour, using tongs (never a fork, which pokes holes that allow juice to run out). Baste meat each time you turn it with juices from pan below. After 8 hours, brisket will look ready to fall apart on its own.

Remove from grill, allow to settle 10 minutes, and slice in ¼–½-inch pieces. Serve with a stack of saltines, a bottle of Tabasco sauce, and a knife.

Serves 6–8.

INCENDIARY SAUCE FOR STEAK

Barbecued brisket is sacred, never sullied with any sauce other than its own drippings. Its only proper condiment is a few shakes of straight-from-the-bottle Tabasco, or maybe a pepper to gnaw on the side. But when it comes to steaks, Texans don't mind a little hot pepper accent. Witness the jalapeño-laden cheeseburgers at Herman Sons in Hondo. Or this eye-popping marinade, suitable for mopping on steaks as they grill or for soaking a London broil a few hours before cooking. Cook the meat over a flaming fire and baste continuously.

8 tablespoons butter
1 cup bourbon
1 cup beef bouillon
2 tablespoons Worcestershire
    sauce
¼ cup lemon juice
1 tablespoon dry mustard
2 tablespoons chili powder

½ teaspoon cayenne pepper
2 tablespoons sugar
1 bay leaf, crushed
3 cloves garlic, minced fine
1 large onion, minced fine
1–3 jalapeño peppers, minced
    fine, or to taste
Black pepper to taste

Melt butter in a large saucepan over medium heat. Stir in bourbon, bouillon, Worcestershire, and lemon juice.

Mix together mustard, chili powder, cayenne, and sugar. Stir into liquid. Add crushed bay leaf. Bring to a simmer. Add garlic, onion, and jalapeño peppers. (Be careful adding jalapeños; their heat takes a while to disperse through the sauce.) Simmer, uncovered, 15 minutes. Add black pepper to taste.

*Makes 2 cups sauce, enough
for 6–8 pounds of beef.*

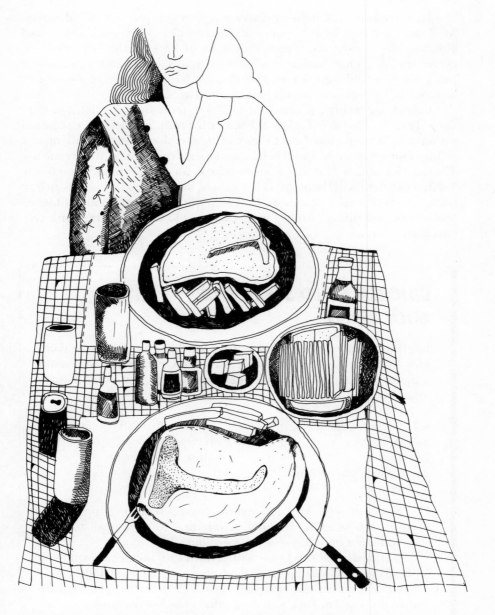

Chicken fried steak is cowboy soul food, evoking images of frontier moms at wood-fired stoves. And yet no dish seems quite so at home in a small-town cafe or truck stop. It has nothing to do with chicken, except that it's fried like chicken and is usually presented underneath a mantle of cream gravy similar to what you get with chicken. It is *beef*, either cubed or pounded as thin as a veal cutlet, dipped in egg and flour, then skillet-fried.

Its ingredients are notably cheap, suggesting it was born of adversity. At Massey's in Fort Worth, where the kitchen dishes up about a thousand chicken fried steaks every day, they trace it back to the Depression: a clever way of giving some appeal to a piece of saddle-tough beef. Only a fancy pants would consider making chicken fried steak out of a *good* cut; so much of its pleasure derives from its transcendence.

One of our favorite places to eat chicken fried steak is a joint in Bandera, Texas, called O.S.T. (for Old Spanish Trail). Bandera is a postcard vision of a Western town, and many of its merchants make their money selling fancy boots and saddles to vacationers from nearby dude ranches. The interior of O.S.T. is *machismo moderne*, an electric bunkhouse of the 1980s, complete with bonging video games, fading blowups of cowgirls, a picture or two of John Wayne, and all sorts of rodeo memorabilia. Chicken fried steaks are dished out at long indoor picnic tables covered with red-checked oilcloth.

CHICKEN FRIED STEAK AND MILK GRAVY

In all its country glory, chicken fried steak is pure Southern comfort. Blanketed with milk-soft gravy, its gnarled tan crust rises in a thousand crisp bubbles, yet hugs the meat, so that every mouthful is a perfect mix of crunch and chew.

4 4–5-ounce cube steaks	1–2 cups lard or vegetable oil
3 eggs, beaten	1½ cups milk
1 cup flour	Salt to taste
2 teaspoons coarse black pepper	

Dip steaks in eggs. Mix flour with 1 teaspoon of the pepper, then dredge each steak thoroughly in mixture. Return steak to eggs, then to flour again. Reserve leftover flour.

Heat lard or oil in a heavy skillet until very hot but not smoking (360°–375°). Use enough fat to have about ½ inch in skillet.

Put steaks into hot fat and cook 6–8 minutes, until golden brown on bottom. Turn and cook other side 3–4 minutes.

Remove steaks from fat with slotted spoon and drain on paper towels.

To make gravy, pour off all but 2 tablespoons of fat in skillet. Return to heat and sprinkle 2 tablespoons of leftover flour over hot fat, stirring constantly for a full minute, scraping up browned bits of crust from bottom of skillet.

Add milk, a little at a time. Continue cooking and stirring until gravy is thick. Add pepper and salt to taste (gravy should be quite peppery).

Serve steaks smothered in gravy, with mashed potatoes and/or biscuits, black-eyed peas or greens.

Makes 4 chicken fried steaks with gravy.

In the spirit of a Southwestern cafe, you ought to serve your chicken fried steak and mashed potatoes on a partitioned plate. You will have one section left to fill. Black-eyed peas, each with a winking black eye in a tan socket, are the most popular companion; fried okra comes in a close second. (In addition, serve iceberg lettuce drenched in a half-and-half mixture of mayo and ketchup. Wrap knife, fork, and spoon tightly in a paper napkin.)

BLACK-EYED PEAS

Don't doll up the peas. Like mashed potatoes, they serve as a pallid counterpoint to the pepper bite of the steak and gravy.

2 cups dried black-eyed peas   1 large onion, chopped
¼ pound salt pork   Salt to taste

Wash peas thoroughly. Place in stockpot with water to cover. Score salt pork and add to peas with onion. Bring to a rolling boil for 15 minutes. Lower to simmer, partially cover, and cook until tender, about 1½ hours. Add water as needed to keep peas from drying out, but not so much that the result is watery. By the time they are tender, the peas should have absorbed most of the liquid. Season with salt.

Serves 4–6.

FRIED OKRA

Because it is fried and ought to be brittle-crisp, okra is usually segregated to a separate little dish alongside the main plate. Don't bother with utensils. Just pop them in your mouth by hand. The cornmeal snap makes them crisp punctuation between potatoes, peas, and chicken fried steak.

☞

1 pound fresh okra (or 20   1 egg, beaten
     ounces frozen, defrosted   ¾ cup buttermilk
     and thoroughly drained)   1 cup yellow cornmeal
1 teaspoon salt   Oil for deep frying

Wash fresh okra and use a paring knife to scrape off furry surface. Pat dry, remove stems, and cut into bite-size disks. Place in a large bowl and sprinkle with salt, tossing to cover evenly.

Mix egg and buttermilk. Dip okra in mixture, then roll in cornmeal.

Heat oil to 335°.

Deep-fry okra, a handful at a time, about 5 minutes, until golden. (Do not crowd the pan.) Drain on paper towels. Season with additional salt, if desired.

Serves 4–6.

Perhaps the most manly dish of all is beans, refried beans in particular. No food—not chili, not barbecue, not steak, not calves' head enchiladas—is as authoritatively Western. Known as *refritos*, they are made by augmenting the substantial starch of cooked pinto beans with lots of extra grease. They look like red clay, they cling tenaciously to a plate, and although their ingredients might sound terrifying, they are one of Tex-Mex's greatest luxuries.

Our model for *refritos* is a legendary eatery in what was once the stockyards neighborhood of Fort Worth—Joe T. Garcia's. Joe T's is a white house that seems to lean precariously with age. Until health department regulations said differently, customers entered through the kitchen. You can still see the chefs back there, wrestling their heavy skillets in a cacophony of fire and smoke. Most people simply order "dinner," a prix fixe menu of classic Tex-Mex grub, including soft flour tortillas, guacamole, tacos, enchiladas, and Joe T's out-of-this-world refrieds.

REFRIED BEANS, JOE T–STYLE

Although few home cooks (and even fewer restaurants) take time to make them from scratch, authentic refried beans are worth the effort, equally scrumptious alongside *huevos rancheros* for breakfast or a T-bone steak at night. Like a Sunday morning baked bean sandwich in Boston, they originated as a way of making leftovers delicious.

2 cups dried pinto beans (1 pound)
1 onion, diced
2 cloves garlic, minced
8 ounces salt pork, cut into small cubes

1 teaspoon whole cumin seed
Salt and pepper to taste
Shredded Monterey Jack cheese as garnish

Place beans in a large saucepan and cover with water. Bring to a full rolling boil for 2 minutes, then remove from heat, cover, and let beans sit 1 hour. Remove beans from liquid with a slotted spoon and place in a second pot. Add enough water to cover beans by at least 1 inch.

Add onion, garlic, *half* the salt pork, and cumin seed, bring to a boil, cover, and boil until beans are tender but not mushy (3–4 hours), adding boiling water as necessary to keep beans from drying. (But you don't want them wet either.) Season with salt and pepper. (Beans may be refrigerated at this point and refried quickly when desired.)

Fry remaining salt pork in a large skillet. When rendered and crisp, add beans, about ½ cup at a time, mashing them into rendered fat with a heavy spoon. Keep adding and mashing until beans are of desired consistency. Most cooks like some beans still unmashed.

Serve garnished with shredded Monterey Jack cheese.

Serves 6–8.

Oklahoma ought to hire Texas's press agent. Say the state's name to anyone from the East and it conjures up either an apparition of Woody Guthrie dust bowl blues or a simpleminded place where the corn is as high as an elephant's eye.

Ever since we wrote a book about truck drivers and discovered that approximately 50 percent of the long haul wildcat truckers in America hail from Oklahoma, it has seemed to us to be the most masculine state of all. Not noisy masculine like Texas or shaggy masculine like Colorado or lonesome masculine like most of the Great Plains, but a land of real men: soft-spoken, hard-riding, gentlemanly sorts of guys who crease their high-crowned hats in a special way that identifies them as Okies—and who thrive on the culinary trinity of beans, corn bread, and onions.

OKIE LUNCH

It was in a Ponca City hash house, long ago, that we first encountered this completely glamourless meal. It is poor man's food, filling and good, like the English ploughman's lunch. Although plain to the point of sadness, the simple counterpoints among silky beans, grainy corn bread, and crisp onion make it a delicious combination.

First, prepare pinto beans as in the preceding recipe, up to the point of refrying them. As beans are simmering and softening, make the corn bread:

Vegetable oil to grease skillet	2 tablespoons sugar
1¼ cups yellow cornmeal	1 cup milk
½ cup flour	2 eggs, beaten
1 teaspoon baking powder	4 tablespoons butter, melted
1 teaspoon salt	and cooled

Grease bottom and sides of a 7- or 8-inch cast-iron skillet generously with oil. Place on center rack of oven and turn on oven to 425°.

Mix together cornmeal, flour, baking powder, salt, and sugar. Mix milk, eggs, and butter. Combine both mixtures.

When oven is at 425°, pour batter quickly into heated skillet (which should be smoking). Close oven door immediately. Bake 20–25 minutes, until golden yellow. Let cool a few minutes and serve warm.

Serve pinto beans in individual bowls, sided by a block of warm corn bread, with a stack of thick slices from a sweet onion on the plate with the bread. Both bread and onion should be eaten by hand; the beans, with a spoon.

Serves 6.

We never met an Oklahoma truck driver who didn't have a few Slim Jims tucked into his rucksack. (Slim Jim, in case you don't frequent the grocery sections of truck stops, is a trademarked name for a shiv of "beef snack" that vaguely resembles jerky.) If indeed independent long-haulers are the last American cowboys, it makes sense that their palates run along lines similar to their frontier forebears; and jerky—leathery strips of air-dried beef—is a pillar of chuck wagon cookery.

Jerky is as primitive as food can be, the strips of beef either gnawed plain or reconstituted to make a crude stew. The honest truth is that we

never even wanted to taste the horrid-looking stuff until one day we saun-
tered into an outfit named Jiggs Smoke House in Clinton, Oklahoma.

Jiggs is a log cabin that sits in a cloud of smoke on the access road to
what was once Route 66. On the wall are pictures of celebrities who have
stopped in—not *People* magazine types, but down-home characters like
Goober from "Mayberry R.F.D." and Chill Wills. Jiggs has a freezer full of
calf and turkey testicles, and a single dining table where you can wolf
down a two-fisted barbecue sandwich on a bun. And it sells the most
delicious beef jerky you will ever eat—big mahogany-colored flaps of beef
that look like they were peeled off an old tree. It is chewy, yet it gives
nicely when you work on it, blossoming with profound beef and smoke
flavor.

The jerky is swell in the context of Jiggs, but even better when you
have some sent by mail. The first time we went to pick up an order at the
local post office, the entire building smelled of the stuff, even though it
was swathed in paper and cardboard. If you want to see what we mean, if
you love to chew and chew and extract a miraculous tidal wave of flavor,
you can send away for your own to:

Jiggs Smoke House
Clinton, OK 73601
(405) 323-5641

JERK-IT-YOURSELF BEEF JERKY

It is easy to jerk your own. Cut round steak into ½-inch-thin strips
(with the grain). Dip the strips in a hot (but not quite boiling) brine
of ¼ cup of salt to a gallon of water. When the meat is gray, drain
it and dredge in a half-and-half mixture of coarse salt and cracked
pepper, then hang it from a tree limb where it will get plenty of
sun and fresh air.

It is also possible to oven-jerk meat by hanging the strips in a
warm (175°) oven from the topmost rack 5–6 hours, until the meat
is tough and very dry (but still bendable). Place a baking pan at
the bottom of the oven to catch any drippings. And leave the oven
door ajar so air circulates. (A convection oven, with the door
closed, is even better; the time will be more like 4 hours.)

Jerky should be stored in a cool place in a glass jar with a few
holes punched in the top. If it has been dried sufficiently, it keeps
indefinitely—that, after all, is the point.

Whoever said that Americans have fallen out of love with meat never traveled through the West. For card-carrying carnivores, no place sets the adrenaline rushing quite as effectively as a cowboy sale barn cafe. On the premises of a livestock exchange, it is where cattlemen come to eat before and after auctions. (You know you've hit a real one if you spot a boot scraper at the door.) At the Stockyards Cafe in Sioux Falls, South Dakota, the dining room is spitting distance from the pens, and there is no ignoring the cattle lowing outside as you slice into a two-pound T-bone.

The first such place we encountered was in Manhattan, Kansas. Its name, with flawless logic, was the Sale Barn Cafe. Its decor consisted entirely of iconographic pictures of men's men: Elvis, the Marlboro Man (whose son worked in the cafe), Roy Rogers. The menu was steak, Swiss steak, hamburger steak, roast beef, chipped beef, wet beef, or beef and noodles. At breakfast, the cattlemen drank endless cups of coffee, accompanied not by the usual cafe cinnamon rolls but by cinnamon-dusted sour-milk doughnut holes called dillybobs.

SALE BARN DILLYBOBS

¼ cup sour cream
½ cup buttermilk
2 teaspoons baking soda
⅓ cup milk
1 egg, beaten

⅔ plus ½ cup sugar
3–4 cups flour
¼ teaspoon salt
Vegetable oil for deep frying
¾ teaspoon cinnamon

Combine sour cream and buttermilk. Mix baking soda into milk and combine with buttermilk mixture. Stir in egg and ⅔ cup of the sugar.

Sift 1 cup of the flour with salt. Stir into liquid mixture, mixing only enough to combine. Add enough additional sifted flour to create a dough that holds together but is still slightly sticky. Do not overmix.

Knead on a lightly floured board 30 seconds. Cover with a damp towel as you heat oil.

Heat at least 4 inches of oil to 375° in a heavy skillet or saucepan. Use a thermometer to get exact temperature.

With floured hands, roll dough into 1- or 1½-inch balls and drop into oil, 4–6 at a time. Turn to ensure they fry evenly. Fry until golden brown, 2–3 minutes per side.

Drain on paper towels. Combine remaining ½ cup of sugar and cinnamon. While dillybobs are still warm, roll them in cinnamon-sugar. Serve immediately.

Makes 30–36 dillybobs.

The king of the sale barn cafes is Johnny's in Omaha. It is adjacent to the stockyards, but once you wrap your fist around the baroque bullhorn-shaped door handle and enter, you lose all sense of place. Johnny's has no windows; it is womb-dark, illumination supplied by television screens displaying futures prices. The Kawa family, who have run Johnny's since it was a small cafe in the 1920s, buy their meat from local packing houses and butcher it themselves—steaks of every shape and size, plus a lush stew made from oxtail.

OMAHA OXTAIL

We used to see oxtail on sale at our local market (it is always a bargain) and wonder what to do with it. Johnny's specialty, oxtail in heavy gravy, inspired this high-seasoned party stew. Make it a day ahead so the fat can be skimmed.

6 tablespoons butter
⅓ cup chopped suet

6 pounds oxtails, disjointed
　　into 2-inch pieces

☞

Flour   3½–4 cups beef broth
2 large onions, chopped coarse   ½ cup red wine
4 cloves garlic, crushed   1 bay leaf
4 carrots, cut into 1-inch disks   1 teaspoon thyme
1 16-ounce can whole tomatoes   Salt and pepper to taste

Melt butter and suet in a large skillet. Dredge oxtail in flour and brown in fat. This will likely have to be done in two or three stages. Remove browned joints and place them in a large stockpot.

When all joints are browned, sauté onion and garlic in remaining fat until onion is light brown. Add onion and garlic to oxtails. Add carrots and tomatoes. Pour in beef broth and wine, adding enough to barely cover ingredients. Add seasonings. Stir well and bring to a boil. Boil 5 minutes, skimming off scum from surface. Reduce to a simmer, partially cover, and cook 3 hours, or until oxtails are tender.

Remove bay leaf and cool. Refrigerate, then skim fat off top. Reheat and serve.

Serves 6.

Real men are not squeamish. They pick up snakes, dead mice, and insects in their bare hands. They eat odd parts of animals, leaving tenderloins to tenderfeet.

Some animal parts are painful even to discuss. Take testicles—please. The men of the West love to eat gonads, gonads off of roosters, sheep, pigs, and bulls. But even rugged guys, or perhaps *especially* rugged guys, don't like to call a ball a ball. It's not polite. So they talk euphemistically of Rocky Mountain oysters or calf fries, but everybody knows perfectly well where the spherical goodies once hung.

Obviously, there is a difference between testicles that once belonged to a rooster and those from a bull. Rooster fries are hardly bigger than colossal olives. We first saw them in the town cafe of Cozad, Nebraska, where they were deep fried and served to a group of overalled farmers gathered at a large table. The men munched from a communal plate, popping the little brown spheres into their mouths like fried okra.

Rooster fries—like their bigger relative, turkey fries—are hard to come by outside the West; you need many pairs to satisfy even a modest hunger. But most butchers can provide you with calf fries; and let us tell you, one set makes a hungry man's dinner. Their texture is reminiscent of sweetbreads—organ-tender, smooth, heavy. Their flavor is subtle, nearly fugitive, and so they are usually seasoned brightly.

Pat Wickel of the Wolf Lodge Inn outside Coeur d'Alene, Idaho, gave us a few tips about cooking testicles. Marinated and deep-fried Rocky Mountain oysters are one of her specialties, on the menu every night. She advised us that many customers like calf fries as a side dish, to accompany the Wolf Lodge Inn's forty-two-ounce porterhouse steak.

BULLS' BALLS

1 set calf fries

Marinade

⅔ cup red wine
⅓ cup olive oil
⅓ cup soy sauce
2 teaspoons brown sugar
2 cloves garlic, crushed

1 teaspoon salt
1 teaspoon coarsely ground
   pepper
¼ cup minced parsley

Flour
Oil for deep frying

Under cold running water, cut and carefully peel away tough membrane from around each testicle. Then take a sharp knife and cut each into ½-inch-thick slices.

Combine all marinade ingredients. Soak slices in liquid, turning frequently, for 2 hours.

Remove slices from marinade and dredge thoroughly in flour.

Heat oil to 365°. Deep-fry slices until golden brown, about 5 minutes. Drain on paper towels. Serve warm with horseradish or horseradish–sour cream dip.

Serves 2.

Note: An easier way to cook testicles is to clean and slice them, as above, parboil them 10 minutes, then coat them with a mixture of 3 cups Bisquick, 3 eggs, and 1 cup milk. Deep-fry at 365° until golden brown.

Hangover cures are a staple of manly cookery. The rugged Basques have Drunkard's Soup (p. 302); every good bartender has a secret potion; and Tex-Mex cooks have *menudo*, a visceral stew made from calves' feet and the lining of a bull's stomach.

Menudo is eaten in restaurants like El Dorado in Tucson, where you slurp it up beneath velvet paintings of matadors, astronauts, and dead

Kennedys. Nearly every Tex-Mex eatery from San Antonio to Yuma sells it by the pint or quart, to go. That way, you can buy it Saturday night and heat it up at home on Sunday to clear your head.

Although not as common as ground chuck, the ingredients are readily available in butcher shops; despite their exotic nature and foul smell, the resulting brew is truly palliative, genuine Southwestern comfort food.

MACHO MENUDO

Start your *menudo* Saturday morning, and by night, it will be tender and ready to go. Given adequate time on a slow fire, it is a marvelous confluence of disparate foods—the distinctive slick texture of long-simmered tripe, the gelatinous heft of calves' feet, and the pillowy earth scent of hominy. Because it's so much trouble to cook, and because it stinks up the kitchen so bad (and because the ingredients are so cheap), we suggest making a lot at one time. *Menudo* keeps well; in fact, we like it best when it stands a day or two (refrigerated) and is reheated. As for its ability to cure hangovers, we assure you that you will forget all about your aching head as soon as the simmering calves' feet begin to perfume the house.

5 pounds tripe
2 calves' feet, sawed into
   chunks by butcher
2 large onions, minced

5 cloves garlic, crushed
4 teaspoons salt
1 tablespoon oregano
3 cups canned hominy

Scrub tripe well under running water. Place in a stockpot, cover with cold water, and bring to a boil. Drain and let tripe stand in cold water.

Wash calves' feet, cover with water in an 8-quart stockpot, and simmer, partially covered, 1½ hours. Drain.

Cut tripe into 1-inch-wide pieces. Combine in stockpot with chunks of calves' feet in about 4 quarts fresh water. Add onions, garlic, salt, and oregano. Simmer, partially covered, 4–6 hours, or until tripe is soft but still has a bit of a chaw. Liquid will boil down, but don't let it get too low. You are aiming for a thick soup. Add hominy after 3½–4 hours—it should cook about 1½ hours.

Serves 12–15.

There is one last branch of manly cuisine, at home on the coast of Southern California. Some may question its authentic manliness, but nobody can doubt that its partisans have taken the idea of masculinity to one outrageous extreme.

We are talking about the cuisine of the body builder. Body builders' natural habitat is the beach. They are tan, their bodies hairless, and they cannot move without appearing to pose: They are American Adonises in Wayfarer sunglasses.

If you want to watch musclemen eat, we recommend a visit to the Orange Inn in Corona Del Mar. It is one of the oldest health-food shacks in the state, a roadside drive-in that serves sandwiches of sprouts and seeds and grains, and an only-in-California drink called a "smoothie."

MUSCLE BEACH SMOOTHIE

Smoothies are like milk shakes but good for you. Instead of ice cream and Bosco, they contain nondairy ingredients that are supposed to make a person strong and healthy. They are as calorific as the thickest soda fountain concoction, suitable for building the muscles body builders need to support their chests and keep their tiny heads steady on those outsized necks.

A good smoothie is *cold*. Chill the fruits and/or add a bit of crushed ice, reducing the amount of fruit juice accordingly. If you cannot find bee pollen, don't worry. Although one nutrition nut we know says it cures allergies, you see, it is more of a thickener than a taste sensation.

1 ripe banana
½ cup strawberries
¼ cup pitted dates
1 tablespoon bee pollen
    (available in health-food
    stores and at apiaries)

3 tablespoons honey
1 cup cold fruit juice of choice
½ cup crushed ice

Blend banana, strawberries, and dates in a blender until smooth. Mix in bee pollen and honey. Add juice and ice and mix at high speed until well blended. Serve immediately.

Makes 1 smoothie.

NOT SO NEW
CALIFORNIA CUISINE

unshine, health, rest and beautiful surroundings . . . scenic wonders, snow-capped mountains, date palms in stately array . . . winter wonderland without the winter": that, not so long ago, was California, as extolled by the brochure of Shields Date Gardens in Indio. It was a time when California wasn't just eccentric the way it seems now; it was downright exotic; it had a culture all its own.

It had its own way of eating too, prior to hocus-pocus notions of "new" American cuisine. Before the ideology of progress crept into our gastronomy—and with it the gimmick that *new* equals *improved*—the West Coast had a slew of colorful, uncorrupted eateries that expressed the bedrock character of old California. It still has them; but they have been eclipsed by the glitter of celebrity chefs and meretricious foodways.

So allow us please to circumnavigate the phenomenon of New California Cuisine. Enough has been written about open kitchen cooking, fast-track urban grills, homegrown goat cheese, and weird ravioli to last into the next millennium.

To taste a Western spirit that transcends culinary trends, take Route 10 through the Coachella Valley and stop at Shields Date Gardens. The Gardens aren't a restaurant; just a dairy bar and souvenir emporium promoting California dates as "Nature's Finest Food." The soda fountain is overseen by timeworn portraits of Floyd and Bess Shields, outfitted in safari gear and pith helmets, surveying their date gardens; hand-tinted pictures depict glamour girls holding bushels of dates. Here is an image of California—"America's Arabia"—as a land of glamour, exotic scenery, and health food.

Date shakes, one of Southern California's venerable regional specialties, hearken back to that early certitude about the confluence of beauty and nutrition under the desert sun. Made from chopped dates or Shields' patented Date Crystals, these luscious smoothies are a nostalgic taste of pre-Pritikin health—when healthy eating implied offbeat, natural, and super-calorific foods.

Date Crystals, and a collection of recipes that can be made therefrom (including date dainties and date dream bars), can be bought by mail from:

Shields Date Gardens
80-225 Highway 111
Indio, CA 92201
(619) 347-0996

DATE GARDENS MILK SHAKE

In this classic shake recipe, finely chopped dates work just as well as Date Crystals. Your goal in blending the drink is to create a luxurious frappe so thick that it *barely* makes it up a straw. The proper attire for drinking a date shake is a swimsuit; the proper location, at the beach or by the side of a backyard pool.

3 tablespoons finely chopped chilled dates	3 scoops vanilla ice cream ¾ cup ice-cold milk

Combine all ingredients in a blender and mix just enough to blend.

In a quest for restaurants with indigenous Southern California character, the premier stop is Musso and Frank Grill on Hollywood Boulevard, built in 1919 when Hollywood was known for its orange groves as much as its movies. The boulevard has hit the skids, but once you enter Musso's (as its friends know it), you have left T-shirt shops and peep shows behind.

You are stepping into Hollywood of the 1920s and '30s, when this Tudor-style, leather-boothed grill was a hangout for movie colony writers who had come from the East. They liked it because it reminded them of a New York steak house, with its aproned waiters and long roster of high-quality food served without fuss in a dining room that was comfortably clubby, its walls decorated with a mural of men and dogs hunting.

Musso's booths are private, but not so tall that you cannot see which famous people come and go; and there is a long counter on one side of the room, set with linen place mats for single diners. Although it is a living antique, it is still a place to spot celebrities: We oogled Bob Seger and two members of his band (they had steaks and silver bullet martinis). When you park your car in back, the lot attendants are easily encouraged to tip you off to the stars inside.

The cuisine, prepared by a chef the menu guarantees is "from Paris, France," is unaffected Americana, ranging from homemade chicken pot pie every Thursday and skinny "flannel cake" pancakes for lunch to sourdough bread and an exhaustive list of two dozen salads.

Salad has long been a primary element of West Coast gastronomy.

Think of crab Louis and green goddess dressing, both born in San Francisco; or the Cobb salad of L.A. What such salads share is a sense of health and generosity. They are not precisely arranged garden bouquets, but rather vigorous presentations of California bounty.

MUSSO'S CHIFFONADE SEAFOOD SALAD

Although chiffonade suggests delicacy, there is nothing froufrou about this mighty mélange of seafood. They hack up the greens, leave the shrimp whole, dole out big chunks of crab, and mix everything with gobs of dressing.

Iceberg lettuce	Fresh lump crabmeat
Romaine lettuce	Small shrimp, cooked and
Watercress	cooled
Hard-boiled egg	Lobster, cooked and cooled
Boiled beets	Thousand Island dressing

Shred lettuce and watercress. Dice hard-boiled egg. Cut beets into toothpick-size sticks. Shred crabmeat. Combine all ingredients and cover generously with dressing. Toss well.

COBB SALAD

Even more than Musso's chiffonade, Cobb salad is a study in culinary chaos, the ultimate hodgepodge, in which all the ingredients are so thoroughly blended that each forkful gets you some of everything, unified yet dissonant.

Contrary to the notion of one waitress we met in San Diego who described the house salad as "coming with an extremely large cobb" (i.e., a jumbo scoop of chopped-up ingredients), Cobb salad was named after Robert Cobb, the owner of Hollywood's Brown Derby, who allegedly invented it as a way to use leftovers.

The Derby presents it with all the ingredients marshaled in separate places in a large salad bowl. Once you've seen them, the waiter pours in the dressing, then mixes like hell. In a good Cobb salad no piece can be too large, no one element distinct. The best one we know is served at the Grill on the Alley in Beverly Hills, where it is properly pulverized, smacks of top-quality bleu cheese, and crackles with freshly fried bacon. Beyond those essential guidelines, use your own taste, leftovers, and imagination when gathering and measuring ingredients. We suggest Cobb salad with a continental flair—mixed with Charles Boyer's favorite French dressing, from *Cooking with the Stars.*

CHARLES BOYER'S FRENCH DRESSING

1 clove garlic
½ teaspoon salt
¼ teaspoon pepper
⅓ cup olive oil

2 tablespoons wine vinegar
1 tablespoon prepared brown
  mustard
½ teaspoon sugar

Mash garlic with salt and pepper. Stir in olive oil, vinegar, mustard, and sugar. Allow to stand 1 hour. Chill.

Makes about ½ cup, enough for 2 salads.

SALAD

⅓ head iceberg lettuce, washed
  and dried
6 leaves romaine lettuce,
  washed and dried
10–12 stalks watercress
2 ribs celery, sliced
½ avocado, chopped

1 large tomato, chopped
1 boned and skinned chicken
  breast, chopped
1 hard-boiled egg, chopped
2 ounces bleu cheese, crumbled
6 slices crisp bacon, crumbled

Place lettuce and watercress in a large wooden bowl. Using a fork and knife, slash at leaves until they are bite size. Now add dressing and continue slashing, until they are nearly pulverized.

In a separate bowl, mix all other ingredients except bacon. Stir into lettuce, adding crumbled bacon just before serving.

Makes 2 salads.

California's greatest contribution to the roster of American salads actually came from Tijuana in the 1920s. It seems there was a restaurant south of the border called Caesar's Place, run by a man named Caesar Cardini and patronized by partygoers from Hollywood. One especially raucous Independence Day weekend, so the tale goes, Caesar ran out of steaks and chops. All he had on hand was romaine lettuce, Romano cheese, olive oil, eggs, and garlic. Guess what Caesar made?

The interesting thing about the story—and about other believable accounts of the Caesarean birth—is that the original version contained no anchovies. In addition, Caesar's salad was made with whole, untorn leaves of lettuce so that it could be eaten easily by hand, without utensils.

ORIGINAL CAESAR SALAD

Unlike the vulgar democracy of Cobb salad, Caesar does not thrive on anything-goes ingenuity. Add anchovies if you wish, but to savor the regal magnificence of the original, follow these instructions to the letter.

15–20 large, unblemished
   leaves romaine lettuce
1 cup stale French bread, cut
   into ½-inch cubes
1 large clove garlic
1 egg
¼ teaspoon salt
Juice of ½ lemon

¼ cup olive oil
½ teaspoon Worcestershire
   sauce
¼ cup freshly grated Romano
   cheese
Freshly ground black pepper to
   taste

Wash and dry lettuce. Wrap and refrigerate.

Warm bread cubes in 275° oven, tossing until they are hard and dry, but not burnt. Set aside.

Mash garlic clove into side of a very large salad bowl. Ease egg into boiling water and boil exactly 1 minute, then crack it into bowl, breaking it up with a fork. Add salt. Add lemon juice, olive oil, and Worcestershire. Add leaves of lettuce, tossing to coat them thoroughly. Add Romano and pepper. Toss again.

Arrange on 2 plates. Garnish with croutons.

Makes 2 large salads.

Musso and Frank's menu is lavish in an unpretentious manner that has disappeared from swank eating places. It is immensely long, the parade of choices reflecting not the exoticism that kitchens of modern fancy restaurants show off but rather the hardheaded good sense of a well-stocked larder aimed to please every taste. "Vegetables," for instance, is a category of entirely familiar things, including creamed spinach, plain spinach, stewed tomatoes, green peas, string beans, and hot or cold canned asparagus, with or without hollandaise. For hors d'oeuvres, you may order any kind of seafood cocktail, as well as a can of sardines ("imported"), stuffed celery, or a dish of olives.

Most main courses are equally, cheerfully mundane: daily specials of minced chicken with noodles or corned beef and cabbage; macaroni au gratin, "spaghetti Italienne," roast lamb and mint jelly, plus a dozen steaks and chops and twice that many kinds of seafood. Tucked among the entrées, between chicken à la king and the low-calorie plate, is this old-money comfort meal:

WELSH RAREBIT, HOLLYWOOD BOULEVARD

1 tablespoon butter
4 teaspoons flour
½ cup warm milk
8 ounces Cheddar cheese, grated
2 drops Tabasco sauce
1 teaspoon Worcestershire sauce

1 teaspoon Spanish paprika
1 teaspoon hot mustard
½ cup beer
1 egg yolk, beaten (optional; see Note)

Melt butter in a small, heavy saucepan. Stir in flour and cook over medium heat, stirring constantly, for about a minute as it begins to bubble. (Do not let it brown.) Add milk, continue stirring, and bring to a boil. Lower heat and cook 2–3 minutes longer, continuing to stir, until thick and smooth. Remove from heat.

Melt cheese in top of a double boiler. Stir in cream sauce until blended. Add remaining ingredients. Cook, stirring constantly, 5 minutes. Serve in a bowl or deep plate, poured over toasted white bread.

Serves 2.

Note: This recipe makes a fairly soupy rarebit. If you like it thicker, add a beaten egg yolk after rarebit has cooked in top of double boiler 5 minutes. Then cook and stir 2 minutes more.

When we first tried to figure out the cuisine of Southern California, one native suggested—only half in jest—that our definition ought to include the phenomenon of celebrity restaurants. True, famous clientele are as much a part of Los Angeles gastronomy as any single foodstuff, and not just in the upscale eateries like Chasen's or Spago. In fact there is an equally venerable celebrity habit—patronizing dives, of which Los Angeles has a healthier population than any other American city.

Chili dogs, garlic burgers, street-corner burritos, and Flying Saucer bar-b-q: the streets of L.A. are a festival of sleazy eats; nearly all of the sleazy eateries display pictures of famous people who come to scarf their chow.

Our favorite dump, and one of the most important on any map of California's culinary landmarks, is Philippe's, which is actually quite blasé about its celebrity patrons. When pressed, they will tell you that Mickey Rooney and Merlin Olsen have come to eat, but the staff at Philippe's is prouder of its French dip sandwich than of any famous customers.

Philippe calls itself "the original," referring to its staked claim as the first restaurant in the West to serve a French dip. Thin-sliced roast beef au jus on a roll: French dips are everywhere today, even beyond the West, and although they hardly seem like a major breakthrough of American foodways, they are an unassailable cornerstone of vernacular cuisine from the Mississippi River to the Coast. Many places serve the natural gravy in a separate cup, for dipping, as the sandwich's name seems to suggest; but at Philippe's, the *original* way of doing it is to *dip* the two halves of the bun in juice, just enough to soften the chewy insides, before inserting the roast beef.

It's a good—and historically authentic—sandwich, but what is most vividly Californian about Philippe's is its mess hall atmosphere, bustling with a clientele reminiscent of Los Angeles as you see it in a 1940s *film noir.* Old-timers read racing forms and newspapers at chest-high communal tables lined up on a sawdust-strewn floor. Waitresses with sculpted hairdos and cupcake caps dish out homemade—but unmistakably institutional—steam table chow such as beef stew, pigs' feet, and giant baked apples. The beverage list runs from dime-a-cup coffee to French champagne.

THE ORIGINAL FRENCH DIP SANDWICH

The real secret of Philippe's good sandwich is neither the roast beef, which is ordinary, nor the torpedo roll. It is Philippe-made mustard, lined up in containers along the tables across the sawdust-strewn floor. "It's hot but it's good" is the mustard's apologetic motto; and it *is* hot. For French dip sandwiches at home, made without Philippe's original mustard, we recommend mixing up a batch of our Red Hot Mustard (p. 246) to complement the beef.

Hard-crusted torpedo roll (to make your own, see p. 249)
Natural, flourless gravy

3–4 ounces warm roast beef, sliced thin and gray
Hot mustard

Slice roll lengthwise and dip each half in gravy enough to soften bread, but not so much that juice soaks through and weakens crust. Pile in roast beef and spread on mustard.

Before it became the Pied Piper of the chic food revolution, San Francisco had a lusty culinary culture all its own, reflecting a heritage of forty-niners, Italian fishermen, artists and bohemians, and seagoing adventurers. It was known for the generosity of its North Beach boardinghouses and the seafood feasts of Fisherman's Wharf, for the highfalutin fare of the Palace and St. Francis hotels, for straight-shooting seafood grills, and for a slew of offbeat eateries such as Mike's Billiards Parlor and Papa Coppa's (home of chicken in a coconut).

No old San Francisco eatery is more self-consciously colorful than Trader Vic's, descended from a wooden beer joint named Hinky Dink's that a peripatetic restaurateur named Victor Bergeron opened in Oakland in the early 1930s. The Trader borrowed his tropical motif from Don the Beachcomber in Hollywood, but brought back recipes from the seven seas, an omnifarious collection of exotic and mundane food that has become the manifest of the Western world's most disparaged cuisine—Polynesian.

The San Francisco Trader Vic's was opened in 1951 and is the flagship of an empire of twenty more around the globe. What is truly amazing about the Trader's Number One Restaurant is how happily kitsch and class coexist there. We discovered this interesting fact one embarrassing evening years ago when, after a day of respectable-looking activity in San Francisco, we dressed down for dinner at the Trader's—loud Hawaiian shirts, tourist garb all the way. When we entered, we were given the house ascot to wear and seated in Siberia, just where our clothes deserved, beneath a scowling Tiki god. We ate gummy sweet-and-sour pork and drank litmus-colored drinks with gardenias floating in the rum.

Next time, we dressed nicely and went with a different attitude. We sat in the Captain's Room, which resembles an upper-crust yacht club, and had an elegant, only-in-San-Francisco meal of Trader Vic specialties that transcend clichés about Polynesian food.

BONGO BONGO SOUP

Bongo Bongo "made us famous," according to the Trader in his autobiography, *Frankly Speaking: Trader Vic's Own Story*. It is a bowl of Pacific pleasure that makes up for all the pu-pu dished out in the name of Oriental cuisine. Not that it is truly *authentic*. Like so much of Trader Vic's far-reaching menu, it was fabricated with a dash of inspiration from the South Seas and a heap of invention. The puréed spinach, for instance, is used to replicate the color that algae-eating toheroa clams from New Zealand gave the original version.

1⅔ cups cream
1½ cups milk
10 ounces fresh oysters,
    poached about 5 minutes in
    gently simmering water (or
    10 ounces canned oysters,
    drained) and puréed
¼ cup strained creamed
    spinach (baby food)

2 tablespoons butter
1 teaspoon Accent
1 teaspoon A-1 sauce
½ teaspoon black pepper
Dash garlic salt
Dash cayenne pepper
2 teaspoons cornstarch, mixed
    with 2 teaspoons cold
    water

Bring 1 cup of the cream and all the milk to a simmer in a large saucepan. Add oyster purée, spinach, butter, Accent, A-1 sauce, black pepper, garlic salt, and cayenne. Return to a simmer, whisking until smooth, but *do not boil*. Add cornstarch mixture, continuing to whisk until soup is slightly thickened. Adjust seasonings to taste.

Ladle into heatproof serving bowls. Whip remaining ⅔ cup of cream. Top each serving with a dollop of whipped cream. Place under broiler a few seconds, until cream is glazed and slightly brown.

Serves 4.

The signature dish of San Francisco is cioppino, fisherman's stew with an Italian accent—at its best when Dungeness crab is available fresh. Grottoes on Fisherman's Wharf shovel it out by the busload, and nearly every seafood house and Italian restaurant attempts a version. Even Trader Vic concocted a "fisherman's spaghetti" with canned clams and shrimp, based on what he referred to as "spaghetti à la something-or-other" that he ate in Amalfi.

But for an authentic taste of San Francisco cioppino the way it ought to be, we consulted John Canepa, chef at Tadich Grill. Tadich's is a land-mark that began as a coffee stand set up in 1849 to serve sailors docked in the harbor of Yerba Buena (San Francisco's former name). Today it is acknowledged as the granddad of the city's renowned seafood grills, specializing in charcoal-broiled fish, steaks, and chops, served in ma-hogany eating hall splendor, leather-crusted rounds of sourdough on the side.

TADICH GRILL CIOPPINO

Chef Canepa's tips for "cioppino delizioso" include using abso-lutely fresh fish and a light, aromatic sauce. He insists that the sauce should be made first; then the fish should be sautéed, the wine added, and the whole thing simmered together only a few short minutes. To cook the seafood in the sauce toughens shellfish and turns flatfish into mush. It is also important, he advises, to sauté the fish over high heat, reducing the wine so that only the bouquet remains.

SAUCE

½ medium onion, chopped
2 tablespoons olive oil
4 tablespoons butter
½ rib celery, chopped
1 medium carrot, chopped
1 tablespoon fennel, chopped
½ medium bell pepper, chopped
½ stalk leek (white part only), chopped
1 28-ounce can crushed tomatoes

1 tablespoon tomato paste
3½ cups water
2 teaspoons salt
¼ teaspoon black pepper
½ teaspoon oregano
½ teaspoon basil
¼ teaspoon thyme
4 bay leaves
Dash cayenne pepper

In a heavy saucepan over medium-low heat, sauté onion in oil and butter until soft, about 5 minutes. Add celery, carrot, fennel, bell pepper, and leek. Braise, covered, 5 minutes over low heat. Add remaining ingredients. Simmer, partially covered, 2 hours, stirring frequently. Discard bay leaves.

SEAFOOD PREPARATION

8 ounces halibut, cut into ½ x 2-inch pieces	2 tablespoons flour
8 ounces swordfish, cut into ½ x 2-inch pieces	1 teaspoon chopped garlic
	2 tablespoons olive oil
8 large scallops	4 tablespoons butter
8 large shrimp, shelled and deveined	1 cup dry white wine
	8 cherrystone clams, washed and cleaned
4 ounces small shrimp, shelled	1 tablespoon chopped parsley
6 ounces crabmeat	

Dust halibut, swordfish, scallops, shrimp, and crabmeat lightly with flour.

In a large saucepan sauté garlic in oil and butter over medium-high heat 30 seconds. Remove garlic with slotted spoon. Add all seafood. Sauté over medium-high heat 2 minutes, until seafood is golden. Add wine and stir, reducing wine. Cook 1 minute.

Add sauce to seafood, cover, and cook 3–4 minutes over low heat.

Steam open cherrystone clams (about 5 minutes).

Serve in an oval casserole or soup dish, garnished with cherrystones and parsley. On the side serve sourdough bread, toasted and buttered, brushed with garlic and sprinkled with oregano.

Serves 6.

Sam's Grill, like Tadich's, represents a heritage of high-quality fish houses, appointed with polished wood and white linen, staffed by manly men in aprons and formal waiter's garb, with menus printed every day to reflect what the morning market offers.

Open since 1867 (when it was located in the old California Market), Sam's is a quirky establishment, open only on weekdays until 8:30 p.m. It caters to a good-looking crowd who work downtown and mob the place at noon, jockeying for a table or crowding three deep against the bar. Reservations are not accepted. Whoever you are, you wait.

As is characteristic of so much new California grill cookery, most of

Sam's seafood is prepared plainly. It is the place to sample Pacific rarities that never make it East, like rex and petrale sole grilled over charcoal and the unbelievably delicate local fish called sand dabs—about a half-dozen sweet little fillets sautéed in lemon butter. It is also the best place we know to eat the classic Northern California omelette known as Hangtown fry.

Hangtown was the nineteenth-century name for Placerville, a hot spot during the gold rush. One day, according to legend, a forty-niner who had just hit pay dirt strode into the town saloon and instructed the cook to make him the most expensive dish in the house. As eggs were a dollar each —if you could get them—the fanciest thing the flush prospector could eat would be an omelette.

Into the pan of precious yolks the chef threw a handful of oysters, which at the time—contrary to this tale's theme of *nouveau riche* profligacy—were cheap and plentiful.

A different story, set forth by James Beard, accounts for the macabre name by suggesting that Hangtown fry was the last breakfast of a desperado about to be strung up, who decided to have all his favorite foods in one meal.

It doesn't matter which tale you believe about who invented Hangtown fry. The point is that both yarns are set in a long-forgotten California that was part of the American frontier, a rugged place where men were men, and a mess of oysters tossed into a frying pan full of eggs was more than a sissy omelette.

SAM'S GRILL HANGTOWN FRY

Sam's Hangtown fry is made with Olympia oysters, the itsy-bitsy rarities from Washington State. If, like us, you cannot locate real Olys, be sure to use fresh oysters *with flavor*, such as Belons or Apalachicolas, because the dish is nothing without their salty marine smack. Size is important too. Large oysters overwhelm the eggs. The point is to have bite-size nuggets throughout the omelette.

2–2½ dozen shucked Olympia
    oysters, or 6–8 large
    oysters, cut into dime-size
    morsels
½ cup flour
1 egg, beaten with 1
    tablespoon milk

½ cup bread crumbs
Oil for frying (deep or pan)
2 tablespoons butter
2–3 eggs, beaten
2–3 slices lean, thick bacon,
    cooked and drained

Roll oysters or oyster morsels in flour and shake off excess. Dip into egg wash, then roll in bread crumbs. Fry at 350° 1 minute, or until crisp and golden. Drain and set aside.

Melt butter in an omelette pan. Pour in eggs. Stir slightly, and when eggs are beginning to set but are still liquid, add oysters. Flip omelette to brown other side.

Slip omelette onto a warm plate and top with bacon.

Serves 1.

More than any other American city, San Francisco has the distinction of being the cradle of Italian-American cuisine. Its North Beach trattorias, sawdust-floored family dinner houses, and exhibition-kitchen pizza/pasta parlors helped define red-sauced Italian-style cookery. You know the meal: minestrone, meat-heaped spaghetti, and garlic bread, served in a dimly lit brick-walled grotto with Chianti bottle candleholders on red-checked tablecloths.

America is now so sophisticated that such peasant fare seems passé, replaced by new, upwardly mobile clichés about what pizza and pasta are supposed to be. Interesting, though, that the *re*discovery of Mediterranean cookery (pesto, sun-dried tomatoes, extra-virgin olive oil, northern-Italian-is-better-than-southern) has been spearheaded by chefs from the San Francisco Bay Area.

We aren't going to give recipes for spaghetti and meatballs or chicken cacciatore or garbanzo salad—although it is really quite delightful, after a decade of *nuovo cucina*, to dig into well-made versions of those time-worn all-American, Italian-American classics.

There is, however, at least one dish that cannot be ignored in any discussion of old California cuisine—the New Joe Special. Although Italian-accented, and served in nearly every old-style Italian eatery in the city, it is unique to the Bay Area, as much a part of Golden Gate gastronomy as cioppino or Hangtown fry.

NEW JOE SPECIAL

If we were academic sorts, we would be hard at work researching a thesis about the many faces of Joe in American cookery. As dilettantes, we know that there was a nine-stool ice cream parlor in San Francisco at least as far back as the twenties named Joe's. New owners—none named Joe—bought the business in 1927 and began serving spaghetti and one-pound hamburgers. Joe's begat New Joe's, then Little Joe's, then Original Joe's. Modern-day *Original* Joe's is a descendant of New Joe's (and only a distant relation, as far as we know, to Baby Joe's or Little Joe's).

This question remains: Did the original New Joe (as opposed to the Original Joe) invent the New Joe Special? (And a corollary query: Was there an actual, living Sloppy Joe?) Was the "special," in the beginning, some kind of haywire Americanization of a northern Italian *spinaci* dish? Or just a stopgap measure by Joe's chef when he ran out of everything but hamburger, spinach, and eggs?

However this eccentric little branch of San Francisco's cuisine evolved, "Joe" has come to signify a dish made with Italian-seasoned ground beef. "Sloppy" almost always means tomato sauce and a burger bun to hold it. "Sicilian" means the inclusion of anchovies, olives, and capers.

Special Joe always implies spinach. We have eaten some New Joe Specials that are hardly more than spinach and ground beef. At Original Joe's in San Jose, the recipe includes onions, eggs, and, as in most Bay Area restaurants, an option of mushrooms. What a mess! Invention has always been the soul of Joe, so feel free to experiment.

10 ounces fresh spinach, washed and chopped, or 1 10-ounce package frozen chopped spinach	2 tablespoons butter
2 cloves garlic, minced	1 pound ground beef
1 onion, chopped	4 eggs, well beaten
⅔ cup sliced mushrooms	½ teaspoon oregano
2 tablespoons olive oil	Salt and pepper to taste
	Grated Parmesan cheese to taste

If using fresh spinach, boil until limp. Drain well, pressing out as much water as possible. Set aside. If using frozen chopped spinach, cook in boiling water until defrosted. Drain thoroughly.

In a large skillet sauté garlic, onion, and mushrooms in olive oil and butter until onion is limp. Add meat, breaking it up with a fork, stirring as it cooks. Depending on how lean the meat is, you may want to drain off excess fat now.

Stir in cooked spinach, mixing well. Stirring vigorously, add beaten eggs. Cook, stirring, 2–3 minutes until eggs set (do not overcook). Season with oregano, salt, and pepper. Garnish with Parmesan cheese.

Serves 4.

According to *A Cook's Tour of San Francisco*, Doris Muscatine's vivid 1963 account of San Francisco eateries, one of the city's most popular and "distingué" desserts was fried cream. She traces it back to an old California recipe for "Bonfire Entree," served in sticks stacked up like a log cabin along with brandy-soaked sugar lumps. Diners were invited to ignite their own. "Things have changed a bit in California," Ms. Muscatine observes. "Now the waiters set the fires." This festive recipe comes from the Veneto Restaurant, whose *Dolce Vita* atmosphere includes a full-size gondola floating in an indoor Venetian canal, plus strolling accordionists. In the quiet of home, a show-off dessert such as this makes a grand finale to an otherwise tasteful meal. And it *is* delicious.

FRIED CREAM

2 cups milk
½ cup plus 2 tablespoons semolina (or Cream of Wheat)
2 eggs, beaten
1 teaspoon vanilla extract
½ teaspoon salt
2 tablespoons plus 5 teaspoons granulated sugar
Flour

2 eggs, beaten with 1 tablespoon milk
Fine, dry bread crumbs
2 tablespoons brown sugar
About 4 tablespoons butter for frying
18 whole cloves
1 cup high-proof rum or brandy, warmed
Whipped cream (optional)

Bring milk to a boil. Add semolina slowly, stirring constantly and continuing to cook until it is very thick and it pulls away from side of pan, about 3 minutes. Remove from heat and continue stirring while you slowly add eggs. Add vanilla, salt, and 5 teaspoons of the granulated sugar.

Line a 9 x 9-inch baking dish with plastic wrap. Pour mixture into dish. Smooth and flatten with a spatula. Cover and refrigerate overnight.

When firm, turn onto a cutting board and divide into 9 squares. Roll each square in flour, then dip into egg mixture, then roll in fine bread crumbs.

Combine remaining 2 tablespoons of granulated sugar with brown sugar.

Fry squares in butter over low heat until golden brown, about 3 minutes per side. Drain on paper towels and place each square immediately into a very hot flameproof dessert bowl. Stick each square with 2 cloves and sprinkle with sugar mixture. Pour 1 ounce of warm rum or brandy over each. Avert your face and ignite brandy. When flame goes out, dollop with whipped cream, if desired.

Serves 9.

INDIAN RESERVATIONS

For those of us who learned about Indians from cowboy movies or in museums with dimly lit dioramas and speakers playing tapes of thumping drums, breaking bread with Native Americans is a shocking taste of cultural dissonance.

The most authentic Indian restaurant we know is run by the Tigua tribe in El Paso, Texas. It is a wraparound environment keyed to tribal culture with pottery and rugs, a traditional stick-and-reed roof, adobe walls, native music in the background. Many customers are Indians, and, yes, many of them wear long wrinkled skirts of faded velvet and centuries-old turquoise jewelry—the characters one hopes to see while tearing into loaves of Pueblo clay oven bread.

But seated next to these appropriately picturesque people are other, equally authentic natives, garbed in rubbery pantsuits and big-lens eyeglasses, looking no more exotic than members of Phil Donahue's audience. They wear K mart headbands and designer jeans; as we visitors clear our sinuses with fire-hot Tigua Indian chili, they plow into hamburgers, German chocolate cake, and cherry pie. Except at tribal ceremonies, Indian foodways are inextricable from peanut-butter-and-jelly pop cuisine.

From the beginning, Native American food was assimilated quickly into the mainstream. Culinary miscegenation began in 1621, after the Pilgrims' first brutal winter in Plymouth, when they were joined by a Wampanoag brave named Squanto. The native showed the strangers (most of whom were city people) how to plant and harvest corn. "Indian corn" they called it, and it saved them from starvation. Cornmeal became a staple of American cookery.

Since then, America's regional cooking has omnivorously absorbed Indian food and cooking technique—from succotash and clambakes in the East to the alder-smoked salmon of the Pacific Northwest.

In the Southwest, it was Spanish explorers who joined their food with the Indians'. They brought chilies north and blended them with Pueblo native ingredients to create New Mexican cuisine. Chilies are the soul of this unique regional style of cooking, but the most distinguishing visual element is its use of blue cornmeal.

Corn signifies life to many Native Americans; their use of festive-colored corn goes back to prehistoric America. And yet, with the exception of ceremonial unleavened piki breads, modern uses for blue cornmeal have a Tex-Mex or New Mexican flavor—such as blue corn tortillas, blue corn chips (like Doritos), even blue cornflakes for breakfast.

Earth-colored bread made with blue cornmeal is a startling sight, but its taste is familiar, a stout cold-weather companion to mutton stew (see p. 293). Of course, it requires blue cornmeal. In the Southwest, most supermarkets sell it; elsewhere, look in gourmet stores. Otherwise, blue cornmeal is sold by:

Casados Farms
P.O. Box 1269
San Juan Pueblo, NM 87566
(505) 852-2433

Blue chips and tortillas are available from:

Josie's Best New Mexican Foods
1130 Agua Fria Street
Santa Fe, NM 87501
(505) 983-6520

PUEBLO BLUE CORN BREAD

1½ cups blue cornmeal
½ cup flour
1 tablespoon baking powder
½ teaspoon baking soda
1 teaspoon salt
¼ cup sugar
1 egg, beaten

1¼ cups buttermilk
3 tablespoons lard or bacon
    drippings, melted
1–2 jalapeño peppers, diced
    fine
2 tablespoons minced onion

Preheat oven to 375°. Mix cornmeal, flour, baking powder, baking soda, salt, and sugar. Mix egg, buttermilk, and lard. Combine mixtures. Stir in peppers (1 or 2, depending on taste) and onion. Pour batter into a well-greased 9-inch cast-iron skillet. Bake 20–25 minutes, or until a knife inserted in center comes out clean. Let bread cool 10 minutes and serve from pan, cut into triangular wedges

Serves 4–6.

Back in the 1970s, for our first taste of authentic Indian cuisine, we headed into the Arizona desert toward Shungopavi, a place known to the Native Americans who live there as the Center of the Universe. It is Hopi land, surrounded entirely by the Navajo reservation.

At the Center of the Universe we found the Hopi Cultural Center Restaurant, an adobe lunchroom no more exotic-looking than a summer camp canteen, Visa and MasterCard accepted. We also found meals unlike any other food in America. To be sure, they are *American* meals—the only true indigenous food this nation has.

NOK QUI VI, AMERICAN STYLE

This primitive-tasting stew may be a not-too-distant inspiration for Tex-Mex chili. As eaten by Pueblo shepherds, it was made with gamy mutton. Supermarket lamb, although lacking the free-range tang, provides good results too. And it is possible—although not true to Hopi cookery—to use chunked beef or pork. At Shungopavi, we ate it served with fry bread and honey, and a copy of the Hebraic-looking *Navajo Times* to puzzle over. At home, we make mild lamb and vegetable Nok Qui Vi, accompanied by blue corn bread (preceding recipe) laced with hot chilies.

1 onion, chopped
3 cloves garlic, minced
3 tablespoons lard
5 cups chicken stock
2 pounds lean lamb, cut into 1-inch chunks
2 cups drained canned hominy
2 large carrots, cut into 1-inch lengths
1 cup diced turnip
1 4-ounce can mild green chilies, drained and chopped
1 teaspoon ground cumin
Salt and pepper to taste
1–2 jalapeño peppers, diced fine (optional)

Sauté onion and garlic in lard in a 4-quart stockpot until onion softens. Add remaining ingredients except jalapeño peppers, bring to a boil, cover, and simmer very gently 45 minutes. For a hotter stew, add jalapeño peppers when stock comes to a boil.

Serves 6–8.

The *pièce de résistance* at the Center of the Universe is piki bread—slate blue, ashen to the touch, like spiral strudels untombed from some ancient sarcophagus. Piki is made on smooth stones heated and greased with sheeps' brains then used to bake the bread in the manner of a crepe. The result is a vaporous sensation so fragile it is fugitive, evaporating as it moistens on the tongue. At the Hopi restaurant, these ineffable delicacies arrive at the table sheathed in Saran Wrap.

We have tried several recipes for piki bread made in Teflon skillets or with a crepe maker, and none come close to piki stone breads. In its place, we suggest you might want to use superfine blue cornmeal to make some of these wafer-thin pancakes.

BLUE PANCAKES

You can do almost anything with blue cornmeal that you do with the fine white variety. These pancakes are a thinned, fragile version of a hot cake recipe we found in Juanita Tiger Kavena's indispensable book of *Hopi Cookery*.

1 cup blue cornmeal
1 tablespoon baking powder
1 teaspoon salt
1 tablespoon sugar
3 tablespoons butter, melted
    and cooled

2 eggs, beaten
½ cup milk
½ cup water

Combine cornmeal, baking powder, salt, and sugar.

Combine melted butter, eggs, milk, and water. Add to dry ingredients.

Pour as 4–5-inch cakes on a lightly greased griddle and cook over medium-high heat until lightly browned.

Makes 10–12 cakes.

Blue cornmeal breads are rare and strange. In Sacaton, Arizona, at the Gila River Restaurant (run by the Pima tribe), the menu is based on another style of Indian bread, closer to mainstream American cookery—fry bread. Ancestor of New Mexico's *sopaipillas*, and perhaps even a distant relation to the fast-food scones of Utah, fry bread is inelegant camp food, traditionally cooked in lard-greased Dutch ovens over an open fire.

The nature of fry bread varies considerably, from the chewy doughnut-textured rounds of the Plains tribes to these airy popoverlike disks served by the Pimas.

GILA RIVER FRY BREAD

Jon Long, director of the Gila River Restaurant, told us that fry bread should never be made in advance. The only way to enjoy it, he insisted, is sizzling hot out of the skillet. We like to drizzle its crusty golden skin with honey, or merely dust it with powdered sugar: great breakfast breadstuff.

2¼ cups flour
2 teaspoons baking powder
1 teaspoon salt
3 tablespoons solid vegetable
    shortening

About ¾ cup warm water
Fat for frying

Mix flour, baking powder, and salt. Cut in 1 tablespoon of the shortening. Melt and cool remaining 2 tablespoons of shortening and set aside. Add just enough water to flour mixture so dough holds together and can be handled easily. Knead on a lightly floured board until smooth, about 30 seconds, adding only enough flour to work dough.

Form dough into smooth 2-inch balls. Brush each ball with cooled shortening and let stand 45 minutes.

In a deep skillet or deep fryer heat fat to 360°.

On a lightly floured surface, with the heel of your hand, flatten each ball of dough out into a round circle about 6 inches in diameter.

Ease into deep fat. Dough will bob to surface. Cook until dough is light brown, a mere 45–60 seconds, turn, and cook other side 45–60 seconds. Remove from fat immediately and drain on paper towel.

Makes 6 individual breads.

Greater things are made of fry bread than simply sugar-dusted pastries. One of the most popular "Indian" specialties throughout Arizona is a one-dish feast known as a Navajo taco—extra-wide rounds of fry bread heaped with chili, lettuce, cheese, peppers, etc.

In our search for the best Navajo taco, we headed for Tuba City, a dusty desert town on the Navajo reservation. Here is the Tuba City Truck Stop Cafe, a squat cinder block building utterly without eye appeal. But it was *real*. With the exception of the blond-bouffanted waitress, we were the only Caucasians in the house. Up front, young Indians played a fierce game of Asteroids; at the counter, one gnarled old tribesman decked out in buckskin and leather gingerly spooned into a bowl of jiggly red blocks of gelatin.

In these true West surroundings, we were served a most amazing meal —freshly fried, flake-crusted rounds of bread heaped with meat-and-bean chili, shredded cheese, lettuce, and tomatoes, the whole shebang crowned with a single hot pepper.

THE ULTIMATE NAVAJO TACO

Make all the toppings first, then fry the bread and dish these out as soon as the bread emerges from the fat. For authentic textural variety, the chili used on a Navajo taco should contain beans and not be too blistering hot.

CHILI FOR TACOS

2 tablespoons solid vegetable shortening	1 teaspoon salt
1 large onion, chopped fine	¼ teaspoon cayenne pepper
2 cloves garlic, minced	½ teaspoon ground cumin
1 pound beef, cubed	½ teaspoon black pepper
1 tablespoon chili powder	1 16-ounce can tomatoes
	1 16-ounce can kidney beans

Melt shortening in a large saucepan. Sauté onion and garlic until soft. Add beef and cook until well browned. Add remaining ingredients, cover, and simmer 30 minutes, stirring occasionally.

OTHER INGREDIENTS FOR TACOS

1 pound longhorn Cheddar cheese, shredded	Chopped tomatoes
Shredded iceberg lettuce	Jalapeño peppers, diced

To make tacos, prepare all ingredients, then make fry bread (preceding recipe). Top bread with chili, then cheese, then lettuce and tomatoes. Add jalapeño peppers to taste.

Serves 6.

At the Tigua Indian Reservation Restaurant in El Paso, Texas, the bread specialty is yeast-leavened from wheat flour and baked in clay ovens. It is soft and earthy-crumbed, suitable for tamping down fires on the tongue, which are begun by some of the most amazing Native American food you will eat anywhere—Tigua chili.

We had ordered two bowlfuls. They were mesmerizing to look at, the red chili like molten cinnabar, the green a lagoon-hued mystery of chili pods and mutton. A few spoons of each and we began praying for our immortal souls. This was the hottest meal we had ever eaten. Perspiration beaded on our brows; we clutched our throats; we yelped; we gulped at tumblers of ice water.

As our faces gradually returned to their normal colors, we were joined by tribal kibbitzer Jose Sierra, who had been enjoying our gastronomic agony from a distance. He relished explaining that hot chili—really hot chili—made this stuff taste like pablum. He then convinced us to give it another try, this time chewing the clay oven bread as a sop for the hot oil in our mouths. With the bread clutched in our hands like little life preservers, we dipped in again and came to know that the heat was only the beginning of the chili, a way of "opening" the taste buds to appreciate the pepper pods as vegetables.

Great chili is surprisingly hard to find in Texas restaurants, yet there we were eating some of the best cowboy chow in the Southwest—on an Indian reservation! It is ultimate chili—plain fire-hot meat, nothing more than that. Beans, rice, and clay-oven bread come on the side.

TIGUA INDIAN RED CHILI

Tigua chili, either red or green, "will bring tears to your eyes," according to the Tigua Pueblo menu. Its secret is dried whole chili pods (not chili powder!), which comes in varying degrees of hotness. Many supermarkets outside the Southwest now carry peppers for Tex-Mex cooking. Taste the chili purée. If it isn't hot enough to suit your palate, jazz it up with finely diced jalapeño peppers. We like to serve this chili with wedges of Pueblo Blue Corn Bread (p. 292), omitting jalapeño peppers from the bread.

10–12 chili pods, about 5
   inches long
10 cups water
1 tablespoon lard
4 large cloves garlic, crushed
1½ teaspoons salt
2½ pounds stewing beef, cut
   into bite-size pieces

¼ cup cooking oil
1 medium onion, chopped fine
1 teaspoon oregano
2 medium potatoes, peeled and
   diced

Remove stems and most of the seeds from chili pods (more seeds = hotter chili). Place pods in water over medium heat. Bring to a slow rolling boil and cook until tender, about 30 minutes.

Remove chilies from liquid with a slotted spoon, reserving cooking liquid, and liquefy in a blender, adding enough of the liquid to create a smooth purée. (Reserve remaining cooking liquid.)

Pour chili purée into a saucepan. Add lard, garlic, and salt. Bring to a simmer.

☞

In a large pot brown beef in oil. Add chili purée; cook and stir so that beef can absorb chili flavor. Stir in onion, oregano, and 2 cups of reserved cooking liquid. Cover and simmer 1 full hour, adding potatoes after 20 minutes. After an hour, test a piece of meat to see if it is fall-apart tender. If so, chili is ready. If not, cook another 15 minutes.

Serves 4.

SHEPHERDS' HOTELS

here are huge parts of this country, especially in the West and Great Plains, where there are no cities, no towns, and no place to eat. That is why we like Route 80 through Nevada. The oases of civilization on this scenic highway are far apart, but nearly every one has a handy restaurant. And it is all thanks to the Basques.

Three-quarters of a century ago, Basque shepherds from the French and Spanish Pyrenees began to immigrate to the West—to Idaho, Nevada, and the California hills—where the high pastures were ideal grazing land for sheep. Most of them were second or third sons; they left home because Basque custom gave family land to the oldest child.

These were mountain men who lived solitary lives for months, coming to town only two or three times a year. When they came—to Elko, Winnemucca, Mountain Home, or Reno—the town's hotels sought their business by serving familiar Basque food. To this day, the best—the only—places to eat in this otherwise barren landscape are those that are descended from the shepherds' boardinghouses and hotels.

Further west in the North Beach neighborhood of San Francisco, where a boardinghouse tradition defined life for bachelor immigrants of Italian as well as Basque descent, the hotels were destinations for sheepherders on vacation in the summer after the herd was brought in.

Basque cuisine, like their language, is unique. In the field, it was nomad food such as Dutch oven bread and untended, long-simmering stews (almost always based on lamb). But a visit to the boardinghouses, after weeks in the hills, was an opportunity to revel in special-occasion fare. Boardinghouse kitchens went all out to make every meal like Sunday dinner, multicourse feasts prepared to satisfy mountain man appetites. That sense of he-man culinary extravagance survives today, despite the fact that Basque immigration has stopped and open-range grazing has fallen victim to environmentalist restrictions and a low market demand for lamb.

The location itself sets the mood. Louis' Basque Corner in Reno or the Martin Hotel in Winnemucca are both near the city train station, where newly arrived immigrants would have an easy time finding them. On the wrong side of the tracks in a Nevada town, or in the teeming neighborhoods of San Francisco populated by foreign-speaking newcomers, these hotel dining rooms still have the flavor of a melting pot West, where strangers came to find a new life, adapting Old Country foodways to fit the frontier.

No Basque boardinghouse is ever fancy. You eat in a plain, ragged dining room, decorated with pictures of the Pyrenees or homilies written in the weird native language loaded with q's and z's that doesn't look like either French or Spanish. Dinner, served once per evening, is announced by the clanging of a bell.

One of the West's great Basque feeds is dished out on Stockton Street in San Francisco, in the DMZ between Chinatown and North Beach—at the Obrero Hotel. Built just after the 1906 earthquake, it was originally a Barbary Coast bordello. "One man showed up for dinner several years ago," current owner Bambi McDonald told us, "and said that as a lad he delivered wine to the place, as a messenger for his father, who was a bootlegger. And for his fourteenth birthday, he was treated to a night with the girls as initiation."

Later, the Obrero became known for its family-style (Italian) Sunday dinners. In the 1940s, it was bought by Spanish Basques as a boarding-house for shepherds on vacation. In the 1950s, it passed into French Basque hands; then finally Bambi McDonald, an upstate New Yorker, bought it. Refurbished and spruced up as a European-style pension, it is a bargain bed-and-breakfast hotel, where double rooms (no bath) including breakfast (ham, eggs, cheese, bread, coffee) go for $30. The heroic dinners, dished out in the large common room, are legendary.

There is a definite shape and rhythm to every true Basque boarding-house meal. There is always red wine on the table. And loaves of hard-crusted bread. Dinner comes in stages: soup, salad or relishes, a dish of beans, a first entrée, a meat entrée, potatoes and/or vegetable, and finally a minimal dessert—usually a plate of cheese, accompanied by Basque coffee laced with brandy.

Boardinghouses buy loaves of bread to go with dinner; but in the old days, in the field, Basque shepherds baked their own. If you want to have a real mountaineer's feast, set the table with a loaf of this Dutch oven-baked bread.

SHEPHERD'S BREAD

1 package dry yeast
1½ cups tepid water (110°)
½ cup sugar

4½ cups flour
1½ teaspoons salt
4 tablespoons butter, melted

Dissolve yeast in ¼ cup of the water with a pinch of the sugar. Mix together flour, salt, remaining 1¼ cups of water, remaining sugar, and melted butter. Add yeast mixture and stir well until dough holds together. Turn out onto a floured board. Let rest.

As dough rests, line a 2½–3-quart Dutch oven or lidded heavy casserole with aluminum foil. Coat foil and inside of lid thoroughly with light salad oil.

Knead dough until it is smooth and workable, about 10 minutes. Place inside Dutch oven, cover with lid, and place oven in warm (about 80°) place. Allow dough to rise until it pushes up lid, about 2 hours.

Preheat oven to 375°. Punch dough down; regrease lid; allow dough to rise again until it just touches lid. Bake, covered, 12 minutes. Remove lid and continue baking 35–40 minutes, until crust is dark brown. Turn out of pan and cool on rack. (The first slice should be fed to one's sheep dog.)

Makes 1 large loaf.

At the Obrero Hotel, once the bread and wine are on the table, the nightly mess begins with soup, split pea the favorite.

OBRERO HOTEL SPLIT PEA SOUP

"I tried to cut down the size of my recipes," Bambi McDonald said when she gave us this one, "since most of my ingredients are measured by 'the small salad bowlful,' or 'the large green pan,' etc." We have reduced the quantities even further, and suggest cooking the peas first. Bambi just cooks everything together. However it is done, with no seasonings other than salt, this soup is essence-of-vegetable simple—totally bland: the calm before the storm of a major Basque feed.

2 cups split peas
1 large onion, sliced
5 carrots, peeled and sliced
    into disks
5 ribs celery, sliced

½ small head cabbage, sliced
    (about 3 cups)
Salt to taste

Place peas in a stockpot and add 6 cups of water. Bring to a boil for 2 minutes and let cool in water 1 hour. Drain. Put in a kettle with remaining ingredients and 2 quarts of water. Bring to a boil, turn heat down, and simmer 2–3 hours, or until split peas are tender.

Serves 8.

On Sunday morning in a Western boardinghouse, or very rarely on a weekend night, you might be privileged to get a different kind of soup—aggressively Basque—known for its ability to cure all kinds of sinus ailments, including hangovers. Its official gastronomic name is *Basuru Zalda*, meaning garlic soup. But those in the know call it *Moscor Zalda*, a.k.a. drunkard's soup.

DRUNKARD'S SOUP

"Please stand downwind from people," inveighs our *From the Basque Kitchen* cookbook, published by the Reno Basque Club and sent to us by Lorraine Erreguible of Reno. There is perhaps no other food that so well conveys the hairy-chested vigor of this cuisine. Remember, Basques consider this soup breakfast food, an eye-opener. Definitely from the kill-or-cure school of mixology, we actually like it—but only when sober.

6 cloves garlic, sliced thin
⅓ cup olive oil
½ loaf day-old French bread,
   cut into large croutons

4 cups chicken stock
4 eggs
¼ cup chopped parsley

In a heavy-bottomed stockpot, sauté garlic in olive oil over medium heat until it begins to soften. Add bread, stirring to coat. Cook and toss bread until brown and crisp. Remove bread with slotted spoon and reserve.

Add chicken stock to stockpot. Bring to boil. Simmer 5 minutes. Stir in eggs vigorously so they get stringy. Return to simmer. Stir in parsley.

Pour soup into individual bowls. Garnish with reserved garlic croutons.

Serves 4.

No Basque meal is complete without an early course of beans: garbanzos and chorizo sausage, string beans and hard-boiled eggs, or string beans roasted in garlic. One of the heartiest such assemblages is the preliminary bean dish served at Louis' Basque Corner, just a few blocks from the lights of downtown Reno.

There is a frontier feel about eating at Louis', surrounded by transplanted Old World memorabilia in a rough-and-ready Western setting. Tables, covered with bright red cloths, are designed for twenty people at

a time. And meals are served in chuck wagon abundance, bowls and platters carried to the table by waitresses in Basque costumes.

Ezkualdun itarrak (Basque beans) are a Louis specialty—nothing
fancy or esoteric, but guaranteed to satisfy. As Louis' wife Lorraine says,
"They are simple food, cooked to perfection."

EZKUALDUN ITARRAK

Although at Louis' these beans are merely one of several courses,
we believe they make a two-fisted meal with nothing more than a
green salad, French bread, and a glass of red wine. The chorizo
sausage called for in the recipe can be found in Mexican grocery
stores. If you cannot get it, substitute a spicy, Italian-style sausage.

1 pound dried pinto beans	2 teaspoons Worcestershire
½ pound bacon, cut into 1-inch	sauce
lengths	1 teaspoon chili powder
½ pound chorizo sausage,	2 bay leaves
sliced	1 teaspoon thyme
1 large green bell pepper, diced	½ teaspoon rosemary
1 large onion, diced	1 tablespoon chopped parsley
5 cloves garlic, chopped fine	2 teaspoons salt, or to taste

Clean and rinse beans. Soak in 4 cups of cold water overnight.
Change water and put beans in a large stockpot with enough water
to cover. Bring to a boil, then reduce heat to a simmer.

As beans simmer, fry bacon and sausage over medium heat
until sausage is cooked through. Add bell pepper, onion, and garlic
and cook until vegetables are soft. Add seasonings (except salt) and
mix thoroughly. Add to beans, cover, and continue simmering, stirring frequently, until beans are soft but not mushy, about 30 minutes. (If liquid is absorbed before beans are soft, you may have to
add about 1 cup of water.) Add salt; remove and discard bay
leaves.

Makes 4 meal-size portions.

GREEN BEANS WITH GARLIC

An Obrero Hotel specialty, this odoriferous way with beans is for
garlic lovers only. It starts with fresh beans, but they get baked
until they are shriveled and limp as noodles—conduits for maximum amounts of garlic, oil, and butter.

1½ pounds fresh string beans,
    trimmed and washed
8 cloves garlic, minced
4 tablespoons butter

⅓ cup olive oil
2 tablespoons wine vinegar
1 teaspoon salt

Blanch beans in boiling salted water (30 seconds—no longer). Drain and rinse under cold water. Layer in a roasting pan or wide casserole.

    Preheat oven to 400°.

    Sauté garlic in butter and olive oil, only until light brown. Pour butter, oil, and garlic over beans. Drizzle on wine vinegar, sprinkle on salt. Toss to mix well.

    Roast beans, uncovered, 40 minutes, tossing frequently.

Serves 4.

After soup and salad and beans and relish and bread and wine, you are ready to commence serious eating. Now comes the most vividly Basque-flavored part of the meal, the first entrée, also known with undue modesty as "the side dish." This is usually a stew or casserole made with one of the favored sauces, either red (peppers and tomatoes), white (wine and broth), green (garlic, oil, herbs), or black (squid ink). The repertoire of ingredients for these dishes include viscera such as tripe, heart, or sweetbreads; or variety meat like tongue or testicles; more often, in modern boardinghouses, you will get paella or a shepherd's stew.

Rice is an essential ingredient in many of these first courses, especially in a wonderful one we enjoyed many years ago at San Francisco's Cafe du Nord on Market Street. It was a Friday night specialty called clams and rice.

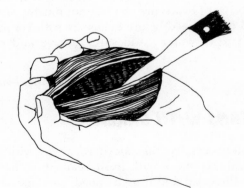

CLAMS AND RICE

Although it is possible to make this dish with the clams in the shell, we find it easier to make (and eat) if the clams are shucked first. If added in the shell, the clams must be grit-free, scrubbed thoroughly.

24–36 clams, depending on size
½ cup clam juice
1½ cups chicken broth
2 tablespoons olive oil

2 tablespoons butter
4 cloves garlic, sliced
½ cup chopped parsley
1 cup converted rice
Salt (optional)

Scrub clams.

Combine clam juice and chicken broth and bring to a boil.

Heat olive oil and butter in a Dutch oven or large skillet with a lid. Sauté garlic until soft. Add parsley. Add clams and rice, blend, then add clam juice and chicken broth. Season with salt, if desired. Cover and simmer 17 minutes, until rice has absorbed all liquid. Serve immediately.

Serves 4 as a main dish;
serves 6–8 as a side dish.

When we needed suggestions of what to serve at a terrific Basque meal, we went to Winnemucca, Nevada, and sought the advice of Frenchy Fouchet of the Martin Hotel ("Fine Food—Slots—Bar"). He suggested lamb cassoulet, an economical concoction of his leftover lentil and chorizo side dish combined with an equal amount of leftover lamb stew. Not having such abundant leftovers, we worked up this recipe the day after a leg of lamb, abetted by *From the Basque Kitchen:*

WINNEMUCCA LAMB CASSOULET

4 ounces salt pork, diced
1½ cups dried lentils
3 cups chicken broth
1 16-ounce can whole tomatoes
½ cup finely chopped onion
2 cloves garlic, minced

1 tablespoon chopped parsley
1 bay leaf
½ teaspoon salt
½ teaspoon Tabasco sauce
2 cups cooked cubed lamb

☞

Brown salt pork in a Dutch oven or large skillet with a lid. Add all remaining ingredients except lamb. Bring to a boil and cover. Simmer slowly 2 hours, until lentils are soft. Preheat oven to 350°. Add lamb and pour into greased 2-quart casserole. Bake 20 minutes.

Serves 6–8.

The best use we know for leftovers is in an Obrero Hotel first-course side dish that is known around the hotel as "budget pie," because everything that goes into it, except the eggs, is from previous meals. It's a mostly potato dish, plenty filling, the spuds accented by ends of roasts.

SHEPHERD'S BUDGET PIE

8–12 cups well-seasoned and buttered mashed potatoes
4 cups ground cooked meat (beef, pork, lamb)
2 large onions, chopped
5 eggs

2 teaspoons garlic salt
1 teaspoon black pepper
1 tablespoon poultry seasoning (Accent, etc.)
2 tablespoons butter, melted

Preheat oven to 400°. Butter heavily a 9 x 13-inch Pyrex baking dish. Pat in a bottom crust of mashed potatoes, using about half the potatoes.

Combine meat with onions, eggs, garlic salt, pepper, and poultry seasoning. (If you have leftover gravy, use it to moisten meat, and leave out 1–2 eggs.) Layer meat mixture onto mashed potatoes. Cover with remaining mashed potatoes. Brush top of potatoes with melted butter. Bake 1½ hours, or until top is puffy and dark golden brown.

Serves 8 generously.

Having plowed through shepherd's pie or clams and rice, you are now ready for the main entrée at a Basque boardinghouse meal. This is usually the simplest and most *Western* of the courses—a steak, pork chops, a slab of roast beef, a leg of lamb. If the side dish is based on beef or lamb, plainly cooked chicken is often the order of the day. This way with chicken is about as plain as the Basque kitchen gets.

BASQUE CHICKEN

1 teaspoon salt
½ teaspoon black pepper
1 cup flour
1 3-pound fryer, disjointed
¼ cup olive oil
4 large tomatoes, peeled,
   seeded, and diced

4 ounces ham, diced fine
1 red bell pepper, roasted,
   peeled, and diced
½ cup dry white wine

Preheat oven to 375°. Mix salt and pepper into flour in a bowl. Dredge chicken pieces in mixture.

Over medium heat in a large skillet brown chicken in olive oil. Remove chicken and place in a 4-quart baking dish. Pour off excess oil from skillet, but do not wipe clean. Fry tomatoes, ham, and bell pepper briefly. Pour in wine and simmer 4–5 minutes. Empty contents of skillet over chicken in baking dish. Cover and bake 20–25 minutes. Serve, accompanied by potatoes and green beans with garlic (p. 303).

Serves 4.

Dessert after such a feed is a mere blip from the kitchen: a piece of cheese, an apple, an orange. But that is not to say the meal is over. After chowing down in the Basque manner, one needs a *digestif:* a glass of Izarra (Armagnac-based liqueur), or a Picon punch, or a cup of Winnemucca coffee.

PICON PUNCH

Enjoyed either before or after dinner, Picon punch is a definitive boardinghouse drink, a bittersweet snootful with all the delicacy of a charging ram.

1½ ounces Amer Picon
1½ ounces seltzer

Lemon twist
Dash brandy (optional)

Fill a 5–6-ounce glass with ice cubes. Add Amer Picon, then seltzer, and stir. Rub twist of lemon around rim of glass; add lemon. Float a dash of brandy on top, if desired.

WINNEMUCCA COFFEE

The goodness of this after-dinner kicker depends on *strong*, freshly brewed coffee to begin with.

Coffee
¾ ounce brandy or Cognac

¾ ounce anisette
Lemon twist

Set a spoon in an old-fashioned or footed cocktail glass. Fill three-quarters full with hot black coffee. Add brandy or Cognac, anisette, and twist of lemon.

WESTERN BREAKFAST

reakfast, not brunch, is what we are talking about here. In case you have forgotten, breakfast is the meal that is eaten first thing in the morning, shortly after waking up and before commencing the day's activities. Breakfast is an eye-opener; it girds you, perks you up. You read the morning paper over breakfast and find out what's happening. Or you share news and gossip with family (at home) or friends (in a town cafe). It is a quick meal, unless you embrace the moment and linger over second cups of coffee. You walk away from breakfast satisfied but not stuffed, ready to take on the world.

That kind of breakfast is why we like to motor west, where the morning meal is elevated to its rightful status as the herald of the day. Oh, sure, there are fine eye-openers back east, including biscuits and red-eye gravy in Tennessee, pancakes and maple syrup in New Hampshire, and ham and eggs at the Ham and Eggery in Miami. But nowhere is breakfast honored with the kind of enthusiasm that infuses it in the West, most especially in California.

Our theory is that the health and well-being of Western breakfast results from a confluence of two culinary traditions: old pioneer vittles, designed to stoke a person full of calories for a hard day's work, plus the cuisine of those new pioneers from the 1960s, counterculture escapees from the East, among whose culinary totems are homemade bread, small farm produce, and large communal feeds.

Big breakfast evokes images of farm food; it was years ago at a now defunct restaurant named the Farmer's Table in McCook, Nebraska, that we first realized there was something plumb different about the way they treat morning eats in the American West.

The Farmer's Table menu had lists of three-egg omelettes, pancakes, and waffles, but few customers paid attention to those piddly things. Hoisted to the tables on platters roomy enough for the daily feed of a one-ton hog were breakfasts entitled "The Harvester Special," "The Feed Wagon," and "After Chores Omelets." One category called "Super Steak" was headed with a thirty-ounce T-bone, served with three eggs, three slices of toast, buckets of jam, and a mountain of country fried potatoes and onions. Having eaten normally the day before, we opted for mere one-pound sirloins, with the works, after which we drove all the way to Oklahoma City without a twinge of hunger.

NORMAL-SIZE
WESTERN-STYLE STEAK 'N' EGGS

Pan-fried is the only way to make a steak destined to accompany eggs. First, prepare any toast, pancakes, or other breadstuffs that will accompany the meal. Get the coffee perking and the table set. Once you slap the steak on the griddle, there won't be time to waste.

A 6- to 8-ounce cut of steak (boneless) should be ample for a normal breakfast appetite, especially if the beef is accompanied by the usual fixings. The best and most authentically Western cut for breakfast is the one known as a "Spencer steak," which is a rib steak (entrecote) without the bone. You won't likely find beef cut into Spencer steaks in the East or South, but it's easy to buy a rib steak and trim it.

Set two pans on the stove: one well-seasoned cast-iron pan, large enough for the steak (or steaks), and a nonstick pan, large enough for the eggs. Turn on the heat to medium high under the cast-iron pan. (And turn on the vent fan.)

As the pan heats, mix 1 cup of coarse kosher-style salt with just enough water to form a thick paste. Plaster one side of each steak thoroughly with the paste. Slap the salty side down on the hot pan. Pat the top side of the steak with another layer of salt.

Meanwhile, melt enough butter in the egg pan for eggs. Scramble them, add milk, or simply remove from the shells so they are ready and waiting to get cooked.

After 3–5 minutes, the underside of a 1½-inch-thick steak should be crusted. Lift the steak, pressing the spatula hard against the pan to pick up as much crust as possible. Slap the steak down on the other side.

As the steaks finish, cook the eggs. When the underside of the steaks are crusted, remove them from the pan, scrape off all the salt coating, and spread the top of each steak with butter. Serve immediately with the eggs.

Note: The salt coating, if cooked over medium-high heat, leaves virtually no salty residue.

We knew before we ever headed west that we were going into steak-three-times-a-day country, but who could have guessed that Denver is a city with an insatiable hunger for eggs? Dozens, the Egg Shells (three of them), the Egg-Ceptional Eatery, the Delectable Egg, Le Peeps (four locations), and Scrambles—all are Denver restaurants that have built menus around eggs! At Scrambles, they even accommodate egg lovers with severe cholesterol overloads by making yolkless omelettes! Another house specialty at Scrambles is frittatas, our own version of which is often part of company breakfast at home.

VEGETABLE FRITTATA

Frittatas have a long history in Western gastronomy, going back to the Italian family-style restaurants and boardinghouses of the Barbary Coast. They are baked omelettes that can be filled with anything imagination conjures. Our version was originally inspired by the combination of ingredients known as a Denver, or Western omelette, which food historian Evan Jones suggests might have begun as a Chinese cook's variation of egg foo young! One zucchini-bountiful summer, it evolved to this cheese-rich vegetarian egg cake.

1 cup sliced and halved
   zucchini
1 cup sliced mushroom
¾ cup chopped green bell
   pepper
¾ cup chopped onion
1 clove garlic, minced
3 tablespoons olive oil
6 eggs

¼ cup cream
1 pound cream cheese
2 cups cubed white bread, with
   crusts removed
1½ cups grated sharp Cheddar
   cheese
½ teaspoon salt
½ teaspoon pepper

Sauté zucchini, mushroom, bell pepper, onion, and garlic in olive oil until barely soft. Cool.

Preheat oven to 350°. Beat eggs and cream together. Add cream cheese in small pinches. Add bread, Cheddar, and cooled vegetables. Add salt and pepper. Pour mixture into well-buttered 10-inch springform pan. Bake 55 minutes. Let stand 10–15 minutes before serving.

Serves 6–8.

New Mexico is one of the great eating places in America. Few other states claim to have their own unique cuisine; no other state, with the possible exception of Louisiana, is so fiercely proud of it. Looking for some place to eat in the Mesilla Valley or in the mountains of the north, you cruise past innumerable small cafes with hand-lettered signs boasting that they serve "native food." It is rare to get a bad meal in these inconspicuous eateries, but you never know which of them will have the lightest *sopaipillas,* or tenderest *carne adovada.*

We knew we had hit a winner when we walked into the Duran Central Pharmacy in Albuquerque one morning, because off to the side of this fully stocked drugstore was a lunch counter perfumed with chili and eggs; behind the counter was a lady rolling out flour tortillas with a wooden dowel.

The Duran menu was brief and spicy: burritos, enchiladas, *sopaipillas,* and for breakfast, *huevos rancheros* (eggs, ranch-style). Although *huevos rancheros* are ubiquitous throughout the Southwest, as common as ham and biscuits in Dixie, really good ones are rare. What makes them special is their freshness—of the chili on top and the tortillas underneath.

So, in order to make good *huevos rancheros,* first you have to make tortillas—either crisp corn tortillas or soft, pliable flour tortillas. As served at the Duran Central Pharmacy on the side of bowls of chili, or as the wrapping for a chili-cheese-potato torpedo sandwich, or as the foundation for a superior plate of *huevos rancheros,* they are one of the easiest breadstuffs to make.

FLOUR TORTILLAS

Instant gratification for bread lovers, flour tortillas smell wonderful hot off the griddle. Although kitchen efficiency experts advise they can be frozen and defrosted, why bother? Do as they do at the Duran Central Pharmacy and fry them up fresh, to order, as needed, during a meal. Have a bowl of drawn butter and a brush on the side, and paint them on their way from the griddle to the plate. Nothing tastes more authentically Southwestern or is a more welcome substitute for ordinary boring toast at breakfast.

3 cups flour	2 teaspoons baking powder
1 teaspoon salt	1 cup tepid water (110°)

Mix flour, salt, and baking powder. Add water slowly, stirring until mixture barely begins to hold together. Work dough with hands to form a single mass, and turn out onto a floured board.

Knead dough until smooth. Divide into 12 pieces. Cover pieces with a damp towel or plastic wrap. Let rest 15 minutes.

Flatten each ball with the heel of your hand onto a lightly floured board. Use a rolling pin to roll each round quickly into an 8-inch circle, turning the round by quarter turns as it flattens.

Place flattened tortilla immediately onto an ungreased nonstick skillet, preheated to medium high. As tortilla cooks, press down with spatula. When lightly browned on bottom, turn and cook other side.

Serve immediately.

Makes 12 tortillas.

The town of Hatch, New Mexico, in the Mesilla Valley, is the heart of chili country, its white adobe homes draped with drying red *ristras*, its cars' bumper stickers advertising the annual chili festival. We first learned about the lore of the pod in a town cafe named Kearney's, a whitewashed building very local in character (with the regulars' personalized coffee mugs hung on the wall), and very proud of its chili.

"It's the best in the West!" Mother Kearney bellowed at us, referring to the house chili, when we first stopped for lunch in 1976. She then gave us a lecture about the different chili peppers of the area, using jarfuls that Kearney's kept behind the counter for just such show-and-tell demonstrations. Since that happy introduction to Mesilla Valley chilies, we always seemed to pass through Hatch early in the morning at breakfast time. We would have a little chili talk with young Jackie Kearney (her mother has since passed away), then whale down plates of Kearney's superior *huevos rancheros* before heading north toward Santa Fe.

MESILLA VALLEY HUEVOS RANCHEROS

Many *huevos rancheros* are spread out across crisp corn tortillas. We prefer our *huevos* Sonora-style, on wheat tortillas. Once the tortillas are made, follow this recipe, based on one Jackie Kearney wrote out for us several years ago. As made at Kearney's, the *salsa* that went on top of the eggs was four-alarm hot. Of course, the spice level depends entirely on the heat of the peppers you use; jalapeños vary considerably. Take a tiny nibble, then cut them in according to taste.

2 tablespoons butter
1 tomato, peeled, seeded, and
    diced
½ cup diced onion
1–3 jalapeño peppers, diced
2 Flour Tortillas (preceding
    recipe), warm

½ cup mashed refried pinto
    beans (see p. 264)
¼ cup grated sharp cheese
2 eggs
Chili sauce

Melt butter and fry tomato, onion, and peppers over low heat until onion is tender. Set aside and keep warm.

Place 1 flour tortilla on an ovenproof plate and cover with mashed refried pinto beans. Sprinkle with cheese and warm in oven until cheese melts.

Fry eggs and slide on top of melted cheese. Cover with chili sauce. Serve with second tortilla on side for mopping up.

Serves 1.

By definition, *huevos rancheros* are always a combination of eggs and chili. Like omelettes, *huevos* possibilities are unlimited, from dainty-palate avocado toppings with scarcely a dot of chili, to fire-breathing jalapeño sauces like Kearney's. Allow us to suggest one peculiarly New Mexican variation on the theme—a specialty of the Duran Pharmacy—that elevates morning cackles from the world of "100 Things to Do with Eggs" into the realm of major good eats:

CACKLING CARNE ADOVADA

Carne adovada is a definitive New Mexican meal—pork marinated in a purée of red chili peppers. It is served as pork chops for a main course at dinner; but it goes great with eggs too, especially if the pork is cut into bite-size chunks. Our formula for making *carne adovada* is based on a recipe given to us by the grandest New Mexican restaurant of them all, Rancho de Chimayo, north of Santa Fe. The Jaramillo family, who operate the Rancho on land that has been in their family since the 1700s, start with dried red chili pods—the only way to go. Fortunately for the rest of us, such pods have recently become available in most supermarkets.

CARNE ADOVADA MARINADE

½ pound dried whole chili
  pods (California *chili de*
  ristras)
1 teaspoon salt
1 tablespoon finely chopped
  onion
½ teaspoon white pepper

½ teaspoon oregano
2 teaspoons sugar
1 teaspoon vinegar
½ teaspoon Worcestershire
  sauce
6–7 cups boiling water

Preheat oven to 350°. Wash whole chili pods. Remove stem and seeds. Roast until fragrant, 3–4 minutes, watching closely to make sure pods do not burn.

Break up roasted chili pods into a bowl. Add remaining ingredients, except boiling water. In a blender mix ¼ cup of the chili mixture with ¼ cup of water. Continue blending, in these small increments, until all the chili is used up. Mixture will be smooth and saucy. Bring to a boil and simmer gently 20 minutes.

CARNE ADOVADA

3–4 pounds pork, trimmed of
  fat, cut into 1-inch cubes
4 cloves garlic, chopped fine

2 tablespoons ground cumin
Carne adovada marinade

Arrange pork in a large baking dish. Combine garlic and cumin with marinade and pour over pork, turning pieces of meat to coat them evenly. Marinate in refrigerator 12 full hours.

Preheat oven to 325°. Cover pork and bake 30 minutes. Remove cover and baste pork with marinade. Bake 30 minutes more, basting several times.

Makes enough carne adovada *for 6–8 dinner entrées or for 8–10 servings of* huevos rancheros.

HUEVOS RANCHEROS WITH CARNE ADOVADA

12 Flour Tortillas (p. 313)
3 cups mashed refried pinto
  beans (p. 264)

1½ cups grated sharp cheese
12 eggs
Carne adovada

Place 6 tortillas on ovenproof plates, spread with beans, and sprinkle each with cheese. Warm until cheese melts. Fry eggs and place 2 each on top of melted cheese. Ladle *carne adovada* on side of plate (do not crush eggs). Serve each plate with an additional tortilla for scooping up *carne adovada*.

Serves 6.

"Bill and Alice Jennison opened the Tecolote Cafe with the feeling that breakfast is a meal that is too often neglected," says the first Tecolote menu from 1980. "It is their desire to serve you a wholesome meal, at a reasonable price, in a pleasant, cheerful atmosphere."

They have fulfilled their ambition for six years, dishing out symphonic New Mexican breakfasts in a casual cafe on the south side of Santa Fe. Here is a demonstration of what we mean when we contend that Western breakfast is something special. Choose from a repertoire of jumbo three-egg omelettes, shirred eggs baked on a bed of chicken livers, Italian frittatas, even New York–style scrambled eggs and lox; plus there are local breakfast specialties, including green chili omelettes and an astonishing breakfast burrito constructed from a wheat flour tortilla wrapped around scrambled eggs and sausage, topped with chili and melted cheese.

"We wanted to have something special to serve Sunday morning," Bill told us, "so we came up with cinnamon streusel, which we make by the dozens every week." On our last trip through Santa Fe, we happened to stop by Tecolote on a Saturday. Bill and Alice were in the kitchen, rolling out mountains of dough and sprinkling it with streusel mix. As they rolled, we watched, and pried loose their streusel recipe.

TECOLOTE CINNAMON STREUSEL

Bill and Alice are not the type of chefs to put on airs about their creative genius. Bill defers to Alice as "the soul of Tecolote," and Alice confided to us, "My first husband didn't even like my cooking. He was brought up on macaroni and cheese." They weren't shy about telling us that when they went on the lookout for that certain special Sunday something, they finally found their inspiration in an old *Better Homes and Gardens Cook Book* recipe for a teatime roll called "Biscuits Supreme." They doctored it up, added the streusel mix and the glaze, and rolled it in a spiral. That's creativity, American-style.

2 cups all-purpose flour
2 tablespoons whole wheat
    flour
2 teaspoons granulated sugar
4 teaspoons baking powder

½ teaspoon salt
½ teaspoon cream of tartar
½ cup solid vegetable
    shortening
¾ cup milk

Streusel mix

3 tablespoons butter
1½ cups brown sugar
½ cup very finely chopped
    pecans

1 teaspoon cinnamon

Glaze

2½ cups sifted confectioners'
    sugar
3–4 tablespoons orange juice

1 tablespoon grated orange
    rind

Sift flours, granulated sugar, baking powder, salt, and cream of tartar. Cut in shortening until crumbly. Add milk and stir only enough for dough to hold together. Turn out onto a floured board and let rest as you mix topping.

To make streusel mix, combine butter, brown sugar, pecans, and cinnamon until crumbly. Preheat oven to 450°.

Knead dough on floured board as little as possible, until smooth enough to roll out to a 10 x 15-inch rectangle about ¼ inch thick. Spread streusel mix across top, then roll up from short side into a tube. Use a serrated knife and a sawing motion to slice tube into ½-inch disks and lay circles about 1 inch apart on a sheet of parchment paper on a baking sheet. Bake 10–12 minutes,

☞

until nicely browned. Remove from parchment paper and cool on rack.

While rolls are still warm, mix confectioners' sugar, juice, and rind and drizzle on top.

Makes 16–20 rolls.

California is the best state in the union for breakfast. Up and down the coast, in swank cafes and roadside beaneries, it is easy to become accustomed to fresh o.j. and hot loaves of bread, to pecan waffles, sourdough French toast, and mimosas made from locally bottled champagne.

Start in San Diego at a local institution called Hob Nob Hill, a pinnacle of three-squares-a-day (except Saturday) since 1944. Every morning, you will have to wait in line to eat there; a wait that is made doubly excruciating by the fact that the line runs through a lobby of display cases stocked with Hob Nob Hill's loaf and Bundt cakes, pecan rolls, fruit breads, and muffins.

Nothing is new about this cuisine. It is classic morning fare dished out by uniformed coffee shop waitresses who *fly* through the aisles speeding meals on their way. Forget brunch-time lassitude. However genteel the plates of food, one cannot help but feel the spirit of celerity that reigns at Hob Nob Hill. We love to grab a table, down our breakfast, gulp that coffee, pay the check, and be on our merry way.

SAN DIEGO PECAN WAFFLES

Nuts on top of pancakes, waffles, and French toast; nuts in the batter; nuts in the syrup—Californians love to customize ordinary breakfast fare with nuts. Seldom do you find a plain waffle on a menu without this souped-up cousin right nearby. At Hob Nob Hill, they put chopped-up pecans in the batter, then shower the top with pecan halves. Syrup on the side is always served warm.

1 cup pecan halves as garnish	1 cup milk
2 cups flour	1 cup buttermilk
½ teaspoon salt	3 tablespoons butter, melted
1 tablespoon baking powder	1 cup finely chopped pecans
½ teaspoon baking soda	Dash cream of tartar
4 eggs, separated	

Preheat oven to 300°. Before preparing waffles, place pecan halves on a baking sheet and put in oven. Toss them and watch them closely as you make waffles; bake nuts until crisp and brown, 15–20 minutes, but do not scorch.

Combine flour, salt, baking powder, and baking soda. Beat egg yolks well. Stir into dry ingredients with milk, buttermilk, melted butter, and chopped pecans. Beat egg whites with cream of tartar till stiff. Fold into batter.

Into *hot*, well-greased (or Teflon) waffle iron pour enough batter to almost cover bottom surface. Cook until waffle is golden brown.

Serve immediately, strewn with toasted pecan halves, melted butter, and warm syrup on the side.

Serves 4.

While breakfasting at Hob Nob Hill, you are faced with a disturbing sight—glass cases at the kitchen side of the dining room, filled with all the coffee cakes, muffins, sweet rolls, and fruit breads you didn't order. Orange pecan Bundt rings, cherry cashew bread, carrot muffins, pineapple cake, pecan sticky rolls—the sight of them makes you hungry all over again, which is why so many Hob Nobbers leave with bakery boxes full of things to take home. The Hoersch family, who has operated Hob Nob Hill since it was a fourteen-stool lunch counter, gave us this prized recipe for one of their regular favorites, boysenberry Bundt cake. We have cut it down and reworked it to home kitchen proportions.

HOB NOB HILL BOYSENBERRY BUNDT CAKE

2 cups sifted cake flour
3 tablespoons instant nonfat
    dry milk
2½ teaspoons baking soda
½ teaspoon salt
1 teaspoon cinnamon
½ teaspoon nutmeg
½ teaspoon ground cloves
½ cup chopped pecans
1½ cups sugar

¾ cup lowfat yogurt
3 eggs, beaten
¾ cup corn oil
½ teaspoon lemon extract
1 cup boysenberries, or
    blackberries, blueberries,
    loganberries, etc. (If frozen,
    be sure fruit has thawed
    completely before using.)

In a large bowl mix cake flour, dry milk, baking soda, salt, cinnamon, nutmeg, and cloves. Stir in pecans.

In a second bowl mix sugar and yogurt. Add eggs, corn oil, and lemon extract; fold in berries; then mix all ingredients into dry mixture, stirring just until smooth.

Preheat oven to 350°. Pour batter into a well-greased and floured 12-cup Bundt pan. Bake 45–50 minutes, or until a toothpick inserted in center comes out clean. Cool 15 minutes in pan, then cool completely on a rack. If desired, ice with Lemon Cream Cheese Frosting (following recipe).

LEMON CREAM CHEESE FROSTING

While we like their moist Bundt cakes without any icing whatsoever, Hob Nob's Stanley Hoersch advised that they usually ice them with a powdered sugar glaze. Or, if they make them into loaf cakes, they are frosted with this thick lemony cream cheese mixture, which keeps well.

8 ounces cream cheese
4 tablespoons butter, softened
4 tablespoons solid vegetable
    shortening
1 1-pound package

confectioners' sugar (4
    cups), sifted
1 teaspoon grated lemon rind
2 teaspoons lemon juice

Whip cream cheese until soft. Add butter, then shortening, creaming until smooth. Add sugar and beat until light and fluffy. Beat in lemon rind and juice. Spread on room-temperature cakes. (Extra frosting may be refrigerated and later warmed to spreading consistency.)

One of the best breakfasts we ever ate was in the early 1970s on the road heading north out of San Diego. It was in San Juan Capistrano, at a truck stop cafe named Mac's Coffee Break, a motley joint that catered to a clientele of surfers, truckers, and CIA types from the nearby Nixon home in San Clemente.

We stopped at Mac's with a hillbilly friend from Kentucky, a string bean–shaped guy who could eat more than a hungry wrestler. We started with oatmeal and thick-sliced toast, mugs of pulpy orange juice squeezed to order, then dug into giant-size platters of sourdough French toast sprinkled with confectioners' sugar, guacamole-mushroom omelettes, and a stack of out-of-this-world banana nut pancakes. The pancakes, steamy hot and dripping butter, contained bits of nut and mashed bananas in the batter; plus the stack (about a dozen four-inchers) was loaded with nuts and sliced bananas between the cakes.

Although Mac's is long gone, those luscious pancakes, their fruit and nut abundance so evocative of California, have a lifelong welcome place on our breakfast table.

BANANA-CASHEW PANCAKES

3 cups flour
1/4 cup sugar
1 teaspoon salt
2 teaspoons baking powder
1 teaspoon baking soda
4 eggs, beaten
1/3 cup corn oil

3 cups buttermilk
1 cup mashed bananas (2–3)
1 cup chopped cashews (salted or unsalted, to taste)
1/2 cup whole cashews as garnish (salted are okay)
2 bananas, sliced, as garnish

Sift together flour, sugar, salt, baking powder, and baking soda. Mix together eggs, corn oil, buttermilk, and mashed bananas. Combine, mixing just enough to blend, adding more buttermilk if too thick. Mix in chopped cashews. Fry pancakes on a buttered griddle over medium heat. Serve garnished with whole cashews and sliced bananas.

Serves 4.

When you get to Los Angeles, there is an entire culture of coffee shops that specialize in hot lunch and quickie breakfast, plus a subculture of ignominious eateries where breakfast stars: Egg Heaven in Long Beach (for an omelette of Persian rice and chili), Eat 'N' Park in Burbank (for two-man "Crazy Omelettes" loaded with chopped-up hot dogs and chili), and the most colorful of them all, Duke's at the Tropicana.

The Tropicana is a hotel on Santa Monica that seems to attract a clientele of aspiring rock musicians and all the human flotsam and jetsam that always come with them; Duke's is the motel coffee shop. Every morning at seven, the pointy-hair crowd lines up to grab their places at long tables shared with muscle boys, would-be agents, gawkers, and geeks.

This group is not normally known for its fine taste in food, but you will find no better breakfast in Los Angeles. Bowls of flawless fresh fruit and berries speckled with coconut, stacks of apple and banana pancakes, omelettes with sourdough toast and crusty hash browns on the side—here is California breakfast par excellence, with the added benefit of ambition-charged ambience that is stone Hollywood.

As in so many of L.A.'s colorful dives, the management of Duke's plays up its attraction for celebrities who like to keep in touch with their humble roots. In fact, they can reel off the famous people who eat there, always identified with their favorite dish. Springsteen gets a Reuben sandwich. Cher's favorite is blackberry blintzes.

CELEBRITY BLINTZES

Duke's almost always lists a blintz of the day on its blackboard: pineapple, strawberry, whatever's in season. The fruit is fresh, and, what is more amazing, the crepes are tender—so unlike the rubbery frozen ones that pass as blintzes in most restaurants between Los Angeles and New York. Our recipe is for plain cheese blintzes —easily supplemented with whatever fresh fruit or berries you have on hand.

CREPES

3 eggs
1½ cups skim milk

1 teaspoon salt
1 cup flour

Combine eggs, milk, salt, and flour, stirring until most of the lumps are dissolved. Let stand 15–20 minutes.

Over medium heat, brush a 7-inch nonstick skillet with melted butter. Pour 3 tablespoons (¾ of a ¼-cup measure) of batter into pan, circulating pan so batter covers entire bottom.

Cook 2–3 minutes, until bottom is pale gold and top is set. Remove from pan. Repeat procedure, stacking cooked crepes, cooked side up, separated by wax paper. (Stack only 4–5 per pile.)

Fill crepes with cheese filling:

CHEESE FILLING

16 ounces farmer cheese
4 ounces cream cheese,
   softened
3 egg yolks

⅓ cup sugar
1 teaspoon vanilla extract
Berries or small chunks of
   fruit, as desired

Beat cheeses together. Beat in yolks, sugar, and vanilla. Fold in fruit. (If using fruit, reserve half to serve on top of finished blintzes.) Place 2 tablespoons of filling in center of uncooked side of each crepe. Fold over once to form a half circle. Fold in sides, and fold once more to form a tube.

BLINTZ PREPARATION

About ½ cup clarified butter
Sour cream and/or applesauce
   as garnish

Heat clarified butter in a skillet. Fry blintzes seam side down over medium heat until golden brown. Turn to brown other side. (This will have to be done in 2–3 batches.)
   Serve garnished with fruit and sour cream and/or applesauce.

Makes 15–20 blintzes.

"The restaurant business is in my blood," Cassandra Mitchell told us. "My great-grandparents operated a restaurant-hotel in San Francisco from the 1880s until about 1940. My own career started in the mid-1960s, working for a friend at his Pacific Coast coffeehouse serving up soup and sandwiches to accompany poetry readings and cool jazz."

Ten years ago Cassandra bought a rundown bus depot in Yountville with hopes of turning it into a restaurant of her own. At the time, she was living on a farm in the Napa Valley, raising poultry, pigs, and dairy animals. "I lived with six gourmets, and we were constantly amusing each other with our latest culinary ideas. Food was our religion, and we practiced it daily."

She named her depot the Diner, and with friends' help planted gardens and fruit trees and rebuilt the interior. The cuisine of the Diner was conceived as of-the-people food. There is a distinctly California spirit about it, but that does not mean the esoteric preparations and precious ingredients so often associated with trendy food. It means whole-grain breads baked each day and an herb garden out back; it means sundaes topped with freshly made double chocolate sauce and cheesecake-flavored milk shakes made from buttermilk and vanilla ice cream; it means a repertoire of inspired Cal-Mex cooking such as chicken and cream cheese enchiladas and guacamole-stuffed *envueltas*. Best of all, it means superior breakfast, "served all day."

Cassandra's breakfast menu lists all kinds of omelettes, and luscious "seasoned potatoes," fried with onions, herbs, and Cheddar cheese, but what makes us weak in the knees are her pancakes. Three varieties: potato pancakes made from lace-thin shreds of potato suspended in an herbed batter; banana pancakes sprinkled with crumbled walnuts; and cornmeal pancakes, served with boysenberry syrup.

THE DINER'S
CRISPY CORNMEAL PANCAKES

"Quite straightforward," Cassandra described this recipe, "yet it transcends its simple composition."

1¾ cups yellow cornmeal   2 eggs
⅓ cup flour   2¼ cups buttermilk
1½ teaspoons salt   ⅓ cup light salad oil
¾ teaspoon baking soda

Sift together cornmeal, flour, salt, and baking soda. Mix eggs, buttermilk, and oil. Combine both mixtures. Batter should be consistency of heavy cream. If too thick, add more buttermilk.

Butter hot griddle and spoon batter onto surface in 4-inch cakes. Cook over medium heat until pancakes are golden brown. Flip and cook other side.

Serve immediately with pats of butter and boysenberry or raspberry syrup (or jam).

Serves 4.

We confess that we never even considered making our own sausage at home: what a pain, when links and patties are so easily available in the grocer's freezer! However, after savoring the Diner's sausage, and getting Cassandra Mitchell's recipe for same, we changed our tune fast. No need for casings, sausage stuffers, and all that paraphernalia to make these patties; they are as easy as meat loaf. And the results are succulent, spicy, infinitely superior to anything store-bought.

CASSANDRA'S HOMEMADE SAUSAGE

This recipe makes a heap of sausage, but why not stock up? The raw sausage freezes well, as either individual patties or 1-pound blocks. (The recipe can be cut neatly in half.) For good juiciness, ask the butcher for pork with about a 30 percent fat content. Cassandra's suggestion for maximum flavor is to grind the spices just before mixing.

10 pounds ground pork
4 tablespoons salt
⅓ cup dried sage
2 tablespoons coarse black
 pepper
1 tablespoon ground cloves

1 tablespoon nutmeg
⅓ cup plus 1 tablespoon brown
 sugar
2½ tablespoons crushed red
 pepper
½ tablespoon allspice

Mix all ingredients together by hand. Form mixture into hamburger-size patties. Fry over medium heat until crisp and brown on both sides.

Makes about 40 patties.

INDEX

A NOTE ON THE TYPE

The text of this book was set in a film version of Aster, a type face designed by Francesco Simoncini (born 1912 in Bologna, Italy) for Ludwig and Mayer, the German type foundry. Starting out with the basic old-face letter forms that can be traced back to Francesco Griffo in 1495, Simoncini emphasized the diagonal stress by the simple device of extending diagonals to the full height of the letter forms and squaring off. By modifying the weights of the individual letters to combat this stress, he has produced a type of rare balance and vigor. Introduced in 1958, Aster has steadily grown in popularity.

Composed by Dix Type, Inc., Syracuse, New York.
Printed and bound by Murray Printing Company,
Westford, Massachusetts.
Designed by Virginia Tan.